The Jedi Compass
A collective works from around the Jedi Community

Symbol created by Jacob Barger, cover art expanded upon by Nathan Thompson

It is a little known fact that the Jedi Community has been around since the mid-90s. Since the early Star Wars Role-Playing Games and Kharis Nyteflyer's website in 1995, our community has been building upon the idea of using the philosophy outlined in the fiction to bring about a real life way of life.

In 2005, Adam Yaw took on the task to document the work which had been done by members of the Jedi Community up to that point. He went to places like Force Academy, Ashla Knights, Institute for Jedi Realist Studies, and The Jediism Way to compile information on being a Jedi, Sith, and even Grey Jedi alongside scholarly works around the internet. This document is over 1000 pages, and is a wonderful introduction to the Jedi Path. But since that time, the Jedi have evolved, taking on more ideas from works that inspired the authors of Lucas Film's fictional universe. Ten years after Adam's project, the Jedi Compass is meant to document where we are today.

We are comprised of members from across the world. We have members from all but one continent (that we know of, first person that truthfully admits they are from Antartica will have made history ;)), and we are finding new things out everyday about one another. Learning to co-exist in a world where the various religions, nationalities, ethnicities and cultures of the world are respected and even learn from. Though, represented in these pages are the works of members from across the English Speaking orders. There are still orders from the Czech Republic, Russia, South America and the Philippines which were not able to be reached in time to contribute.

So what is the Jedi Compass itself? The document was written with the aide of members from Church of Jediism, Jedi Academy Online, Chicago Jedi, Jedi Church (the Original), Force Academy, Temple of the Jedi Order, Ashla Knights, Temple of the Jedi Force, and so many more. The document can be used by anyone to develop their own teachings, meditations, or training program to become a greater Jedi, much like what we as a community have done in these pages.

When you open this book, we hope that you learn something about who we are today, and who we will become in the future. But more importantly, we all hope that this book can help you awaken the knight within.

-Setanaoko Mizu Oceana
Force Realists Radio Host at Knights of Awakening.

THE JEDI COMPASS
BY THE JEDI COMMUNITY

The Ineffable

The Force- "The Force" is a loosely adapted term to explain a something which all cultures agree exist, but disagree on exactly what it is. As such, a Jedi dedicates themselves to understanding of all things within and through "the Force". As a rule, no Jedi can set down in law a concrete definition of "the Force" for all to follow, only for themselves.

Core Ethics

Loyalty to the Jedi Code- This has a few different variants depending on what order a Jedi attends. A Jedi is bound by the code. By maintaining your loyalty to the code, you are able to keep your actions in check through the moral integrity of the Jedi Path outlined in the Jedi Code. It is important that a Jedi checks their own version of the code against the original codes (Jedi Code and Skywalker Code) before they adopt it.

Duty to the All- A Jedi's mission is to support their community through service. A Jedi is charged with acting, objectively, when they recognise a situation where someone needs help. Jedi put their lives above the lives of others, even when facing danger, but know that they can help through direct action or indirect action as per the situation.

Respect the Law- A Jedi knows enough of the law to operate within it. Jedi should respect, and do their best to live by, the laws of the land they are living in. However, these are man's law, and like man, subject to flaws. A Jedi must act for the best interest of mankind as he/she sees the situation.

Defense- A Jedi understands that defense is not purely physical, but that there are many ways to defend a person or property. As such, it is important to understand that Jedi are not vigilantes. If, however, they are in a position where they are called to defend themselves or someone else against loss of life, limb or senses, they are allowed to apply the appropriate amount of force necessary for defense.

Action- A Jedi recognizes that there are times when getting involved with a situation is against the will of the person they are seeking to assist, or that helping them may be more detrimental in the long run. As such, a Jedi seeks inner wisdom to determine when to act and when not to act.

Self Awareness

Interior- A Jedi works to become aware of their emotions and things which make them "tick". They learn of their flaws and strengths, seeking to reconcile a life with those flaws which they cannot change and the strengths they have been blessed with. In this a Jedi must be constantly looking inward for their motivations, their directions, what moves them, and why they allow it to do so.

Exterior- It is important that a Jedi be aware of the person they present to those around them, and how that will affect the dynamic of the groups they find themselves in. How one's presence is received will determine whether or not the next steps will be met with hostility or acceptance.

Virtues

Tolerance- You do not need to agree with someone's religion, their nationality, their career choice, their dress or anything else for that matter. Tolerance is not about agreement, it is about showing respect for the freedom of a persons choices and to respect their choices, until it reaches a point in which a reasonable person would consider the individual's actions as a/an (emotionally, spiritually, financially, and/or physically) abusive threat to you or another person.

Responsibility- Responsibility is at the heart of learning to overcome our problems. A Jedi should be held responsible for all of their actions. Without it, we cannot grow, we cannot help others and we cannot justify why we are to be taken seriously.

Discipline- In order to walk the Jedi Path, you need to live by your training and by the philosophy. It is your responsibility to continue your growth throughout the rest of your life. Even while you are training with a mentor or taking a course at an order, it is discipline that will get you through to your knighthood and beyond.

Fortitude- Fortitude is the emotional strength and conviction to press forward in any given situation which poses an internal or external adversity. Developing fortitude allows a Jedi to show that they are not willing to give up until they have drawn their last breath.

Integrity- A Jedi seeks to maintain their integrity to the Jedi Code at all times. A Jedi should hold themselves to a high standard knowing that what they do when no one is looking is just as important as what they do when people are looking.

Objectivity- A Jedi trains themselves to gain as much relevant information as possible before drawing their conclusions. Once intelligence has been collected, they approach the problem with as little cultural and emotional bias as possible so that they are able to develop a decision on their next action.

Overcome

Aggression- To build on the Jedi Virtues, a Jedi must keep themselves open to the world. Through the misuse of aggression, they miss out on opportunities to further their cause. This does not preclude being assertive. A Jedi needs to learn to find the most effective means of resolving a conflict through the least bit of hostility possible.

Recklessness- A Jedi does not take unnecessary risks, knowing that their life is important to the Jedi Mission of bettering the world around them. In overcoming recklessness, a Jedi acknowledges and is mindful of how small the impact is perceived to have on themselves or others.

Attachments- Overcoming your attachments is not about getting rid of all your possessions or even denouncing your family, instead this is about forward movement. In overcoming/subjagating your attachments, you are acknowledging what value these things have to you, and you recognize that there comes a time when you should no longer fight for your attachments, and you must let go. For a Jedi overcoming attachments can extend to bad habits, unhealthy obsessions, and connections to people that make us less who we have chosen to be.

Prowess

Defense Art- A "Defense Art" is not necessarily physical in nature, it can be through speech, writing, diplomacy, art or a number of other options which lead to an active method of curing the world of oppression. Like many of the other disciplines, you may find that your Defense Art is the same as another art (Physical, Scholarly, or Spiritual).

Physical Art- A Jedi should seek a physical art within their capabilities which keeps them them in shape and focuses on maintaining discipline of their body. . Part of the physical art, which can be observed by all Jedi regardless of their mobility, is health. A Jedi should eat right, and maintain their health to the best of their ability.

Scholarly Art- A Jedi should seek out skills that provide benefit to them and the people around them. The search for knowledge is fundamental to Jedi as one never stops learning, seeking knowledge or bettering their skills.

Spiritual Art- A spiritual art may be as simple as developing meditation, but can go far beyond this. A Jedi may choose to develop a spiritual art aimed at connecting them with "the Force" through healing, seeking guidance, or simply developing their own self awareness.

"How To" For Jediism
Octagon
Temple of the Jedi Force

1. Ask yourself why. Know why you're here and what your goals are. Let the answer serve as a reminder in difficult times of what you've set out to do. OK, you want to be a Master one day, well why? How will achieving such a goal change your life for the better? The more detailed you are with your goals the better.

2. On a scale of one to ten what is your level of passion to reach your goal? In life the people most likely to reach their goal tend to rate their passion level at eight and above. What happens is that all those things that are at eight or above above already take over and you will end up dropping out.

3. Set your learning ability at ten. Those who are most successful at what they do find someone who is where they want to be. That person becomes their role model. They learn everything they can from that person in order to duplicate that persons achievement. They know that if you want to be an expert car driver you don't get advice from a person who starts out by saying, "Well, I've never driven a car...but I think..." You want to learn from somebody who is where you want to be. Anyone can give you an opinion but you want to follow an experts opinion.

4. Set your action level at a ten. Don't over think advice. Just do it. Learn the skill through practice.
If you're not constantly practicing what you learn then you should stop and re-evaluate you level of commitment to your goal.

5. Always be aware of your mindset. If you want to be a Jedi Master one day, you should be constantly asking yourself, 'What would a Jedi Master do in this situation?' To change your life you have to change how you react to situations. This raises your level of awareness, about yourself and about the situations you find yourself in.

6. Visualization. Visualize yourself at the completion of your goal. Do it as often as you can for short or long periods of time as brief meditations as needed. Thoughts create things. Write down you goal and put it up

somewhere around the house where you can see it. Let it serve as a reminder of your goal.

7. As you learn new techniques realize that it takes three months for a behavior to become a habit. Be willing to commit yourself to the new practice for three months, (mark it on a calendar, make it official).

8. When you fall or fail at something don't beat yourself up. Just get back into it as soon as you can. Don't focus on the mistake, focus on getting back into practice.

Follow these tips and you will be in harmony with the Force and your goals will be reached.
May the Force be with you

THE FORCE

What is the Force?
Silas
Jedi Knights

My view of what the Force is relates to states of balance and imbalance. I don't view it as a power or energy.

I suppose you could say I view life and occurrences in it like a scale. When everything is balanced, there is peace, contentment. The "Force" is a state of peaceful being. When something disrupts the peace, there is imbalance which could be called a "disturbance in the Force". For example, a person easily carrying a bag of groceries is in a balanced state. The "Force", their "Balance", is steady. A person who is struggling with their groceries is imbalanced. As a Jedi, we should restore that balance to a peaceful state by helping that person with their groceries. Likewise a person in a peaceful state is balanced yet a person can become imbalanced when their peace is disrupted due to becoming angry or afraid.

A Jedi should train with the "Force/Balance" and find their personal balanced/peaceful state of being. Recognizing it and maintaining it should be essential to their training. Meditation can help in this case. A Jedi who allows themselves to become constantly imbalanced by uncertainty or nervousness in the face of danger or need cannot effectively help or aid others; watching someone struggle but being too uncertain if you should help makes you hesitate and probably end up not doing anything. A Jedi learns and knows how to overcome that imbalanced sense of being and do what is required of them.

States of balance (the "Force") exist everywhere; they are internal and external. They are within our reach, limited only to the Earth and what we can do in it. A distraught person in need on the other side of the world can find peace if you send them an email with kind, gentle words. The person in line next to you who doesn't have quite enough money to buy clothes for their child can have their stress reduced if you offer up a bit of your own money to pay for the remaining amount. So the Force to me is a mere concept that we can learn from, not something we actually use as a power; it is not something you can really train with. The basic teachings of Force are simple: find peace, understand balance, aim to restore all imbalanced states to their peaceful states.

I suppose all of this comes from what I saw in the Star Wars movies.

The Chosen One was said to be able to restore balance to the Force meaning the Force could be imbalanced but should be in a balanced state. In Star Wars, the Force connected all living things in the galaxy but we are limited to one planet, the only one known to harbor life thus our "Force/balance" relates to what goes on here and here only. We can manipulate the balance but only so much. People die the moment new people are born. Someone commits themselves to living a life of evil while others change to live as a child of light. The way people and this world are, there is always a general sense of balance yet it doesn't mean we should stop aiming for what is good and true. For every good deed I do, there is someone else balancing that act with something foul. That doesn't mean give up – it means work even harder, become a better person, and dedicate yourself even more to doing what is right.

So that may not be 100% correct but I am trying to go by what I see and what I can actually do. If a power like the ones in Star Wars existed (even a variation of it), I doubt it wouldn't have been discovered by this time and age and known to people before Star Wars came out in the late 1970's. Ten to twenty years ago a touch screen seemed incredibly futuristic and now it's commonplace. Knowledge and wisdom are the only true lasting powers. From one man came a theory, later electricity, then a light bulb and it went on and on to create the iPods we see today. Scientists discover thousands of new things every day and we can discover just as much by sitting back and thinking for a while. I personally plan on thinking more about my view of the Force soon because I know there is more to it. I will never completely view it as an essential part of Jedi training (as being able to "wield" or "use" it) but it is an interesting concept nonetheless.

Thanks for reading. *bows*

Possibilities Within The Force
Dave Jenson
The Nomad Jedi

As a Jedi I do not discount any things as not possible. Faith is an important thing in our life, no matter what that faith is in.

Faith in ones self and own abilities, faith in humanity, faith in friends, faith in the Force, and even faith in a God. All are important to the well being of mankind, and we find that one mans faith may be another mans fiction, and visa versa. It is not up to us to discredit another's faith in what they have faith in, but to add to that faith our own, for the betterment of mankind. Would we drive away a prospective Jedi that by not accepting the premise of god? That very Jedi might be the very salvation of millions of people through an idea, or a word spoken to one that is.

I cannot discount that the Force is the spirit of God that flows in, around, and through us, and the fabric of space in all things, guiding all thing creating and destroying things to remake. As for the dark and light side of the Force, that concept has been around since man first felt the Force and called it God, or the spirit of God.

The battle of good and evil has raged for eons. Some would call the light side of the Force God, or Angels as well as the good in man, and the dark side of the Force Lucifer, Satan, Demons, and fallen angels, or the evil in man, which gives entities to either side with both sides having a guiding spirit in either and both sides of the force.

It has and will remain my contention that the Unifying Force Does have a will of it's own, and does guide mankind to decisions, What we do is choose the side we get our input from.

I remember Yoda the fictional Jedi master saying to Young Skywalker when you look into the dark side, you will see it looking back at you. This too can translate in to our real existence and reality of our lives.

What is the Force?
Kyp_Durron
Temple of the Jedi Force

The Force is described as "an energy field created by all living things. It surrounds us, penetrates us, and binds the galaxy together." The Force, in part, is the energy associated with life, and life is associated with the Force. Most Jedi adhere to the ideology that the Force has a Will of it's own, and it guides those who would listen to it's subtle whispers.

The Force is primarily made up of the "light side" and the "dark side". These are concerned with the moral compass of the Force in its various manifestations of Balance. The light side of the Force is the facet of the Force aligned with good, benevolence, compassion, and healing. The dark side of the Force is aligned with fear, hatred, aggression, and malevolence; this side of the Force can seem more powerful, though it is just more tempting to those that can touch upon the power as it doesn't impose any restrictions on its use, often granting almost inhuman strength to those who would give in to hatred and anger. These "sides" of the Force are tied directly to the eternal Balance of the Universe... "Without Darkness, there can be no Light". By the same token, the "side" of the Force one chooses to follow depends on that individual's true intent within their heart.

The Force has also been described as having three additional aspects: The Cosmic Force, the Living Force, the Unifying Force. These aspects are defined by prominent Jedi philosophies. The Cosmic Force essentially embraces space and time in its entirety... It is quite basically what "binds the Galaxy together", and keeps the cosmos in Balance. It is what drives the Cosmos, and what keeps it in Order. The Living Force deals with living things... the Energy created by and connected to all Life itself. "Life creates it, makes it grow... Luminous beings are we, not this crude matter". It is a scientific fact that Energy changes form, but never truely ceases to exist. It is in that science that we are able to understand that the Living Force is the "pool of energy" that embodies all living things. It is theorized that when a living thing dies, it's life force joins the Living Force... likewise, when new life is born, it draws energy from the Living Force. The Unifying Force is what keeps the Cosmic Force and Living Force in Balance. It's energy exists on the molecular level throughout all matter, "unifying" everything in the Universe. Through it, we are connected to not just all living things, but all things. "Feel the Force... between you, me... the rock, the tree, even the ship".

The Force contains many similarities to other existing philosophical and religious principles. Many have related it to the concepts of Qi (also "chi" or "ki"; China, Japan, and Korea), Prana (India), Mana (Polynesia) and other similar traditions focused around the idea of spiritual energies that exist throughout the universe. From Taoism, we take the primary focus for the idea of Yin and Yang... the two diametrically opposed Forces of the universe. Everything from good and evil (as metaphysical concepts) to hot and cold temperatures are considered as being part of this, and it is from here we see the most prominent comparison to the light and dark sides of the Force, and the constant struggle for Balance within the Universe. There are also some parallels between The Living Force and the use of Qi in Chinese martial arts. In the more internal arts (such as Tai Chi, Hsing-Yi, Pa-Kua and Qigong), the maintenance and use of Qi is an essential element of training. Such Qi is sometimes referred to as Empty Force, meaning that it is not seen, but its effect can be felt with time and training. Some manifestations of special abilities are reported to have been attained by high-level kung-fu masters. Other, more rare examples of special abilities attributed to the Force are often catagorized as "paranormal activity". Some individuals show an apptitude for healing, telepathy, teleknesis, etc.

The Jedi refer to two "sides" of the Force, a dark side and a light side. This echoes the concept of Yin Yang in Eastern philosophy, but is not a straight translation, as the emotional dark side is denoted as a Force of evil by the Jedi. The dark side is not made up of specific "parts" or "abilities" of the Force: the dark and light sides of the Force exist inside of the life form which uses it, made from their emotions. A follower of the light side strives to live in harmony with those around him or her. Mutual trust, respect, and the ability to form alliances give the Jedi a distinct advantage. In contrast, a follower of the dark side is only interested in his or herself. To strike down a living creature out of anger, fear or another emotion is of the dark side. To refrain and clear one's self of these emotions is of the light side. Use of the dark side of the Force is forbidden within the Jedi Order.

Traditional Jedi are taught to keep the Force "in balance". They attempt to achieve this by denying the dark side — essentially "keeping balance" by denying balance, as they view dark side as "corruption". This involves the control of negative emotions such as aggression, anger, and hatred, since they can easily bring on acceptance of the dark side... "To become a Jedi, it is not the Force one must learn to control, but one's self". A Jedi strives to maintain control over their emotions instead of allowing negative emotions to control their actions. A Jedi acts when calm and at peace. In contrast, positive emotions such as compassion and courage nurture the light side of the Force. The Jedi Code compares such feelings and provides insight into the ethical use of the Force.

The "fictional" Jedi approach to emotions may be seen as one of the key reasons for their fall during the movies and the Knights of the Old Republic games. Abstaining from passion and love, many Jedi often fell under the sway of them when finally exposed. Unfamiliar with such emotions, they failed to see how they can come to dominate the personality and eventually became the personality through the imbalance wrought by over-compensation. The repression of the emotions merely caused the fall of a Jedi to be even more violent and complete. In this real universe, all sentient beings feel Emotions... the Jedi merely learn to maintain control and Balance.

The Heart of the Force
Octagon
Temple of the Jedi Force

PART 1

The center of the living force is the heart. The closer we get to heart the more understanding, knowledge, wisdom, and truth we gain. The closer we are to the heart the easier our life. It is within the center of the heart we gain mastery of our life in all it's aspects.

How do we know if we are actually getting closer to the heart of the force or if our very ego is deceiving us? Simple. Look at your life a year ago and look at it today. If there has been little change then you were following the path of the ego.

The ego is afraid of change and seeks to keep us from growing. It will provide us with all kinds of excuses of why we shouldn't or can't. If you look back however and have seen improvements in health, wealth, and wisdom then you are on the path to the heart, the center of the living force and no explanation is needed or can really be given of what that's been like.

PART 2

Also in the heart of the Force we realize that being alone is not an option. We are all connected in the heart of the Force. The closer we get to the heart the more we realize the truth in this. We begin to know when others need us. We begin to feel the hurt or joy within others no matter how far away from us they are. When we miss them, we visit them, and they visit us, in our dreams and meditations.

In the heart of the living force we have spiritual guides, teachers, friends, loved ones, councils, master teachers, master guides, and legions of souls who by their very nature love and care for us, just because, we are who we are. How can anyone feel lonely or unloved when surrounded by such a crowd?

May you continue to experience knowledge, wisdom, protection, and victory in the heart of the living force. *bows

What the Force is to Me
Shadouness
Temple of the Jedi Order

    I have been a Roman Catholic all my life (although not *strictly* Catholic; that's why I'm here). That means I am a Christian and I believe in the Holy Trinity: God the Father, God the Son, and God the Holy Spirit. Most of my understanding of the Holy Trinity I have derived from Leo Trese's book *The Faith Explained* (a gift from my uncle, a priest of the Congregation of the Mission (C.M.), St. Vincent de Paul's congregation).

    However, like most Catholics, as I imagine, I have had my periods of doubt, periods of losing faith (even St. Therese of Calcutta as she's written in her journals). During one of these periods, I have mused on the possibility that God may not exist, but somehow experienced the "reality" of His power. In short, I doubted God's existence, but believed in His power.

    I have referred to this Power as "Fate" (which I differentiate from "destiny"), and also "Power", but I now refer to it as "God's Will".

    Regarding God's Will, I see it as something not apart from God Himself. I believe that God being a perfect Entity (if I could refer to Him as that) is a Being whose every manifestation of any aspect of Him is Himself in whole. For example (and strictly only as an example), if we can imagine Him to have a scent or a sound or size, whenever we smell Him, or hear or see His size, we are not only experiencing his scent or sound or mass, but are experiencing Him as a whole, although we may not realize it. He is complete, He is Unity. As another example, when He talks, *He says Himself*, and it becomes real. And this real created thing or event is Him as well. (In light of this, everything He has created therefore is essentially Himself.)

    Then in this sense, when I talk about God's Will, I also talk about God Himself, *not just an aspect* of Him. However, why do I say "God's Will" instead of straight out "God"? Because my experience of Him is limited, and this term that I use is describing this limitation -- i.e., I experience *God* as *His Will*. For example, I may probably experience Him as comfort or forgiveness and call Him the "God of Joy" or "God the Merciful". "God is Love" is one such aspect, I suppose.

    When I say that the Force is the manifestation of God's Will, I am more inclined to regard it as not really God as the Holy Trinity, Who is a being, but as an event -- an event that happens within God or outside of Him (if such events occur), and that *affects* me or *acts upon* me and most other things (if not everything else).

I see the Force therefore not as a being (God) but as an event or an action (God's Will) -- something that happens, something that has the potential of happening, or something that makes things happen, whether inside or outside the realm of time. As I believe that I am an instrument of the Force, as the universe dictates, then let the Force be done through me.

LOYALTY TO THE JEDI CODE

the original Jedi Code and the Skywalker Jedi Creed do not belong to the Jedi Community, however many of our orders use it as the basis of our teachings. The Jedi Code and Skywalker Jedi Creed are copyrighted to Lucas Films and as we understand it Disney.

THE JEDI CODE: AN ANALYSIS
Katie Mock
California Jedi

The ideals of the Jedi laid out in the code are simple, yet extremely difficult to practice, and meaning is conveyed not through the words themselves, but through the contrast of word pairs. Words have power; if we go about changing them to suit our means instead of trying to learn through the process of analysis, we rob ourselves of a learning opportunity and are left with a text that yields little if we meditate on it.

Granted, the text in this case was written by someone as a piece of fiction. Maybe he or she put thought into it, maybe they simply thought it sounded cooler this way, but either way it still can act as a valuable tool and reminder of what being a Jedi is about. Besides, we who call ourselves Jedi don't really balk at taking inspiration from fiction, now do we?

The core of the code consists of contrasting word pairs: no X, Y. Emotion is opposed with peace, ignorance with knowledge, passion with serenity, chaos with harmony, and death with the Force. In the usual fashion of these essays, I'll go pair by pair and explain what meaning can be derived from the comparison.

Emotion is something innate to human nature; all of us have it, and that is a normal natural *good* thing. So why does the code say "there is no emotion"? The answer lies in the juxtaposition of it's pairing. The opposite of emotion is apathy, yet the code says "there is no emotion, there is peace". If peace is taken to be the opposite, then the word emotion isn't talking about our basic and vital ability to feel and react emotionally, but a serious kind of emotional turmoil: emotions at 'war' instead of at 'peace'. This line doesn't tell Jedi to repress their emotions, but to bring them into peaceful balance and interaction with their being. This is the first line and one of the most vital; Jedi are called on to be peacemakers and resolvers of conflict, and objectivity and clarity of mind are essential to that calling. So many people get hung up on the idea of emotional repression, when the code is just stressing inner peace and emotional awareness. We must be aware of our internal emotional leanings, turbulences, and biases in order to come to terms with them and do our job.

The next line is easier to understand; a Jedi should seek knowledge and not hide in ignorance or let ignorance cloud his or her judgment. If we don't know all the facts, we make uninformed decisions, which can lead to disaster and unintended consequences. The more aware and informed we are, the easier it becomes to interact with and influence the world around us for the better. The juxtaposition of ignorance and knowledge stresses that a Jedi should be constantly learning and seeking to convert ignorance to knowledge and understanding. We are never done training.

The following line juxtaposes passion and serenity. Since these are not words that see regular usage or are usually tied to a particular connotation (such as passion is with romantic love), a dictionary definition should shed some light on the difference between passion and serenity. Passion is defined as "any powerful or compelling emotion, such as love or hate", while serenity is defined as being "calm, peaceful or tranquil; unruffled; clear, fair". Although this is similar to the first line it is important not to conflate the two, for they have different messages. The first line is about the importance of emotional balance and peace. This line is about how to deal with the surges and tempests of emotion that our species is prone to. Whether it is love, hate, obsession, greed, or sorry, we often cannot help but be affected by them. A passion is an emotion that can either fire and motivate you to greater heights and accomplishments, or can drown you. Serenity is not being overwhelmed or drowned by those emotions. Again, serenity is not the natural opposite of passion, but an instruction on how to keep passion in the realm of the vital and motivating as opposed to letting it rule your life. If we are sailors on the sea, passion is the wind and waves. Without them, we sit and go nowhere, slowly dying of thirst and hunger, unable to reach our destination. However if we cannot ride them effectively, we will sink and drown. Serenity, the act of being 'unruffled' and clear minded is our boat and our sail. With serenity we can navigate the driving power and joy of our passion without drowning in it. Serenity can cut the damaging power of sorrow and hatred as the rudder cuts the waves, and channel the vital power of joy and love as a sail channels the wind.

Chaos and harmony is, at least to me, fairly straightforward. The world seems to be a chaotic place, but it is not. Everything affects something, which affects something else, creating an intricate web of cause and effect. We may not see the web, or understand how our lives have been shaped by the forces of the universe, but we are all connected through the force. Chaos means disconnection: a disjointed and unpredictable world. But there is no chaos, there is harmony. It is up to a Jedi to make connections among the apparent chaos of the world, to pull together people and ideas and to see the harmony in the natural and inherent chaos of both the universe and humanity.

There is no death, there is the Force. This is the core of the code. Everything is the force; all our emotions, our physical beings, the universe around us. We are all connected and the same. There is a Carl Sagan quote that say "we are the way that the cosmos can know itself". For indeed the cosmos is in us, literally and energetically. In this way, there is no death, only a transmutation, a fading of what we think of as our Selves into the Living Force.

As a whole, the code requires analysis and focus, but that is how it should be I think. Its purpose is not as 'rules' for the Jedi, but a guide, one that helps us keep in mind the most basic principles of the Jedi and helps us overcome the hurdles common to all humankind. The code has a fictional source, just as our inspirational Jedi do, but they both have value. They are not to be worshiped or codified or made sacred, but treated as useful tools for betterment and learning that we can take pride in.

Analysis of the Code and Creed
By Knight Ziphin
Temple of the Jedi Force

The Jedi Code

When we allow emotion in to our lives we take the risk of being influenced by it. By removing emotion from the situation we are able to realize that the situation is neither good nor bad. These are emotions we attach to a situation. By removing out emotion we are able to find peace because what is simply is and our emotions cannot change that. For example many years ago I had a person who I thought was my friend try to shoot me with a revolver. I knew the revolver was loaded and was honestly in fear of my life. For the following couple years I hated him for doing such a terrible and bad thing to me since he could have killed me and honestly i know he intended to. But the fact of the matter is simply that the act was not terrible or bad it was simply the way that the interaction between him and I happened to go. He thought he was in the right and I knew I was in the right. As a Jedi we have to learn to forgo emotion in order to obtain peace.

Lack of knowledge is ignorance. I choose to know everything that my brain will absorb and constantly try to absorb more. If a person does not seek knowledge then they will never be able to escape their position in life. Every day we are faced with challenges that require us to use our knowledge of the world around us to make choices that impact our future. In the previous example I stated that I knew the revolver was loaded. I knew that information based on my knowledge of firearms and how they work. Knowledge is one of the main tools we have that keeps us safe and allows us to keep those around us safe. If a Jedi does not constantly strive for knowledge his ignorance will be his undoing.

Passion is an extremely powerful and reckless emotion. Passion is an emotion that once it has a grip on you will sneak up and over power you without you realizing its happening. Many people become blinded by passion which leads them down a dark path of destruction. As a Jedi this is a path that is self-serving and will only bring you pain. Serenity is the ideal state for a Jedi. When a person lives in serenity they are calm and capable of using the knowledge that they have obtained. Since there is no emotion there is peace a Jedi must always keep passion in check and where ever possible remove it from there life.

We are born in to a world of constant decay. Even before conception our cells are starting to age and is gradually breaking down. Yet we have the ability to reach out beyond our heart, mind and body. We have the ability to touch people with our essence. While a body is a vessel that carries our essence it in no way can contain it. While our physical bodies can be destroyed our essence is made of the force it is not capable of being destroyed. So there is no death there is only the life essence of the living force.

Chaos is destructive, unpredictable, disorganized and confusing. Hurricanes are considered to be a chaotic even since we do not know where it's going, what is going to destroy, what will be left alone. As a Jedi I am to be a servant to those in need. I will never be capable of serving anyone it I am so disorganized that I don't know what I'm doing and likewise if I am confusing to those around my they will not trust me or respect my advice. This is where harmony comes in to play. A harmonious person is pleasant, consistent and orderly. It is much easier to listen to advice if it has order and is consistent and even more accepted if the person is easy to like. As a Jedi I am an ambassador of peace and a servant who helps others along their journey, and the only way to do this is to live a harmonious life. Beyond our interactions with people living in harmony with the living force helps us keep our emotions at bay, which allows us to find peace in a chaotic world. And since we are of the force and shall return to it again being in harmony with it now can help guide us along our own paths.

Fear is a dark emotion that can crush and destroy a person from the inside out. When we are gripped by fear it prevents us from thinking clearly and sometimes at all. If we are living our lives without allowing emotion to control us and prevent us from finding peace and we are seeking out knowledge and living in harmony with the living force then we have nothing to fear. We know our future is to return to the living force. Since we fear not and we only wish to serve then we should live boldly. Where others back down or cower in fear we push forward courageously utilizing the knowledge we have obtained. If courage comes from the mind and spirit of a person and their ability to overcome difficulties and pain then we as Jedi who feel the force around us and feel it flow thru us do not live by the mind alone as we are masters over it.

A foolish person does not use forethought or caution when they act upon a situation meaning that they just rush into things and don't think about the recourses of their actions beforehand. Instead we as Jedi think about the outcome of our actions and its impact on those around us. Instead we have gained knowledge of our world and of the living force. We continue to do so; on a daily basis it is when we utilize this knowledge after we have determined the consequences that separates us from the fools. A person who uses there knowledge only after realizing the outcome is a wise make. An example would be as follows. A foolish man sees a bank robbery in process. He is carrying a fire arm for self-defense. Knowing that he knows how to shoot he does and kills the bank robber. But what he didn't know since he choose only to act on impulse is that there were 3 robbers and one had a hostage. The foolish man not only jeopardized his own life but has now killed a hostage by his actions and potentially all of the people in the bank. The man of wisdom on the other hand would have thought to check for additional robbers/hostages and would have realized that he could not tackle this task alone. Now obviously this could play out 1000+ ways but the point is we have to be wise in our decisions and utilize the knowledge we have in order to help and serve those around us.

The Jedi Creed

I am a Jedi, an instrument of peace. Where there is hatred I shall bring love; where there is injury, pardon; where there is doubt, faith; where there is despair, hope; where there is darkness, light; and where there is sadness, joy. I am a Jedi. I shall never seek so much to be consoled as to console; to be understood as to understand; to be loved as to love; for it is in giving that we receive; it is in pardoning that we are pardoned; and it is in dying that we are born to eternal life. The Force is always with me, for I am a Jedi.

An instrument is something you use for a purpose and our purpose as Jedi is to bring peace. We can bring peace to a person's soul, there heart; we can give them peace of mind. In order for use to bring peace we must first carry peace with in our selves; seeking always to be at peace. This is our driving purpose then by the call of our very nature we will help people to overcome the hatred they harbor and help them replace that hatred with love. But we must always remember that in order for use to find peace we must abandon our hatred and replace it with love. Like the personal story I told about the revolver. I hated my so called friend for trying to kill me for years, but i was never at peace. The hatred raged through me and I tried to taint it with drugs (which didn't work), but one day I let it all go and can honestly say I love him for it.

Being instrumental in a person's life will require us to forgive those who have hurt us and help those who have been hurt to forgive as well. This can be extremely hard to do if we allow our emotions to control our thoughts which is why we must look past the emotion and find peace knowing that what happened happened and there is nothing we can do to change that. Once you get to this point it is much easier to forgive.

Doubt prevents you from moving forward. No progress leads us in to frustration and even anger. Imagine you sit down to watch a movie and it comes on and says loading. How long could you honestly sit there without getting frustrated because the progress bar hasn't moved for the 25% mark for 20 minutes. You start to doubt that you will ever get to watch the movie. Often times in life we are faced with the 25% progress bar so it is important that we remember that if we have faith we will get to watch the movie. In my example the 25% doesn't move for 20 min. but 30 seconds later it jumps from 25% to 100% and starts playing. Just like life it's about patience and faith.

Despair is often times felt when it seems like life cannot go on. We feel it when loved ones die, we lose our possessions, ect. Despair is a deep deep hole that once we sink in to its extremely hard to get out of. Two years ago my best friend and his wife found out they were pregnant with their third boy. He lived on this earth for exactly 26 minutes and 12 seconds. I could see the despair in my friends face. I lacked the words to express to him how much I was sorry for his loss. I attended the wake of his baby son. I watched as other expressed verbally their sorrow and could not find a single word to say to him. The only thing I could do was give him a hug. It was about 2 months ago when we had a memorial birthday party for his baby, and he told me that my words of compassion spoke louder to him that anyone elces. Funny I don't remember saying anything.... He told me that my friendship and lack of words gave him hope. That if I could feel that same sorrow he felt and manage to still be there that there was still something to hold on to. I guess my point is that we bring hope to people by just being there for them.

I like to think that the force is a mist of bight glowing light that surrounds us and flows through us and like despair the light we give off can penetrate the darkness of a person's life. My friend di not recover from the loss of his child quickly and honestly is not fully recovered even as of yet. There were several months where he did nothing but climb in a bottle of whatever he could find, and I made it a priority to be present when he did so. Because I knew and so did he that me just being in the same room as him pushed the darkness that tried to encompass his heart away. That experience has changed him but every time I see him his face fills with joy.

In counseling my fiend through the death of his baby I realized that I was touched just as much as he was. I actually dealt with some of my issues about losing my grandfather Jim. Once I was able to understand his position I was able to understand my own and how I truly viewed death.

I love my wife and I have found that the more I love her the more she has grown to love me, which makes me only love her that much more. I stopped seeking love when I married her. I know that love is often thought of as a two way road but honestly it's not a 50/50 relationship is 100/100 relationship. I give it my all and expect nothing from her. I get back whatever she gives me. And when she gives back more I step my game up. I think that we should look at all relationships this way. When I stopped expecting things from my friendships they became stronger just like my marriage. I have found that it is better to love then to be loved.

Part of it being better to love then to be loved is that if you truly love someone then you are incapable of holding a grudge and by the very nature of your relationship you have forgiven them or given them pardon. Most people when forgiven are likely to forgive back as well. Often times we find those who will not pardon but those people are usually not in your life long enough for it to be a problem. When you learn to forgive people it lifts a weight from your heart mind and soul that opens you up for great things in your own life as well as in others.

I can feel the force extending beyond my body moving in the world around me. I know that beyond death there is more. You can see it in the faces of the people you pass on the street verses the faces of those who have passed. The force lives and flows through each one of us.

Jedi Creed 101 Assignment
StormyKat
Institute for Jedi Realist Studies

Initial Thoughts on the Jedi Creed.

I have been thinking about it for months actually; even before I started the Creed 101 class. To me the creed is grounding. When I look at it, it reminds me that I am working towards being a Jedi. Which, in turn, means I am working to expand and grow beyond myself. Beyond that I am not sure I feel much of anything. When I contemplate it, I try focusing on the last word of each line-- peace, knowledge, serenity, the Force--to help bring me back to the now.

Responding line by line was hard for me. I am not sure if this is what I WANT the lines to mean, or what I actually think they mean. If that makes any sense.

There is no emotion, there is peace.

I take this to mean we are more than emotions. We need to find peace within-or perhaps beyond, our emotions. We can chose how to respond to our emotions. When someone cuts me off in traffic after a long, difficult day at work my emotional response might be to honk and curse at that person, calling them a jerk. or I might just say "jerk" or "ass" outloud. I have a choice how I am going to respond. I also have a choice how to proceed from there. Maybe I have the more emotional response, afterwards I have the choice to hold on to those emotions, to get angry and aggressive in my driving, cursing at everyone. Or I can let it go. I can acknowledge my emotions and move on.

There is no ignorance, there is knowledge.

Every opportunity is a chance for learning. Don't know something, ask! Someone else doesn't know something? Try to teach them. Educate, learn, grow, expand your mind and your horizon.

There is no passion, there is serenity.

Try not to act in moments of passion. Try to find a calm, peaceful place before acting. It relates back to the first line, about emotions, we need to try to think beyond our emotions.

There is no death, there is the Force.

This was perhaps the easiest one for me. Since we are all part of the Force and the Force is part of every living thing, there is no death. We may die in a physical sense but our essence, our spirit and our essence will live on. Maybe it will take different forms---I will nourish the grass if I am buried. My body will feed other life forms, etc. But I will live on. My spirit will live in another form too.

Life Lessons of a Jedi: The Loss of One Dear and How it Works Through the Jedi Code and Jedi Creed
Neaj Pa Bol
Temple of the Jedi Order

In Memory of my Husband Robert, who stood by me in my Journey into Jediism, whom I see as well as a Jedi. This is for you. You believed in me and now I am alone physically, but I have your memory to help me share this with others.... Patty

Taking a step back and re-evaluating things in my life is one thing I did with the loss of my husband. It was not done out of thinking my faith, my beliefs or any thing on that line was not to see if everything was right or wrong. Grieving the loss of someone very dear to one; a parent, a spouse or even a child, does make one ask questions, searching for more meaning to the why's, etc. It's human nature to think, even when something sad happens. My path was where to incorporate my beliefs into what was happening to me and around me. What my Christian beliefs would be, what my belief in Jediism would be. How do I plant these seeds of emotion into that belief system for myself. Yes, a little selfish on my part, these thoughts also do affect those around me as well, but it is my emotions, my grief.

I have found that the more I have studied the Code and what I am going though, I see out there that too many Jedi loose track of what it really means. We're not meant to be rocks or concrete and as hard as one in life. Emotions are human and we are meant to feel them. That is how we're defined as Empathic beings. It is when we let those substances rule the day and become so uncontrollable, that's when we fail the code....

Now uncontrollable feelings or an emotion does not mean that we are against the code or not following it, adhering to it, etc. The depth of a loss runs not just in our hearts or minds. It runs deep into our souls of who we are. As Human beings, this is what makes us such a life form, similar to each other, yet different as well.

Now, this is just my point of view in this matter, but it may help others to understand life within the code when dealing with emotional issues...

Each line of the code has more than one directional point. One is for the Jedi themselves and one is the view to help others.

For Review, (my personal choice of the code is the 5 statements)

The Jedi Code

There is no emotion; there is peace.
There is no ignorance; there is knowledge.
There is no passion; there is serenity.
There is no chaos; there is harmony.
There is no death; there is the Force.

Let's take the first line: There is no emotion; there is peace.

If we were single minded, closed to anything other than just what the words that are written.... Well we all would fail... This is a statement of balance as I have learned. When one is balanced in their emotions, one can find peace. In that peace and balanced emotions, we can understand others in their time of need...

This line does not place where one would be if there was something that was emotional. But if you look at this, like in a Humanistic way. \"There is no Emotion,\" one could believe that we feel emotions but we do not let them dictate our actions and thus, \"there is peace\" with the understanding of emotions, living with them and learning to handle them in the right way, one will find peace....

In The Grieving process, it takes time; it is not over night. We must give ourselves the time to adjust, be upset or as they say, even angry. Yell at the world that you are sad and hurting, missing the one you have lost. Even just sitting down at moments when you need to, to just cry and let yourself feel the pain of loss and cry of that loss.

When we do not let those feelings emerge and do what is natural, we tend to bottle them up, later on, down the road we become Apathetic and then we can not help others when we can not feel...

Let's take the second line: There is no ignorance; there is knowledge.

This line speaks about one seeking to gain further knowledge so that ignorance can not be an excuse to not help others or ones self. Ignorance is not being less educated, it is also learned and shared knowledge that may not have been passed down from one to another. Knowledge is where it all comes into play. Handed and passed down information's and teachings, learned knowledge by study and understanding. With Jedi, this all comes into place in the search for knowledge. That is why one starts as a youngling, then apprentice and then a knight.... Then through all, one still seeks further knowledge through the same methods as well as learned lessons throughout life. Even Masters continue to seek further knowledge by experience and learning. It's a cycle that when it starts continues on throughout life.

Let's take the third line: There is no passion; there is serenity.

Passion is an emotion, a strong one. It goes beyond Compassion. When one is said to be passionate about something, it means they strongly believe in something. Here we once again fall into where emotions play a part in life. To have \"no passion\" suggests that one has compassion for something but knows where to draw the line and not get obsessed with it. Once that understanding is learned, then the final line: there is serenity is truthful...

Everything we do, we will find strong emotions toward that subject or topic. As long as we keep from obsessing or feeling too much for it and noting else, serenity can be found.

Let's take the fourth line: There is no chaos; there is harmony.

Chaos is a word for complete loss of control or organization. Simply, learning to take things one at a time, learn them and practice them, keep your mind focused clearly, so that you can organize yourself, one can find harmony. But remember, in all things, it takes time and does not happen over night. One must practice and learn each and every day and apply the lessons each and every day.

Let's take the fifth line: There is no death; there is the Force.

Death is a natural thing. We heard this spoke by Yoda in the Ep. III to Anakin. But it is inevitable. I remember my Nursing instructor telling me, that dealing with death, one must come to terms with his or her own mortality. None of us want it, none of us can escape it we must come to terms in our own ways. Every religion has its belief that there is a Heaven, Paradise, Eternal Plain, etc. The Jedi call it the Force. How every you choose the words, it will still happen. But once again, we see, that emotion has its hand in this as well....

Everything in the code ultimately has to do with emotions, no way around it. But the lesson I have learned the greatest of is this, as all things are, one must let them happen to learn from and be a part of. If we try not to in any way, we trully can not understand or live by the code. Let alone truly be human to help others as well....

In Ep. I Obi-wan says to Gui-Gonn, \"Not again Master, If you would only follow the code you would be on the Council.\" Gui-Gonn's response was, \"I will do what I must Obi-Wan.\"

In Obi-Wan's view Gui-Gonn was letting his emotions for young Anakin interfere with good judgment, yet, Gui-Gonn was actually following the code by allowing the Force to directed him.

No matter what each Jedi perceives, the understanding truly becomes one of your own. But the lessons in life that you will come up against, using the code to help you will often bring you back to one word of thought; Emotion.

It is in everything that we do, are and will be, no matter if we choose it or not...
Even in the Creed you will find it refers quite often to that word as well....
EMOTION

The Jedi Creed (Temple of the Jedi Order)

I believe in the Living Force of Creation;
I am a Jedi, an instrument of peace;
Where there is hatred I shall bring love;
Where there is injury, pardon;
Where there is doubt, faith;
Where there is despair, hope;
Where there is darkness, light;
And where there is sadness, joy.
I am a Jedi.
I shall never seek so much to be consoled as to console;
To be understood as to understand;
To be loved as to love;
For it is in giving that we receive;
In pardoning that we are pardoned;
And in dying that we are born to eternal life.
The Living Force of Creation is always with me; I am a Jedi.

May The Force Be With You Always And Forever

The First Year..... A Shared Lesson...
Neaj Pa Bol
Temple of the Jedi Order

Soon it will be the first anniversary of my husband Bob's passing. I have learned and experienced so many things since that day. My open letter to him is beginning to look like the beginnings of a book. There were so many things that have happened or I have had to learn in this new life after our time together. Hospice has been there to guide and support myself and Shannon through all this, knowing full well that the steps would be so much like baby steps for me and the physical, emotional and mental feelings that I would experience would be at times overwhelming for me.

I know that friends with good intentions mean well when they say to get on with my life, but to be honest, it is not as simple as the words sound. Every holiday had it's own set of things that I would have to deal with, just like our anniversary and Bob's birthday as well as mine, Shannon's and Zackary's. And soon, the arrival of Shannon's second baby, Ayden. I tried to be strong and still do, but, even though it does get a little easier, it has been a real tough experience.

Married at 16, I've never really known what it was like to be on my own as an Single Adult. So, being on my own now it is a whole new world for me. I find myself trying to figure out what the next step would be a times, find the things that I use to enjoy to relax or just have \"My\" time is stressful at times when trying to figure out what I want...Read, write, listen to music or wishing I had my Bass guitar that Bob made me give up. After being together for 27 years, all the rough times. hard times, bad times and all the good times is all I have left to remember and hold on to. Dealt with the remarks and comments as well as the looks when it came to the age difference between Bob and I, not as bad as it is today or the nutzy way people look at people being together or approaching to be together when there's an age difference.

There have been the days that the depression and missing him so much, I would just be zapped of all my energy or episodes of just crying that exhausted me. No matter how strong you try to remain, love is really an unfathomable thing. You can't measure it, or try to figure out how deep it is, it's not meant to have boundries.

So, since the first year is almost here, all I can say is this. Don't try to undermine or evaluate what a persons feelings are when they are going through the steps of loss. There are no set rules or steps that are specific when you loose a loved one. There is no set time or how long when one should deal with grief, it's not over night, it's not one month, etc. It comes down to when you in your heart is able to take the next steps.

When writing this, I've taken a step back and looked outside myself and thought about Human emotion and then while watching a litter of wolf-dog cubs we have, I observed emotions in them. They say there are many things that separate humans and animals, but emotions even run in them. I watched the mother and how she is tender yet stern with the cubs. How she mothers them by licking and caressing them. We know they can show pain and sadness, yet when I look into their eyes, my mind tells me there is so much more. Intelligence, inquisitiveness, mischievousness, playfulness and more... We are not the only ones that feel things...

Things that took time to learn and appreciate, yet most of that was with another that is now gone and how I appreciate all of that so much more.
For my Jedi Friends.....
For the Jedi part of this, one may say that I am not following the code, yet I disagree and I will explain why...

Being Jedi does not mean you can not feel. Emotions is what is essential in being human. When we loose complete control of our emotions to the point that they dictate or rule everything we do and cannot pull back and restrain ourselves is when that part of the code as a Jedi have failed. In my moments of dealing with grief, it did not get to out of control. Grief allows one to express the loss. Knowing that it is normal to grieve in a world where we do feel things is not a bad thing, nor against the code. We live in a world where we have been brought up as humans with feelings. Even the fictional Jedi had feelings, its how we manifest those feelings and what do in our lives with those reactions.

To say strictly no emotion would be saying Jedi were apathetic, (without emotion). That is not what Jedi are. Emotion is not just sadness or grief or depression, there is happiness, glee, joy, etc. So the Code in general speaks out to the Jedi, reminding he or she that through all these things we experience in life Jedi seek the enlightenment of all, knowing where to draw that line to maintain a balance between all things, but with reverence, respect, knowledge and insight to find that balance in true Peace, continued gaining of

Knowledge, to live in Harmony, reactions that are calm and with Serenity and of all things, the never ending balance within the Force for all time....

One can say I showed weakness by my grief of the loss of my husband, maybe so. My only reply that I can make is, as a loving wife of almost 27 years, to not be effected by my husbands death means that I would not have been true to who I am and to experience all the things because of that loss, to grow more each day to be that better person I choose to be.

There are many things as Jedi that are the other unseen things to add to the constant knowledge one seeks.

Ideals Of A Jedi:

1. Respect yourself. Without self-respect, you will never be able to respect anything.
2. Respect life. Life is what gives a Jedi his/her power, therefore it is to be cherished always.
3. Respect others. Respect all those around you, for they are part of the Force. Even enemies are part of the Force.
4. Respect Nature. \"Intelligent life\" is not the only life, and through the Force a Jedi may learn sources of wisdom from many places, not all seen as \"intelligent\"
5. Respect death. Death is part of the Force, since everything happens in cycles. The cycle of one life affects another, that is the way of things. The way of the Force.
6. Respect the Dark Side. He who does not respect his greatest enemy will BECOME his greatest enemy. With respect comes, objectivity, insight, seeing how things are done and how to oppose them quickly and decisively.

Jedi Behavior: (In Brief)

Self-Discipline, Conquer Arrogance, Conquer Overconfidence, Conquer Defeatism, Conquer Stubbornness, Conquer Recklessness, Conquer Curiosity, Conquer Aggression, Responsibility,
Practice Honesty, Honor Your Promises, Honor your Teacher, Honor the Law, Honor Life, Public Service, Duty to the Government, Render Aid, Defend the Weak, Provide Support.
(Ideals & Behavior, These words taken from a lesson by D. M. Thompson, Jedi Master)

Exercise Five: The Other Codes
Amelia Long
Institute for Jedi Realist Studies

Odan-Urr Version add-on "There is no chaos; there is harmony"
Assignment: Look for some physical clutter in your life. When you see it, confront it. Tell yourself, 'There is no chaos, there is harmony.' And then work to find a home for everything in that pile of clutter. If it's not serving a purpose, recycle it or throw it away. Keep telling yourself 'There is no chaos there, is harmony.' Once you have finished take some time to use the space and see how you feel.
Please take the time to record your thoughts and experiences on this in your journal.

    This is actually a perfect assignment right now as it draws closer and closer to that time where I move back to the USA from Germany. In such a short time, so much has happened which has caused much chaos to enter my life, and I have had to tackle these issues one at a time in order to bring...well, 'order' back into my life. Or as the author of the course wrote: "Find a place for all the clutter in your life."

    Moving to another Country is stressful, especially when you are trying to do things as someone who needs help via the military but is a non-dependent because you are not married to the person you came to the Country for. So, naturally, things have been stressful.

    The first bit of chaos came with getting my plane ticket. Originally the Army said that they could get me a ticker for around $300 and I could fly with my partner so long as we got the signature from the Commander. The people said this should not be an issue, but it was. The Commander said that it was too much liability and too much paperwork and refused to sign. So, instead of paying $300 for a plane ticket back home, I had to pay $870, and it was my fault for not budgeting it because I just assumed everything would be okay. So that was a major flaw on my part. Naturally, I just took a deep breath and accepted it how it was. I knew that I should not have assumed things would work, and merely told myself there was no reason to be stressed. I had the money and would just save more on the next paycheck. Everything was going to be okay.

    It was actually my partner that ended up getting the most stressed out after this little ordeal and I found that I was easily able to brush this off. To me, it was not a big thing, something I would not have been able to do over a year ago. A year ago I would have freaked out, cried and complained, but, I merely breathed in, thanked my partner for trying her best, bought my ticket for back home, and continued to be happy because I would soon be back on familiar soil.

More stress and clutter came with my moving...I had to ship my stuff back, and while this ended up working out great, there did come a point where we were not sure if the Army would be able to ship my things. We had to pull some strings and for awhile I was frantic. I lost sleep, barely ate because I had so much stuff I would either have to pay to ship or throw away.

But eventually, I took action and came up with a plan B and made sure that no matter what, my things would get home.

The thing is, I do stress...but I don't let the stress keep me from solving problems. I do not let it completely wreck me, and I continue to push forward, out of the shadows, into the light where things are clear and sunny. A deep breath and then the making of a plan is how I handle most things. Not only has moving been stressful, but as usual, my relationship is stressful. While originally I had plans of being married once home, those are not going to go through as planned. It has really messed up some other plans I had in place, making me have to rethink all the things I had mapped out before, it left things scrambled, and, it had me in pieces for a couple of weeks. t was only this week that I finally decided it was time to stop.

I could see that a lot of things that had been stressing me out were actually caused by myself (once I took the time to really lay down and analyze things). Laying down and collecting my thoughts, I could see the landslide effect happening as my actions caused a chain reaction of things to happen, all of them coming back to hurt me in the end.

But, once this was finally realized, I could calm myself down, and again, make a plan. It was time to clean up the clutter from the fallen pile and reorganize them again, stack them more neatly this time and hope things don't fall. We are human, and I feel this is all we can ever do but to keep stacking things differently in hopes that they stand firm and steady, and ultimately they do not fall.

I agree that were we to say there cannot be chaos in the lives of a Jedi then not a single person could call themselves a Jedi. But it is also true that chaos leads to destruction, and therefore it has to be met with something to stop it in its tracks before it destroys ones body, ones mind; before it destroys that very person inside and out.

I'm not really sure what the exercise expected other than this...other than how I deal with stress. It said to clean the clutter and this is how I handle things. A deep breath, warm drink, some time in a dark room to think and relax, and then a plan. I will forever keep moving forward. I refuse to sit still and become stagnant.

The Jedi Code
By Jedi Shea
Temple of the Jedi Force

"There is no emotion, there is peace."

Many people mistake this for meaning that the Jedi cannot feel emotion, that it's forbidden for a Jedi to feel emotion. That's not true. Feeling emotion, feeling angry or sad or happy or what not is a part of being human. Controlling your emotions or keeping them bottled up inside isn't good for you. It can stress your out and create a lot of turmoil inside of you, so much that it will eventually cause you to have some sort of nervous breakdown or something of that nature. So to prevent that from happening, we need to, instead of bottling the emotions up inside, instead release them. We need to understand that it's okay to feel emotion, its okay to feel angry or upset every once in a while. If you're sad and all you want to do is curl up in a ball and cry, go ahead. If you're angry and want to scream off the top of your lungs into a pillow, go ahead. Its perfectly normal. However, when you're done, don't stay in that state of mind. Pick up the pieces, put them back together, leave those emotions behind, and continue moving forward with your life. Leave those negative emotions behind and replace them with happiness and joy. If you do this, then your life will be so much better and peaceful.

"There is no ignorance, there is knowledge."

There is always going to be ignorance in the world. When we die, we are still going to have at least some ignorance. Reason being is because there is more knowledge that the universe has to offer than we can take in in our entire lifetimes. So yes, when we die, we will still be somewhat ignorant. There is nothing we can do to change that. One thing we can change is how ignorant we are. To do that, we must continue to learn all throughout our lives. Some say that once you finish high school or college, that you don't need to learn anymore, that you already know all that you need to know. That's not true. There will always be opportunities to learn more and grow throughout your life. We must take advantage of those opportunities because the information we gain can help us in the long run.

"There is no passion, there is serenity."

Just like with ignorance, there will always be passion, we will always have something or someone that we are passionate about. And just like with emotion, its okay to feel it, its okay have passion. It is a form of emotion after all. But here's the thing. Passion is a very strong and intense emotion. In some cases its so strong and intense that its uncontrollable. If it gets to that point, if it gets too intense, then it can negatively impact the person and they are going to be in a much worse state of mind then they were to begin with. So to prevent this, we need to keep our passion from getting to be too intense. That doesn't mean that we have to get rid of it completely. Life I said, its okay to feel passionate about something. Its a part of life, its a part of being human. We just need to make sure it doesn't get too intense. Instead of letting it bring us to a chaotic state of mind, we need it at a point that will allow us to stay at a calm and serene state, if you know what I mean.

"There is no chaos, there is harmony."

    I don't think we are ever going to put an end to chaos completely. Even if all wars were to end, and we went 100, 200 years without there ever being a war, there would still be at least some chaos within countries: crime, protests, even disputes between friends. I know that that we are not going to be able to put an end to all this completely. However we can minimize it by working together, helping each other out, and creating a sense of harmony and peace between each other.

"There is no death, there is the Force."

    We never truly die. Our bodies may die, but our souls and energy continue to live on in the force, places we've lived, places we liked to go, etc. We will continue to live on in the hearts of those we knew and as memories and in stories that our friends and family will tell to people that they know. In reality, there is no death. Our bodies may die, they may not live forever, but our souls and energy are immortal, they will continue to live on forever.

Heartland Jedi Creed
Heartland Jedi, 2012

I am a Jedi, a guardian of peace.
I acknowledge all life is sacred.
I choose to serve others,
I use my training to defend and protect, never to assault.
I will present a professional demeanor.
I will be mindful of my thoughts and control my actions.
I know myself and am aware of my surroundings.
I will approach all situations holistically.
I will seek knowledge with the understanding of self-ignorance.
I will find peace in the midst of a storm.
It is through understanding of the Force I am transformed.

Jedi Creed
Used By Temple of the Jedi Order and Temple of the Jedi Force
2005

I am a Jedi, an instrument of peace.
Where there is hatred I shall bring love;
Where there is injury, pardon;
Where there is doubt, faith;
Where there is despair, hope;
Where there is darkness, light;
And where there is sadness, joy.
I am a Jedi.

I shall never seek so much to be consoled as to console;
To be understood as to understand;
To be loved as to love;
For it is in giving that we receive;
It is in pardoning that we are pardoned;
And it is in dying that we are born to eternal life.
The Force is always with me, for I am a Jedi.

Jedi of the Noble Order Creed
Rick Baker
Jedi of the Noble Order, 2015

I am a Jedi, an instrument of peace;
I choose to serve others,
I use my training to defend and protect, never to assault....
I will present a professional demeanor.
I will be mindful of my thoughts and control my actions.
I know myself and am aware of my surroundings.
I will approach all situations holistically.
I will seek knowledge with the understanding of self-ignorance.
I will find peace in the midst of a storm.
It is through understanding of the Force I am transformed.

Where there is hatred I shall bring love;
Where there is injury, pardon;
Where there is doubt, faith;
Where there is despair, hope;
Where there is darkness, light;
And where there is sadness, joy.
The Force is with me always, for I am a Jedi.

Rivan's Code of the Jedi Way
Rivan Elan, 2010
Coelescere Enclave

There is emotion, there is peace,
there is passion that can be felt in the midst of peace,
peace is not a lie but it is rare.

There is indeed ignorance but there is knowledge in the midst of ignorance
and ignorance in the midst of knowledge.

Through Passion I can gain strength
and yet in that strength I do not see as clearly how to use it
and, perhaps more importantly, how not to.

In the midst of strong passion
I seek Serenity that does not slay passion,
strength that does not obscure truth, and
Power that does not crush questions
but removes the barriers to truth.

There is apparent chaos, there is apparent harmony,
there is true harmony in the midst of chaos,
There is a pattern for true order

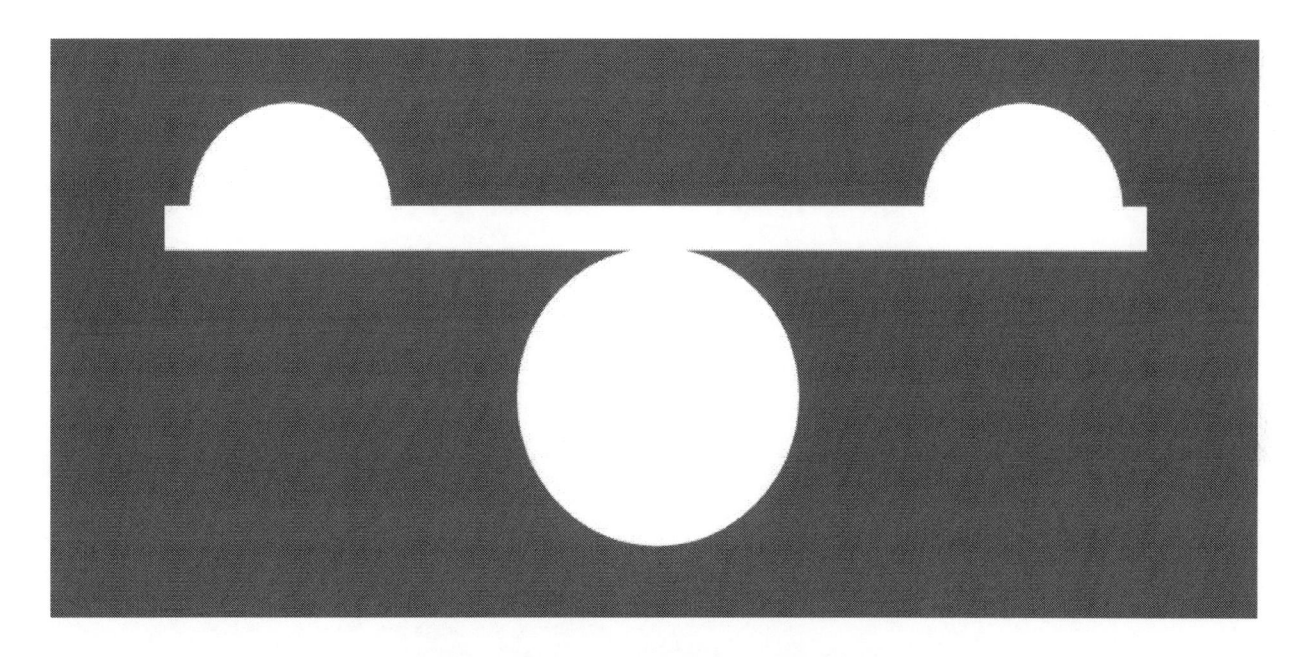

DUTY TO ALL

Picture by Mark Brereton, Temple of the Jedi Order

The Importance of the Everyday Jedi
By Michael Southernskies
Force Academy

This is a lecture that anyone should be able to appreciate, but one I believe is of paramount importance to the Jedi Path. Jedi in the Ordinary World. Not those extreme situations where martial arts or emergency response procedures are of use. Unless we pursue a lifestyle and career centered around security, military, police or medical services, we'll hardly ever need those skills. But when we do, we will be eternally grateful for them.

No, at this time I'm talking about any given day, at any given time. Jedi are supposed to be beacons of light, upholding honour, hope and virtue. My secondary role is that of the Health and Safety Representative (HSR). The main task of the HSR is to communicate between the management and the workforce. We have a small collection of legal powers to do this. We are able to bring serious legal and political pressure on the management to ensure the safety of the workforce, to the point where a job can be totally stopped until a problem is sorted.

In the training course for the HSR I was trained in negotiation, strategic thinking, reading the opposition, and given the courage I need to stand up for those who I represent.

Is this not the expression of the Jedi in the every day?

Learn your rights at work. Learn your rights to life. Many a time I've seen a profit-driven company exploit their workers because they weren't aware of their rights, or because the workers were too afraid to stand up. These men could have been placed in potentially dangerous situations due to the foolhardiness or penny-pinching nature of the management. Jedi, the Bringers of Light, in these times, are to be Beacons of Light.

As Jedi, we must stand up. As Knights of the Twenty-First Century, we must be able, and willing to stand up for those around us. Not just against our own inner dark, or against a mugger in the street, but our own friends, family and co-workers.

Bring the Knightly Virtues into your every day, not just to the forum community. Apply bushido in your life, not just your status updates. Be the Jedi your signature says you are.

Duty to All
Anirac Morgan
Temple of the Jedi Force

A Jedi's existence is to be of service to others

It's easy to write or say these words. At the core of the issue lies the fact that we are still human beings, Jedi or not, and we also have the same basic human needs as those around us. Do I think we should follow our duty to the point of self-destruction? No, I don't. However, I'll get back to that question. As Jedi we are also human beings, which means we require certain things to live, and that what we give ourselves will affect what we give others. For example, if we don't live healthy lives, if we don't find peace and contentment, if we don't have happiness, and instead live unhealthy, add to chaos, are depressed or whatever, that will have an effect on what we project and how people feel around us.

About 5 years or so ago, I worked as a moderator for a Mental Health forum with quite a huge number of members, all in need of guidance, advice, support and most of all: compassion. I served there, and I enjoyed serving there. I enjoyed giving of myself to aid others, because it felt good. Since it made me feel good, I can hardly say it was completely selfless, but perhaps the answer is in why it felt good. Making a difference, knowing that your existence serves someone, it can be a very fulfilling way to feel that your life has value. I do believe in genuine selflessness, I am simply not sure if I have ever been genuinely selfless. I do see it as a great virtue though.

I think that down the line, when all is counted, you'll look back at what meaning your life had, and feel regret at what you leave behind if you're not satisfied with what you see. I don't want to feel regret, and I want to be able to look back and see that I did serve, that I leave behind a mark of positive influence and positive actions.

However, I don't believe that complete and utter altruism is always for the best. At a point you might have to choose between the needs of yourself, and the needs of others. For a while I neglected this, I neglected my own needs and it resulted in a worsening of my depression, as well as me not being able to finish my education. For a long time I was without a job, without an education and with a steadily worsening mental health. Who did I serve? At that point, I could hardly be of use to myself, far less anyone else.

I learned an important lesson that if you want to be of use to others, you must make sure your own basic needs are met. Sacrificing your job, your education or your sanity won't make you that much bigger a saint, it will render you useless, and with less means to help others around you.

By enabling the self and taking care of the self, you enable it to help others, to guide others, to give compassion and effort. If you give yourself no compassion, you'll soon not be in the proper state where you can pass it along to others.

I feel that we are all very connected. That we affect each other mutually, a part of the same ecosystem, so to speak. When a colleague has a bad day, I feel it. I am affected by how he or she deals with her bad day. I can in turn try to affect back, perhaps try for a positive effect that might make both our days better. This I usually try. In any case, whether you're among family, friends, colleagues or complete strangers, our emotions and our projected energies will inevitably have an effect, and we all play off each other like parts of a giant machinery. So, if we wish to serve, we must first ensure that we are in a proper state to serve well. We must enable ourselves in any way we can, to ensure that we are equipped to serve others in the best way possible, through taking care of our own needs as well.

Note, I am not saying that in order to serve I need that second house, the vacation home and a couple of additional cars. As it is, I don't own a house nor a car, I rent a small apartment and my most prized possessions are my SW EU books. Not because they have money value, but because I have collected them for a long time, hence they have sentimental value.

No, what I am saying is that if I skip lunch to help a colleague with a problem, sleep terribly due to my sister's issues with her boyfriend, let the GF abuse my willingness to help her out, eventually I'll end up very tired and mood-managing will be very difficult. I'll not be enabling myself, I'll be limiting myself.

So, service is essential for Jedi. It should be integral to our core, that we do what we can to serve and aid those around us, this I believe in strongly! However, we also need to keep in mind that in order for us to serve well, we must ensure that we take care of our own basic needs and tend to our own mental state, so that we are best possible equipped to serve others in the most helpful way. Me running errands for my GF all over the place doesn't aid her. She needs the physical exercise more than me, and it would do her good to combat her tendencies towards laziness. This she agrees with herself, and last we spoke she said it's because I enable this behaviour. So, we made an agreement that I will "serve less" in the future, and hence serve her better. Besides, being used as a servant made me feel resentful, and although I took the blame for this myself, it clouded my judgement from seeing that I wasn't really serving her at all, running around doing everything she asked me to.

For a time I lived at home. It should be mentioned, I am the oldest of six siblings. My mother was a single mother for a long time, and we had a difficult childhood due to our abusive father. For a while, I took the role of "second parent". In my teens I served my mother through taking extra responsibility for the new baby and the rest of my siblings. What started as servitude became problematic when my mother finally found a new boyfriend. I had ended up becoming quite co-dependent and territorial, and it caused a lot of problems. He wouldn't accept my role as protector, guardian, with the responsibilities following, and I didn't trust him enough to let go of the reins. Eventually, it was him or me, and he moved out. I manipulated events to make this happen, and I am not proud of that. In therapy I was told that my home environment was far too full of triggers for me to be able to fight through the co-dependency and the depression. She recommended that I moved out, and found my own place and started fresh. That it was the only way to heal old wounds and get through some conflicts I was living with.

They are married today, and all is well. However, now that my mother has been sick for a long time, I have considered moving home to "serve". We live quite far apart, but although a Jedi ought to serve so part of me feels I should go home, I know from therapy it won't be good for me, and it won't be good for my family. My mother is better off with my brother to help her, and her husband. I don't trust that I could go back home, to serve there, without my mental state declining due to certain triggers in my home environment. And I know that if I was to let go of my job and my GF, I would become far less of use to them. At least as it is I can give them money when they have difficulties paying the bills, I can be a listening ear when my mother needs to talk, and so on. I serve in the way I think is best for the family, as well as for myself to be able to serve.

Next summer they'll be moving far closer to where I live now, and I'll be able to do more, without having to move back to a place where it's hard to get a job and a place to live, and I won't have to give up my relationship either.

But I am going off topic here! Having touched the self VS others issue, I think the essential is balance. Tend to own basic needs, so you can better serve others. Self-extermination serves none!

As Jedi though, we must find ways to serve, ways to make our lives be a positive contribution for other people. I think there are a lot of ways to do this. Some work in the military, some as doctors or psychologists. Some work as teachers, or guidance counsellors. Regardless of what your occupation is, I think there are still ways to serve others if we look for the possibilities. I am a paper pusher, so I don't exactly feel that my job is vital for other people. However, even though that's not what I want to do for the rest of my life, that's not an excuse not to serve. So, I serve my colleagues, through working on being a positive influence in the work environment, I lend out my ears frequently when I see a colleague is stressed and need to talk, giving support, advice, help out in any way I can. Also, I work on giving good service through the phones. Sometimes people go through rough times, and need to feel understood, heard. Sometimes you don't need to do all that much to brighten someone's day.

I also feel I have duties regarding LGBT matters, but that's in the thread above, so I think that I've covered already.

Albeit my current job isn't particularly meaningful in the great picture, I also do try to volunteer with other things, so that I can serve. I help moderating the Jedi Church, I respond often when people post who are struggling with something, my experiences has proven to often be useful in that regard. You live daily with a medical diagnosis, the negatives can be turned to something positive, the experiences used to help others, to show them that they are not alone in experiencing what they are going through. Being Bipolar type II means that I struggle more with mood managing than some, and that I'm not always the easiest to live with. However, that and my previous experiences with abusive parent, toxic home-environment, struggling with unemployment and depression means I am carrying a large bag of experiences. And if a negative experience can be used to help someone else, it becomes a positive. I live my life after that philosophy. My negative experiences can be used to serve other people, hence they have positive value.

I should conclude this somehow, but I feel I've made a few conclusions already. It's our duty to serve within our capabilities and within what is healthy for the self, also it's our duty to serve in the best possible way, not just blindly without thought or reflection. The exact how, I feel is less important than that we do serve, one way or another, in whatever way we can, and after our own individual strengths. As individuals we are different, and our contributions often too are different. This I think is actually a positive thing, because the community and the people in it has various different needs. People have different needs, so servitude with variation would cover more bases than servitude in one direction.

A Light in the Dark
RyuJin
Temple of the Jedi Order

All too often in recent years there have been tragedies in which the lives of innocents are cut short. Many times the perpetrators of these terrible events are unfortunate souls that have been lost in the dark. In the end we are left mourning the loss of loved ones, angry at the inability to protect them, confused as to why these things happened, and searching for meaning.

Grieve for the loss, but remember they are not truly gone for they have returned to the warmth and comfort of the all embracing force and are therefore with us always.

Do not be angry, for anger does not lead to answers, nor does it ease the pain.

Do not be confused, instead seek the knowledge and gain the understanding needed to prevent such tragedies from occurring again.

If you must have meaning consider this;

There are many who are born into the dark, or cast into the dark, or have wandered into the dark where pain and suffering are all that they know. For them every day is filled with fear, fear of being alone, fear of pain, fear of suffering, fear of being weak, and fear of not having control over the course of their life.

These sad souls are not always easy to spot, for many learn to hide their suffering behind a mask of serenity. Unfortunately the mask does not last forever, eventually it breaks and unleashes the darkness that has been hiding and growing. Usually by this time it is too late to prevent tragedy.

So how do we prevent such things? We must learn to identify the warning signs of suffering. We must be ever vigilant of the hidden darkness if we are to alleviate pain and suffering thus preventing tragedy. We must treat everyone with the respect and dignity they deserve. If you know of someone that is suffering, whether it's bullying, abuse, or loss, extend a hand of friendship to them. Talk to them, and listen, don't just hear them, but listen to them. A lending hand and a friendly ear can cast a bright light in a dark room.

Many that are lost in the darkness are looking for the light, be that light. Guide them from the dark.

It's no secret that I've been in that same darkness and felt that same pain. I know all too well how wonderful it feels to have someone, anyone recognize your existence enough to reach out a hand and lend an ear. These were the moments I held onto that provided the faintest glimmer of light and during the moment when I felt my worst, the force broke through the darkness and enabled me to find my way out. Not everyone has the strength to escape on their own; their eyes become closed preventing them from seeing the flicker of light, robbing them of the strength needed to escape their torment, which is why it's up to everyone to share their strength. We are all connected through the force; when one suffers, we all suffer, even if we do not know it.

Reach out a hand, lend an ear, be that light in the dark for someone.

Happiness and Service
Michael Southernskies
Force Academy

In my life I have met those who serve, and mourn their service. They lament it, but continue anyway, feeling obliged to serve others, guilt-ridden if they don't. Theirs is truly a live of servitude, and for some, eventual bitterness. I was once like this; "sworn", to use my own word, to help others... and at what cost? My happiness. My wasted time. And eventually, I withdrew. Screw other people, I'm in it for me now! I kept on like this for awhile. Got my life in order, got my priorities straight... because balance is key here.

I once talked with a novice Jedi, who claimed that true selflessness, the epitome of the Jedi Path, was to act without any self-interest. If you enjoyed helping others, it wasn't selfless, and a betrayal of this tenet of the path. I called him an idiot and carefully explained to him the ways in which he was wrong. I was there for awhile.

There is a Duty to All in the Jedi Compass. One of our tenets states that we act to support our community, to act objectively to help those in need, and be mindful of our actions at all times, as we can affect others without knowing. Just as one can be an inspiration to others, so can one be a depressant to others. But we have a Duty to All; even ourselves.

For if we are not satisfied by helping others, if it doesn't fill us with that warm, fuzzy feeling... why do we do it? Guilt? Pride? Duty? The Knight-Errant of the old times, an icon often mentioned by those in the Path, was sworn to protect the people of his realm. To uphold the weak, to smite the wicked. In simpler times. They were trained well. Their values? Fortitude. Discipline. Responsibility. Our values? The same.

But for all our training, for all our values, they will stand to nought in the face of a life spent dissatisfied. The path should make us happy, not wear us down. It should fill us with joy, not mourning. The same for our work. Passion, happiness, emotion... all part of the human experience. The human race. Being a Jedi doesn't mean rejecting what makes us human. It simply means keeping the human elements in balance, so that we can create a better world for others to live in.

"I find it hard to believe people can truly be on a path they mourn rather than celebrate." -Khaos

From Reacher's Journal
Reacher
Temple of the Jedi Order

I call myself Reacher because I believe in constantly evolving who I am. I want to continually reach beyond what I think I know and re-evaluate in an ever-changing world.

"By serving each other, we remain free."

Every time I read that, my heart warms. It's concise. It's *clean*. And it sums up my approach to life. Sure, I fall short just as much as any other man, but it's an ideal worth striving toward. And there's beauty in the working.

I knew at a young age I wanted to do something in service to others. When I dreamed, it wasn't of money or women or fame. I dreamed of working with a close group of friends towards a great goal. For a time I thought teaching would be a great fit. I still think that, but back when the time came to choose I committed to military service. I heard the call and answered. I don't love violence, but I respect it and acknowledge its capacity for good. Surgeons injure, but only for the benefit of the patient. My father is a surgeon. I believe he and I are similar in the essence of what we try to do. I also believe that warriors can be more than just entrepreneurs of violence. I consider myself more of a problem solver than anything. I have many assets at my disposal, and not all problems are solved with weapons.

I graduated from university with a bachelor of science in English and minor in engineering. I knew that my school was heavy into engineering already, and I thought exposing myself to some of the greatest literary minds in the world would be more important to a warrior-leader than knowing the tensile strength of a tank's armor or the thermodynamics involved in ship propulsion. Whatever else the job requires, I have to be a communicator.

I entered my chosen service and began learning in earnest. I served as an infantry platoon leader overseas in 3rd Brigade, 101st. That may not mean much to some unfamiliar with the US Army, but it means a lot to me. The 101st has a tradition of putting a card suit on the helmet of each brigade so everyone knew who you belonged to. 3rd BDE bears the japanese torii. It is the only unit in service with a torii as its symbol. I discuss this because of the torii's significance. It translates roughly as 'Gateway to Honor'. It's a reverent symbol of elegance and respect. It agrees with my sensibilities, and the unit lived up to its tradition.

I was afforded an opportunity to serve in a less conventional capacity, and am enjoying learning new things each day. Like others here, I know I will fade in and out as life permits me. I want to express gratitude in advance to any who I share this path with, if only for a short while.

Service and Training as a Religious Observance
Andy Spalding
Heartland Jedi

We come together and what do we do at our gatherings? Train (and hang, but officially train). People ask, what makes the Jedi different than other religions? Is it the Force? EVERY religion has the force in one form or another. Is it our connection with the force? All religions Meditate, pray or commune with spirits in some way. Is it the fact we are a melting pot of religions? Could be, but that just makes this a path anyone can follow.

I feel that what makes this path different is the fact a Jedi serves. We gear our every act toward it. Every time we serve we are following the religious observance of our path. Some pray, others meditate, we serve others as best we can.

Deep down, all activities of the Jedi are dedicated to service. We might say well what about the act of achieving enlightenment? Is that not a wholly internal practice? It is not. We meditate and find peace so we can be of more use when we act externally. We train martially and physically to be stronger and faster so we can serve harder. We push ourselves mentally and challenge our limits so we can quite simply do more.

Training among Jedi is motivated by a desire to put it to use. Why cultivate wisdom if your just going to sit in your temple? Why find oneness with the force only to keep it to yourself? I say that every action that we pursue should be geared toward the service of others.

Sith and darkies though, don't feel that service thing need apply to others. They serve them selves ultimately and that I feel is the basic and most fundamental difference between the two outlooks, where the motivation is.

Every Action Matters
Michael "Akkarin" Kitchen
Temple of the Jedi Order

This is adapted from a sermon of the same title given by myself in February 2013.

How often are we reminded of the little things in our world? The little things that go largely unnoticed except by just one or a few people and the little things you aren't thanked for doing. On the opposite side of course are the grand gestures, those things which get all the media attention and attraction, these things everyone knows about.

What action is worthy of a Jedi? Should Jedi try for grand gestures of small acts? Is there one best and only way to help the world?

This Jedi does not think so.

Grand gestures are good, don't get me wrong, they can do wonders for raising awareness about an issue. But life should not be one long series of grand gestures if that person is ignoring the little things.

It is easy to get caught up in doing some kind of grand gesture and forgetting about all that happens in between. If one sets out to do well one could find that in their pursuit of success, in whatever endeavour, one forgets the little things, perhaps even confusing your priorities of what is important.

One can easily carried away with doing something when one involves oneself with it. But sometimes time may better be spent taking a step back and having a look from a different perspective, if only to stop one from losing sight of one's original goals.

Think about how much difference these little things could really make to someone: you can make someone's day by being polite. You can prevent someone getting into a bad mood by simply holding the door open. You can be a miracle for someone else by helping someone stranded by the side of the road with no mobile phone. You can offer someone your jacket in the cold when you have several layers on and they do not. You can help dig someone's stranded car out of the snow. You can take the time to be there and listen to someone desperately in need of a friendly chat.

What is listed above is just a tiny part of the thousands of little acts one can perform each day to help make someone's better. These are not grand gestures, they will not go down in the history books and will not be counted amongst the great achievements of human kind.

But then again while individual acts might not be particularly noteworthy, the idea of kindness, compassion, altruism, empathy and understanding – all Jedi qualities – being performed by individuals every day to complete strangers is an achievement in itself! The little things themselves might not be remembered, but the fact that assistance and service is provided to those who need it is an achievement nonetheless.

A Jedi does not need to be a great warrior or the wisest philosopher to make a difference, in a positive way, to someone's life. A Jedi should do what they can to help. That is what matters. Can you spare the time to do a grand gesture? Go on a marathon run for charity and raising awareness? Great! But don't forget about the day-to-day things, don't forget about the little things. Every action matters.

RESPECT THE LAW

Living in Reality
Talon Trevor MacDonald
Aurora Borealis

I see, all the time, prospective Jedi that spend much of their time spouting the sayings from the Star Wars books and movies.
This, in itself, is not a bad thing, but It can GROW into a lack of connection to the real world.
I also see many thinking that owning the title "Jedi" makes one automatically one that can go out, stop bad guys, and act as Adjunct Police Units.
This, My learners, can get one killed or arrested.
We are in the Birth phase of a New Philosophy, based on a set of Movies and Books, yet buried in the distant past as well, in many philosophies and faiths that have been around for Millenia.
Our thoughts are not all new, but the way some deal with them can be fairly dangerous to us all.
There are important things to remember at ALL times, Learners.
1) We are NOT Police. Few of us are trained for Combat and Intervention. If you are not trained thus, Those of us that are would prefer that you use a Cell phone, and call the police. We prefer you alive, unharmed, and not charged with crimes for vigilantism.
2) Live in the reality. We cannot perform Telekinesis, openly read or control thoughts, or block bullets with "real" lightsabers. Attempting to brag about such things only distracts our learners, and does not make the speaker look any better. Also, IF you can do it, AND show proof (Not doctored video please) I will watch and decide then.
3) Represent the Jedi diplomatically. Act polite and appropriate at all times. Do not strut. Do not puff out your chest. These things are NOT Jedi. It is enough to say that you represent or follow the Jedi faith. Braggadocio and haughtiness, improper actions and attitudes affect how the outside world will see us all.
We seek acceptance, and the ability to teach and spread our words, We do NOT seek to be shunned and ostracized for our actions.

Respect for the Law
Anirac Morgan
Temple of the Jedi Force

I think this is a complicated question as well. Having never broken the law in my life, I find it hard to imagine a scenario in which I'd feel forced to break one. I have a somewhat exaggerated respect for authorities, be that teachers, policemen, bosses at work. I am neither military nor a member of the police. Also, I am quite aware (thank you Alethea, lol) of the potential consequences of vigilantism, how they can destroy important evidence and impede an investigation so that the police don't get to do their job the way they need to do it in order to bring a criminal to justice. However, what if the police is the criminal, and the government corrupt? We actually had a recent case here in Norway, where the police themselves impeded an investigation, by burying important evidence and declaring that an eight year old girl had killed herself, causing the mother to begin a years long fight for justice. When the police-department was finally forced to reopen investigations, the experts found that crucial evidence had been locked down and forgotten about, and eventually the killer was found and put to trial. In this case, the mother was able to fight the system legally, by contacting private detectives, lawyers, all to pressure the police-department to reopen a case they wanted to remain hidden. I think, in a democratic country mostly there will be ways to pressure the system into working, if it doesn't. There will mostly be legal ways to handle issues, so that over-stepping the law won't be necessary.

However, there might come a time where this might not be possible. Norwegians don't like to talk about it, but during the Nazi occupation in 1943 we were awarded by the Germans for "outstanding co-operation". Although a few resisted and the king fled, truth is that most of the authorities co-operated with the Nazi's both when it came to maintaining power and killing Jews. And those who resisted was breaking Norwegian law at the time, ignoring instructions from the police and local authorities. A lot of people did break the rules, helped smuggle Jews out of the country, and even helped keeping them hidden. So, yes, in some instances I do think it's right to break the law of the land, but I think this applies in rare and extreme cases, like the one mentioned above. Causing a riot can cost more lives than you attempt to save, not to mention loss of property and all over chaos.

Would I intervene if I saw something terrible in another country, that technically wouldn't be illegal in that country? Well, not sure there'd be much I could do. Some countries still practice stoning, de-capitation and human trafficking. What could I do about that? I doubt that anything I could do would make a difference. However, I must believe that the world is changing for the better, and vote/demonstrate/pressure my own government in acting in a way that might somehow affect others for the better. I have very limited power as a sole individual, as is right, but it's my responsibility to use whatever power I have in the best possible way. As it is, that's mostly through voting and participate in political debate, keeping track of what my own government do to not contribute to those things. For instance, I know our government tried hard to save that one woman in Iraq or Iran who was condemned to death for killing her rapist. They failed in this, but if I had gone down there single handed and guns blazing, all I would get would be landing my butt in jail. Either theirs or my own. And it wouldn't make a difference either way for women down there in similar situations.

Basically, at the core I believe in using the power of the people to affect the government if you're not content with the situation. And that the legal way takes longer, but is eventually the better method of making positive changes when the law isn't protecting and serving as it should. Also, I think it ought to get fairly extreme, before it's right to start breaking laws to change them, and that the better way is to work to change them, so that they eventually won't need to be broken. In a democracy the power ought to be with the people, and although you can't always trust the people to make the right decision, nor trust that the government will work as the people wanted it to work, becoming apathetic and throw away your responsibility as a citizen isn't an alternative. You vote, you organize and you put pressure while still working within the law, not creating chaos through breaking the law and create anarchy.

Respect for the Law
Alethea Thompson
Setanaoko's School for Jedi: The Uniniated

Within the confides of any philosophy, I have found that there are some things that people exemplify more than others. Within the Jedi Path, I would probably be identified more with the tenet of "Respect the Law" than any other. Certainly you can find how I incorporate the other tenets into my life, and even find where I still need work- everyone has these and we all work on improving upon them. But it's respecting the law that I am best known for in my instruction.

Over the years I have been given questions of how this plays into the Jedi Path when there are obvious atrocities which may warrant stepping outside of the law. Following Sharia Law would be quite difficult, fortunately I am not obligated to do so. But at one point in time I had the opportunity to be subjected to it, with no choice but to allow it to happen before my eyes. But what could I do?

The question isn't one of admitting defeat, but rather a question of "is it my place?". If the answer is yes, than working within the law to change it is more within the interests of getting the desired effect. While I could interject into this one incident, it does not mean that it will spread. Therefore I've only spared one life against the reprimand of Sharia. It is also something to note that the rules of the middle east is rooted in their culture to keep order. Who am I to intervene, unless it is something I am willing to put my all into the project, it simply is not my place to intervene. Their laws, regardless of how horrifying they are to me, all I have to do is abide by them and reject anything that causes me to act in such a way that encourages the problem.

An example would be- as a Jedi if I see someone committing adultery, and I know that they will be stoned to death for the mere accusation without any real trial, I would not bring it forth. In this, I am respecting the law, but not stepping forward to enforce it as they are not the laws I personally am subjected to. I, as a Jedi, have to refrain from committing the crimes of the law- but I do not have to go beyond that.

It brings about an interesting conundrum though- what if it is going to cause the loss of life, limb or eyesight? As I said before, it is not the place of a Jedi to step in to enforce the law, or to stop the enforcement of the law. But if I saw a muslim woman getting stoned to death, would I be obligated to step in? It is a little known fact that some of the muslim countries where honor killings are practiced, it is actually illegal. If a Jedi were to witness such an incident knowing that it was illegal, then they are perfectly acting within the tenet of "Respect the Law" by stepping forth to save the victim.

Another question that is often asked is: What if the system is broken? Can I not break the law then to build a better world? The answer is… complicated. Prior to the American Revolution, the British Empire demonstrated their inability to be rulers of the people. They were committing injustice upon injustice to the people. Eventually the colonies decided to strike back to earn their right to break free of Britain and govern themselves. Americans see this as a justified war. Today, however, it is becoming more confusing as to where the line should be drawn on what the government has done that would warrant another combative revolution. So when would it be appropriate for a Jedi to jump on board with a revolution- or even start one? For that we need only look as far as places under control of terrorist organizations or dictators. It is my belief that the point a revolution is necessary is when a government begins to wrongfully take the lives of others. The government, not individuals within the government/terrorist organization (such as individual police, but rather an entire police department is called in to be lethal firing squads on the masses).

At that point, I can see a combative revolution is warranted. But even in this there are laws to abide by. They are called the Geneva Conventions and Hague Laws. These are laws that were agreed upon at one point by a good chunk of the nation's leaders that should ensure the moral and ethical high ground of combat. Any Jedi that followed a revolutionary group that did not abide by these basic laws of war, would not be able to refer to themselves as a Jedi- as they are now following the beat of "the ends justify the means". While on the surface these may produce better results (or at least appear to do so- that is an entirely different discussion altogether), a Jedi should never sacrifice the moral and ethical high ground for mere results.

Ultimately, we encourage Jedi to work within the system to change the system. There are times that this just does not work, which is why in another article I have stated that I fully support anyone willing to fight against the Islamic State of Iraq and the Levant- but I will add here "only if you abide by the Geneva Conventions and Hague Laws in doing so".

Although the book has a lot of Deus Ex applied in it, to understand better how strong a Jedi's resolve must be to maintain the moral high ground, I highly recommend picking up Shatterpoint by Matthew Stover. I may not be very much into the fiction, but I do believe that Shatterpoint drives home the point far better than I can in a simple lecture.

DEFENSE

Response to Pacifism vs. Fighting for Peace?
By Talon
Real Jedi Enclave

Seek peace in all things and seek out the root of conflict and deal with it as best as possible. But if that is impossible and violence has been initiated or threatened ... or the situation calls for violence ...

I believe that the concept that the Jedi are against violence is a fallacy. Violence is a tool that has its appropriate time and place. Like all things, the Jedi must not become consumed by it so that violence is their state of existence rather than just a tool that they use. -- But I am also one that believes that being a Jedi is about being part of a warrior culture, something that others deny.

Some Jedi choose pacifism and that is their right. There are many ways that a person can help others that don't involve fighting. A healer that takes the oath 'do no harm' should take that oath very seriously - but I'll not look down on any healer that is willing to pick up a weapon and defend a patient who can not defend themselves.

Now - I personally believe that most people SHOULD NOT fight. Simply because they don't have it within them to be the type of person that fighting requires. If you approach the concept of defending yourself as if you should be as gentle as possible and use only aikido moves with the goal of not truly ending combat as quickly and decisively as possible -- then you aren't cut out to be a fighter. Leave it to someone who knows that fighting may mean kicking someone in the groin, hitting them in the throat, poking them in the eyes, using any weapon available and otherwise doing everything within your power to stop them as soon as they can -- and train hard with that in mind. Warfare isn't nice, it isn't fair, it isn't romantic, it certainly isn't pretty. The warrior must know how to thrive in that environment and come out emotionally unscathed -- a bulletproof mind. 99% of Jedi; even those that are/where soldiers and police officers are not of the right mindset.

Oh, and anyone who says that Jedi shouldn't use guns because 'a Jedi should look someone in the eyes' when they fight -- they shouldn't be fighters either because that is a romantic but thoroughly ignorant notion of someone who is utterly clueless about the psychology of killing and combat.

In this I'm talking about people who want to, as Jedi, pursue justice. Law Enforcement and Investigators. The average person needs to learn at least the basics of fighting and I do believe many should strive to get the mindset and the training that I described if they are serious about self defense. But just learning to resist is a good thing. Studies show that the majority of attacks (self defense) are thwarted by simple resistance.

Jedi respect life in all its shapes and forms -- including their own. They will not throw away their life uselessly. I believe it is better to kill in your own defense and live to help others than to die as a pacifist and allow a criminal to walk free. That is tipping the scales to the dark on purpose in my opinion.

Just like a person should be trained to fight and use violence as a tool -- it can not be the only tool that they have in their kit. ALL Jedi, no matter what their specialty is, should be trained in proper communication and conflict resolution. In the US the FBI crime statistics show that the majority of crimes are committed by an acquaintance (someone you know) in an argument -- generally over property or money -- and the weapon used is a weapon of opportunity; whatever is at hand to grab. It sounds to me like the majority of violent crimes could be prevented simply by being better communicators and be able to resolve conflict peacefully. Strange that out of the millions of martial artists and self defense experts only a few focus in this area. Most simply provide the tool of violence and nothing more.

Defense IJRS Assignment
Jedi Baru
Institute for Jedi Realist Studies

The Assignment

What is your experience with defense?
Are you trained in physical defense, or mediation and conflict resolution?
Could you intervene in a skilled manner?
If none of these, what areas do you feel are most
important to train in over the coming 5 years or so? If you are unsure, talk to someone about it. If you are trained in defense, are you familiar with your legal rights and protections?

Response

I have a lot of experience with the concept of "defense". I do my best to practice defenses for all of my quadrants.
Presence I feel is the number one defense. If a person walks with confidence and reassurance, they can bring calmness and security to most situations. I relate this to "form Zero". Because I either have "no sword" or I have an "internal sword", I do not need an external sword to gain others respect. It be intimidation or it can be "compassion", but people feel the authority and honor it with respect. Developing one's spirit is crucial for this.

Communication skills are the second best defense. I do like the practice of Niman because it acknowledges that words can only go so far. Having a lightsaber on your hip or knowing martial arts to back up your words, can go a long way. Knowing how to defuse a situation is very helpful. I have been trained in various styles of verbal conflict resolution. Developing one's mind is very helpful for this.

Physical can be seen as the easy area to protect. I believe if everyone knew martial arts, the world be be a safer and happier place because people would walk with confidence in their world. I feel that we need to honor the requirements of the lower chakra and to respect Maslow's pyramid. (Maslow's hierarchy of needs). If find that most people reject or ignore their lower functions and try to build a foundation-less tower that focuses on "spiritual things" and self actualization. People prefer to remain in the theoretical and ignore the reality of the physical – which we all chose to live in. In order to be whole, we need to honor all of our quadrants and all of our chakras. They are there for a reason. Developing the Body is helpful here.

Emotional connections are very helpful for defense. I feel that this quadrant is even more shut down and "misunderstood" than the spiritual. Especially in the States is this area ignored and rejected so there is very little information to be found here. I do like books like emotional intelligence and others like that (I am forgetting their names) that are about embracing the wisdom contained in our emotions. Learning how to protect them is very helpful. I find the trick here is – how does a person protect their heart while still remaining open and fluid.

Now environmental protection is difficult to "almost" impossible. Our environment is so filled with toxins and pollution that our bodies are filled with inflammation and disease. We need to stay focused and raise our vibration even high just to keep our bodies healthy and working. I do my best to keep my area clean. I pick up cigarette butts and trash constantly. I live in a place that does not spray and avoids chemicals. I do everything I can within the law to protect my environment from harm. I do wish I could do more. I feel the only thing I can do is to raise people's awareness to the impact that we are having on our world. If we respect ourselves, we need to respect our surround.

Defense; beyond the physical
Anirac Morgan
Temple of the Jedi Force

As learners we will at times stumble over inner conflicts. However, these can be a great source for learning and lead to much needed reflection. One such conflict has been between the advocate in me VS the Jedi. As Jedi, we speak of peace and yet also defence. At times I have felt this might be a contradiction, because although the goal is peace/end of conflict, in the moment it might require the opposite; responding to a potentially harmful situation/attitude in defence of whomever this might be harmful to. A master spoke to me of escalation and de-escalation. Granted, many issues we can work through without escalating a potential conflict, and yet the risk of escalation will be there as soon as we choose to interfere or add our voice as opposition to that of another.

First I should clarify what I believe lies in the term "defence". Many Jedi I have spoken with seem focused mainly on physical defence; the act of protecting another human being against physical harm through either physical force or even a weapon. It is common (and needed) when debating defence that there are also debates around what kind of action is ethically correct depending on what the situation at hand require. The golden rule being that you do what is required to preserve innocent life/property, but only what is required.

However, what about emotional/mental defence?

The fact is that words can kill. Words and harmful attitudes take innocent lives every day in many different countries. Young and/or vulnerable individuals who take their own lives because they feel like they don't belong, that they don't have value. It should be informed that I worked at a Mental Health forum for about 2 years as a volunteer moderator/support giver. This forum had at that time about 60 000 members, today it has over 80 000 members. I spoke with perhaps hundreds of people during that period, and my main responsibility was the LGBT forum. I couldn't count the number of despairing LGBT people I talked to, some who was considering suicide, some who regularly self-harmed or had struggled/did struggle with eating disorders. The young found themselves growing up in a world filled with hate, and they had struggled for a long time with shame and despair. Some had lost their homes, due to being discarded by their own families. Some had struggled with bullying for years, and consequentially suffered from conditions ranging from depression, anxiety, even PTSD in some cases. Weekly we (moderators there) would discuss the latest suicide, and renew our efforts in giving what help we could to our members, encourage them to seek help, encourage them to see beauty and hope rather than the potential for hate and abuse.

Due to this, you could say I am an advocate at heart. I have spent years working against harmful attitudes and seen it as a duty whenever I come across potentially harmful words or attitudes, to be an opposing voice, presenting the other view, hoping this can somehow counter the negative message of the words I am reacting to. I consider working for social justice, as well as countering negative attitudes as being something very much needed to preserve life and health. This is likely due to me repeatedly witnessing how deep wounds emotional/mental harm can cause, and how abuse can affect a human being for years after. Bullying is the foremost reason for suicide among the young, whether LGBT or not. Negative attitudes in LGBT context is also the reason why in many countries in the world being a homosexual or lesbian is punishable by death/prison sentence. In other countries (as well as occasionally still in my own, progressive as it is) LGBT people are still frequently experiencing violence, examples being the 3 young men who were killed by friends/family in Russia in recent time, and a man fleeing persecution in his own country who was beat up and landed in the hospital as late as this week here in Norway.

Hence, why I feel advocacy is so important, not only as defence, but preventative defence. By combating harmful attitudes and social injustice, we create a safer future as well as possibly balm fresh wounds in the present.

However, as a Jedi, I have to be very careful about how I step. The aim is to de-escalate, not escalate, and this I work on keeping in mind when speaking with people who have an opposite opinion or who expresses harmful messages. My aim is not to convert, nor insert my will. My aim is simply to present another view, to aid the other in growing an awareness over how potentially harmful the things people say can be for other people, because if people were simply evil, it would be easy. We could throw on our super-hero costume and go battle the evil with our swords and spears. However, people are usually not evil (unless they are psychopaths), simply unaware. Being different doesn't automatically mean one is less moral than the other, and I don't enter an argument thinking that the other person is intentionally trying to cause harm. Sometimes the person writing or speaking is simply trolling, other times this person has a very strong sense morality, but is unaware of the damage he or she can cause through his or her view.

An example; someone posted on Facebook something that clearly stated;

"Why does it have to be at least one LGBT person in every TV show? Why can't we have at least one TV series without "those people?"

This I see often! Pretty much the exact same message in different form uttered by a new individual.

When I added my comment, the OP immediately said; of course, this isn't against your community, hon. I meant no harm.

But the thing is; meaning no harm doesn't guarantee you won't do harm. In fact; this kind of attitude, classifying LGBT people as "those people" and "why have one of those in OUR TV show" contributes to bringing up a barrier between us and you, and the message young vulnerable LGBT people will get is: "You aren't as valuable as the rest of us, and we don't want to see you on TV."

This message repeated will do damage. It will cause harm. Repeated negative messages will gradually have an effect on the person reading/hearing it, which is why I feel it's so important to be an opposing voice even if the negative message seems small and unimportant at the time. Do I wish I could waive the magic wand and ensure all young LGBT were as durable as me? Sure. Will that happen? No. I can only speak up with a positive and supportive voice, one that speaks the message that LGBT kids don't have to feel they must hide away, that they're not worthy. And I can redirect conversations so that the focus turns to the human aspect and the potential consequences of harmful attitudes without causing harm myself to the other party whoever that is. To defend, never to attack.

I am under no delusion that I alone can change the world, or that I am always right in my views. And I have no interest of making a "win" on the expense of someone else. Maybe walking away would mean nothing in the big picture, and that I am making such a small difference it's not worth doing. Then again, I am not sure I could choose to simply let go of my efforts, to become a more "correct" Jedi, for the sake of ego or respect in the community. I feel that would be incredibly selfish, because although I am a lesbian, I am neither a vulnerable teen nor particularly receptive to negative messages. Due to therapy and Jedi training there's very little you can say to me that would actually hurt me. In addition, I live in a country where there are equal rights, successful efforts against mental health stigma and effective anti-bullying programs. I am incredibly blessed. So, combating negative stigma and harmful attitudes isn't for me, hence I wouldn't be giving up something I do for myself, but something I do for others. I would be sacrificing work I do for others to promote myself.

As my conclusion was that I cannot give up my advocacy, I began to see it isn't a matter of one or the other. It is a matter of uniting these two essential parts of myself, the advocate and the Jedi, in a way that further both aspects of me. Being a Jedi can make me a better advocate, and being an advocate can make me a better Jedi. Allow the strengths of the two to counter out the weaknesses, and find wholeness in this integration. So, the issue isn't whether or, but how!

I know that by presenting the opposite view, by working to bring awareness of the harm this can cause, I am taking the risk that the other will react in a very negative way; hence I might escalate "hostilities" even as I work not to. However, if shooting someone in order to save an innocent can be morally defensible for a Jedi, can risking escalation be morally defensible for a Jedi as well, if the purpose is mental defence and all that can be done is done when it comes to being polite, showing respect, all in order to try and prevent escalation, instead breed awareness and mutual understanding?

As a side note, the person who I spoke of in my example, we had a good conversation in the end, and she did end up removing the post she had posted that caused the reactions. She didn't at all seem upset with my comments, and we ended up wishing each other well. I told her I respected her Christian views, and that my intentions were just to present another view and the reasoning for why it affects people so strongly. So, in this case there was no escalation and we ended on a friendly and civilized note. This was a successful exchange, but I have had other exchanges being far less successful in the past.

Being an advocate for LGBT rights doesn't mean I am negative towards certain religions. I am not, and I feel attacking someone's religion in order to better things for LGBT people is the wrong way to do it. Combating fear and harmful attitudes through being fearful and hateful is never the way to go, because repeatedly I see people do it only to achieve further conflict and raised defensiveness. In my advocacy, I still follow the Jedi code. I do not attack, I merely defend. Despite of whatever emotional reactions I might experience, I will not attack the other person for who he is or what he believes. I present the issue from another angle for them to consider.

Particularly LGBT matters (but other matters as well!) can become a battle of ideologies. This is a problem, because at the core of the issue this is about real people. Human beings and their lives/health. Real flesh and blood people whose lives are affected. When we focus on beliefs and ideology, we tend to forget the human being at the core. My aim is not to wage a kind of war. I simply want to redirect the discussion back to the core of the matter, the actual real life consequences it has for real people. Planting a seed of awareness, I have seen miracles happen through opening a dialogue of mutual respect and understanding. Kindness can be an equally effective weapon as a sharp tongue, sometimes even more so. It is a subtle and non-harmful way of combat, which often succeeds because it is so unexpected. People are so accustomed to certain hostility, they are often caught off guard when what you present is the opposite, when you seek to understand and respect, rather than judge or criticise.

Ridiculing certain religions to support LGBT issues is ineffective and useless. You do not achieve planting a seed of empathy and understanding if all you give is ridicule and offence. Instead, respect and kindness breeds healthy conversation. In addition, religion or orientation tells me nothing of who a person really are. Muslim, Christian, Atheist. Gay. Straight. All just words that tells in truth very little about a person's qualities and character.

To conclude this; I think the aspect of emotional/mental defence is as important as physical defence. Perhaps it pertains to me more personally having experienced both major depression, suicidal ideation and anxiety, and spent years working through it.

My conclusion all in all is that I can't stop advocating for social justice and against stigma, both in regards to LGBT issues as well as mental health stigma and equality issues. It is far too integrated in the core of who I am, pertaining to my own experiences and history. I know the potential consequences of harmful attitudes and social injustice, not to mention bullying, emotional abuse and mental illness. However, albeit being an advocate is integral to who I am, equally so is being a Jedi learner, someone striving for peace and de-escalating conflicts, rather than causing them. My duty dictates I must defend those who cannot defend themselves, and I consider preventative work the best kind of defence. A somewhat equivalent or comparable analogy for my take on "preventative emotional defence"- can be explained as talking down a potentially violent man, in order to avoid needing to use physical force. By combating these expressions of harmful attitudes, by being vocal instead of silent when we see words written that can cause harm, we might achieve that we avoid for the future having to talk someone out of ending their own life, because depression and experience tells them they have no value in this society we live in. By fighting for equality and social justice through building bridges, rather than tearing them down, we might achieve that one day people will work harder on searching for reasons to unite, rather than reasons to divide. That's my hope.

Is There Murder in Your Heart?
By Alethea Jolene Thompson
Heartland Jedi Knight

There is a lot of belief in how astronomy influences metaphysical attributes. That a full moon causes people to become crazy. The Blood Moon of April 2014 brought about an interesting string of events, and the next morning I was called immediately after a shower by two Force Realists (for those of you which are unfamiliar with the term, it encompasses all philosophies and religions which have their root in the Star Wars Mythos) wanting to see blood for what had occurred. It was interesting that as a Jedi, my immediate reaction was much different from these two individuals. Where they wanted to see blood, I wanted to know every detail possible, before I could make a judgment on the next course of action. None of which involved the mystical concept of really damaging the guy that instigated all of these problems.

What was more intriguing was the fact that as we discussed things, a scene in Episode III came to mind:

Anakin: You can't kill him, Master. He must stand trial.
Mace Windu: He has too much control of the Senate and the Courts. He's too dangerous to be kept alive.
Palpatine: I'm too weak. Don't kill me. Please.Anakin: It's not the Jedi way...

Would you believe me if I said one of the people on the other end of that call is someone that I have come to know as a Jedi? Which is what made this scene come to life for me. Shove aside any disbelief you have in whether or not someone can energetically/magickally kill someone. That is not the point of this article- it's the morality behind the actions that I wish to address.

I recognized a fundamental difference between myself and both these individuals. While each of us cared about the victim- our responses with how to deal with the subject were quite different. Where these two wanted to kill, I was more keen on the idea of excommunicating the subject, and having the rest of the group decide what their own actions would be in regards to it. Given the nature of the "crime", you can't really do much of anything, beyond bindings, well aside from kill or attack. But really there is no legal recourse, only verbal, ban hammers, other distancing mechanisms and if you want to go the magickal route- binding.

But what are the differences between Windu and the two that I was in conversation with? Well for one, Palpatine had multiple followers by this point. He had already demonstrated his ability to control others and oppress them. Seeing all of this, Windu concluded that he would be able to turn the people towards his position. In doing so, he foretold the future. Or perhaps, he made it happen by being the pivot point for Anakin. Once Anakin killed Mace, there was no turning back. He betrayed his master. So you might say that Mace pretty much caused it- but hey, anything is possible, right? It also helped that Mace lived in a universe that allowed him to have a shatterpoint which told him why an individual's death was necessary, what would happen if he did not put him in the ground. But we live in the real world, where such things cannot be quantified or proven beyond a shadow-of-a-doubt. There will always be a question of whether or not our answer to act was the right action. The exceptions to those rules, I will get into later.

In order for you to fully grasp what had happened on that night, I need to explain a little bit about the situation. The phone call came in, and what I had learned was that a woman with a healthy self-esteem had been cyber-bullied into committing suicide. The persons related to the case are all, with the exception of the Jedi I mentioned and myself, part of a coven. It is their belief that the subject enhanced his cyberbullying technique with energy. Perhaps to test his own ability or perhaps he really did have it out for this woman, as I do not know the nature of the relationship between the two, I cannot account for the motive. But this coven and Jedi both came to the conclusion- if the subject did this, "he's too dangerous to be kept alive".

If we take what was in the movies at face value, and ignore Mace's shatterpoint, we understand that Mace had a collection of data on Palpatine from everything which had occurred during the previous two movies and up to the point in Episode III that this particular scene takes place. Here is the collection of data we have on the cyberbully- he is not 20 yet, and this is the first incident where his influence had serious implications. As I learned more on the subject, it seems that there were a number of other factors which contributed to the consequences on that night. Such as the fact that her husband and her had a serious fight. Now these things may or may not have had anything to do with the cyberbully influencing both parties (as both were leaders of the coven in question), but the problems already existed and ties were being frayed little by little.

So the question comes down to- it is one incident, what if the person continues down this path of destruction and commits more acts against others? The question now becomes- why didn't we do something when we first saw the opportunity? Again, I will point to the fiction by drawing on the original trilogy. There is always an option to allow someone the opportunity for redemption. Obi-Wan's decision to not kill Vader was more about giving Luke an opportunity to grow and develop the Jedi Order once more, by allowing him to find his own answers. And in the end, Anakin was saved by his son's actions and becoming a full-fledged Jedi.

At the heart of being a Jedi in the real world, is acknowledging there is room for forgiveness and lessons to be learned by all parties involved. That does not necessarily mean you forget, and sometimes it means you are not the person that can effect change in the individual (just as Old Ben realized he could not save Anakin, but perhaps Luke could, and left Anakin in Luke's hands).

Now that you have a little bit of background on the fictional events and the real world events which contributed to this piece, let us examine the ultimate question: In the real world scenario, what are you left to do with the cyberbully? How would a Jedi approach the subject? For me, I look to a sort of escalation of Force. In the Army it was developed like this:

Escalation of Force (or EoF):

Physical Presence (just you being on the scene)
VerbalVisual/Hand-to-HandNon-
Lethal
Show (Demonstration of intent to use weapon)
K-9
Lethal

The Rules for Engagement (or RoE) are as follows:

A: You have the right to use force to defend yourself against attacks or threats of attack
B: Hostile fire may be returned effectively and promptly to stop a hostile act.
C: When U.S. Forces are attacked by unarmed hostile elements, mobs and/or rioters, U.S. Forces should use the minimum force necessary under the circumstances and proportional to the threat.
D: You may not seize the property of others to accomplish your mission.
F: Detention of civilians is authorized for security reasons or in self-defense.

There are a number of other little things that can go into an RoE, such as not firing into a crowd when a subject has made his/her way into one. Or some things may be clarified, such as the fact that defending yourself does not mean against people causing you minor injury (throwing pebbles at you). Or that you are to defend crucial property and/or supplies. But in general, what is provided above is fairly standard.

Looking at these, they are not far off from how I would develop an EoF or RoE for a Jedi.

Jedi RoE:

A: You ave the right to use force the minimum amount of force necessary to defend yourself against attacks or threats of attack.
B: You have the right to use the minimum amount of force necessary to defend others against attacks or threats of attack.
C: Detaining others is morally, though may not be legally so, acceptable if it is for reasons of both your own and/or their security.

Jedi (Civilian) EoF:

Physical Presence - Just your presence, as long as you are a confident individual, may be all the defense you need. Make yourself a "hard target".
Verbal - Can you talk the problem out? There may be more going on than what meets the eye.
When the Physical is not an Option (e.g. on an internet forum) - You could also use the options of banning, reprimanding, etc.
Hand-to-Hand – Do not assault, let them assault you first, then apply only what force is necessary to ensure they will not attack you (or the individual you are defending) again. This doesn't mean you need to put them in the hospital, it may be just enough to demonstrate that you are the stronger of the two. The moment they stop moving to attack you, you must also to discontinue the fight- lest you become the assailant.
Non-lethal – Namely, Oleoresin Capsicum (Pepper Spray) or a taser. This would be based on what you are legally allowed to carry. Japan, for example, classifies OC as chemical warfare, and as such it is illegal to carry. In this respect, Non-Lethal may not be available to you. Or, if you want to go the magickal route, this would be the point that you most likely would apply such- bindings.

Lethal – The point when you can reasonably prove that you are defending against loss of life, limb or eyesight. Either your own, or that of another.

Military or Police Grade EoFs and RoEs would be dictated by those organizations. If at any time you, as a Jedi, felt that the organization's EoF or RoE was somehow immoral or illegal, then I would hope you would have the fortitude to stand against such and either leave the organization when you got a -legal- opportunity or work to get it changed.

Now that we have the ground rules for my own perception of a decent Jedi RoE and EoF, let's exam how I would hope that a Jedi would react to the given cyber bullying issue that came across my desk that April morning.

With the understanding that the information flowed to these two upset individuals after the incident occurred.

First and foremost, can I communicate with the subject? If I could, and on this particular matter I am not 100% sure they could, then my first directive would be to approach the individual and get their side of the story. As they say, there are always at least 3 sides to a story- your's, mine and the truth. But in order to find it, you need the stories of all which are in direct know of the problem. In this case, those which were in the chat room when the bullying occurred. And the victim's roommate. After that, I would need to compare all stories and develop an understanding of what had transpired. There very well could have been a number of factors, some of which may not have been privy to the bully. The bully may very well have orchestrated everything, but only after a proper review could such be founded or unfounded.

Unfounded: What would happen next would need to be reviewed by the coven. As a number of people have formed their own opinions at this point, it would need to be discussed with the group as to whether or not they wanted to keep the bully in their halls. If they said yes, then the next step would be corrective training. Given the particulars of this case, I would probably have them go through a psychological first aide course- with some additional assignments. And that's even if they wanted to stay after everything was said and done.

Founded: As there is nothing to definitive to suggest that the bully may do this again, the only thing left to do would be to ban the him from the group, informing everyone of why the decision was made, and as such they could decide for themselves if they will keep in communication with the him from here on out. I would also keep a log of everything that transpired. If there is legal precedence to launch a cyber bullying suit, then the records would be available for the family to pursue such matters.

Here's the thing, this was done online. Things were discovered after the fact, which makes the individual a non-active threat. If the subject (successfully) attacks the group through magickal means, send a message back- a show of force by attacking magickally back. If it happens again, cut them off- but a Jedi should not do so by means of murder. Shielding and Binding should be our only means of magickal recourse (until such a time when you can successfully sue someone for magickal attacks, to which- then take it to the courts [and yes, that's meant to be sarcastic, well...to an extent, I guess, there are some areas in the world you can be charged with witchcraft...]).

Now, when it comes to your front doorstep. They are in your face, and you can physically hit them- by all means, the moment they open up an attack on you with harmful/deadly intent, protect yourself and those in your immediate vicinity- with the minimal amount of force necessary.

EXCEPTIONS TO THE RULE: It may seem as though I keep harping on the fact that this bully has only been known to harm someone psychologically once to the point it became a serious problem, and that there was a large difference between Palpatine and this guy by sheer volume of how much of a threat they posed. And there is a reason for this- because there are people that just need to be eliminated before they cause serious issues. A prime example of someone in recent history would be Saddam Hussien. The system he was tried under determined that he needed to be hanged for his crimes, and part of that was to keep him from being able to accomplish any more harm. His sphere of influence was established after years of dictatorship. The same can be said of Hitler. Knowing what we know now, we can say "someone should have killed them before they got to where they were", but really look at it- when they started out, was there not a possibility for them to be different people? Would it have been right to kill them off before they got big, with uncertainty that they would get to the point where they would need to be dealt with?

In the real world, we do not always have the answers- intervention is important, but you have to begin somewhere, to try and resolve the problem of one succumbing to their inner evil slowly until you reach the point where you no longer have viable options.

Something to consider: What is your own answer? Do you have murder in your heart? Do you try to justify it by claiming you are defending others, but really your jumping too fast to conclusions?

Regardless of whether or not magick is real, whether or not you can kill someone through mere thought and ceremony- would you still go through the motions to perform it? Just by making the decision to attempt such...knowing that you are putting forth an effort to actively harm someone...Is that truly the Jedi Way?

ACTION

Knighthood and the Will to Act
Andy Spalding
Heartland Jedi

When I think about the path, I am constantly coming back to the concept of the knight. In the fiction, knighthood is the training goal of Jedi. Most of the fiction is geared toward the attainment of this end. We follow Anakin on his quest for knighthood, then we follow Luke on his quest. That is all fine and good in a world with lightsabers and space ships, but it really does not answer the question of why we, in the real world, would want to attain this end. So, I would like to look at what being a knight means for us as Jedi realists.

When we talk about knighthood for a Jedi what are we speaking of? For most sites around the web, it is a rank given for completion of a number of courses. The assumption is that these courses will give someone the necessary skills to be a knight in the real world. There are usually also a set of "trials" one must be put though in order to demonstrate proficiency with this skills. The question then becomes do these requirements create the character of a knight if they are internalized?

I would argue that proficiency is just that, not knighthood. To me, one becomes a knight, when they have developed the will to act. This is of the utmost importance because it does not matter how much training someone receives, it is all wasted time when the time to act arises and they do not. For the knight, it is having the will to do something when they are pushed out of their comfort range into an event that causes other people to shut down. It is important for a Jedi to know if they have the will to act or not. This is the purpose of the trials. To put the Jedi in a situation that will cause them to act and be successful or do nothing and fail. Deep down the trial is not of their skills, but if their will to apply them.

A Jedi becomes a knight when they know that in an emergency they will be able to act in a positive way instead of in a panic or shut down all together. The training that they have received is not as important as the will to use it. All the training does is make it more likely they will succeed when they do act. You can be a very inexperienced knight and still be of more use in an emergency than people who have taken years of classes and do not know to apply them.

Not everyone will develop this ability. Hopefully with time it becomes something they can work on, but not everyone is cut out for knighthood. That is fine because there are many roles to play in life. Knighthood is the path of action.

If you believe yourself to be a knight; ask yourself, when the time comes to act, do you know, not think, know that you will do what needs to be done? It is not an easy question to answer, but if you have a yes, then you are ready mentally to become a knight.

Patience vs. Action in Defense
Talon Trevor MacDonald
Aurora Borealis

It has been said:
"*A Jedi uses the Force for knowledge and defense, never for attack.*"- Yoda

It has also been said:
"*Karate ni sente nashi*" *(There IS no first attack, in Karate)*-Master Chas Yamaguchi

Today we will discuss when an Attack is also a defense.

Picture it: a Thug is standing, holding a knife, threatening others, and there is that one person in the crowd that has received training. The problem is that this person has always been told that One must NOT attack, but always defend.

Here is where many get it wrong. They wait for the knife wielder to strike before making any move to deal with what is already a dangerous situation.

The trained person, by his or her hesitation, is already increasing the danger level to all around them, by not perceiving the attack that has already happened.

When the thug pulled out his knife, and began to threaten others, The potential for harm began. This is true whether the thug is holding a knife, a gun, a stick, of simply in a fighting stance with fists raised. Even by definition of Law, The thug is already considered to have acted threateningly, and response is justified.

By "waiting" for the thug to then lash out, swing his knife, pull his trigger, swing his bat, whatever, the responder is multiplying the possibility that they thug may harm someone, whether it be the responder, or another nearby victim.

When an attacker has his weapon drawn, and there is danger to anyone, it is the responsibility of the responder to act, now, not after the fact. The first attack has already begun. It is up to the responder to see to it that the first attack does not complete it's cycle.

This is true for Police, Military, and Civilian responders, be they our Jedi, or simply some civilian trained to react. DO NOT ALLOW THE FIRST ATTACK TO COMPLETE.

If a thug has drawn a gun, and you are also carrying one, It is legal, and appropriate to fire first, to end the threat.
If said thug has a knife, It is legal and appropriate for the responder to disarm and render the threat null.

If said thug has a stick, bat or other blunt weapon, the same rules apply.

If you wait for the thug to act, you are as responsible for the harm caused, If there was a chance you could have stopped it, and did not.

ACTION
OB1Shinobi
Temple of the Jedi Order

Becoming a Jedi is first and foremost an issue of character, and character is an action.

Jedi is a VERB

Whatever we may feel about psychic abilities and spiritual wisdoms, or martial prowess or social influence, the reason that the Jedi archetype is so universally admired and desired is not so much for their power, as for what they do with their power. And how we ACT is what develops our character.

In fact that's the very definition of Character; what we DO, how we ACT in whatever situation we find ourselves.

The intuitive assumption is that if we act a certain way it is because we have character or do not have character, but this is backwards; our actions are not the result of our character, our character is the result of our actions!

Its all about action; ACTION is where all training begins and ends.

It's not an issue of what we know, or what we believe, or what we are capable of, or how smart or wise we are, or even how "nice" or "good" we are. That THING which is known as CHARACTER is a blend of different ideals which we can only say we have as a consequence of our ACTIONS. The results of our actions over time create a pattern of BEHAVIOR that either makes us valuable to the rest of the world or burdensome. If you want to be a Jedi, then start by being acutely aware of your ACTIONS. Especially their motivations and consequences.

The ideals to act in accordance with in order to be a person of high character, in other words, a JEDI, are generally; courage, honesty, responsibility and accountability, loving kindness, self discipline and self sacrifice, generosity, loyalty, and long term commitment.

Have you ever seen the way tuning forks work? Strike one and the sound it creates will cause another one nearby to vibrate. Spiritually, WE ARE JUST LIKE TUNING FORKS; and our ACTIONS create the resonance which activates others.

If your actions ACTivate these CHARACTERistics from within yourself, then you are a person of exceptional character and you will inspire others to be so as well. If not, then you have a choice to make; what kind of person do you wantto be? What kind of INFLUENCE do you WANT to be in the world?

We activate others no matter what we do; our resonance is felt and experienced by those around us regardless of its nature. You cannot change who you have been in the past, but you can take control of who you will be tomorrow by choosing to act in a way that produces the resonance you want the rest of the world to pick up on.

If you don't know where to start, then start with HONESTY. Honesty is the foundation upon which all of the rest of the ideals - the resonances - are built.

It is absolutely impossible to be a Jedi without having made a sincere commitment to honesty.

This begins with self honesty above all else but it extends afterwards to include those most directly around you. This is a specific action that you can take, today and every day, as genuine Jedi training; BE HONEST with yourself and BE HONEST with everyone you come in to contact with. Simply put; DO NOT LIE.

This does not mean you have to be "brutally honest", in fact I've found that in most cases "brutal honesty" is more about brutality than honesty, and "loving kindness honesty" would serve much MUCH better. And certainly there are

times to simply be silent.

A tip; if you want to avoid being honest because it is inconvenient or embarrassing (for you) then you're allowed to remain silent ONLY if there are no consequences for others, but you are not allowed to lie at all.

This is one a way to take action that will transform your life from average to exceptional, because the "vibration" becomes stronger as you maintain it, and the effects of your acts accumulate to raise the overall vibration of your surroundings

in a way that activates the people around you to match.

And that is a very Jedi thing to do.

INTERIOR

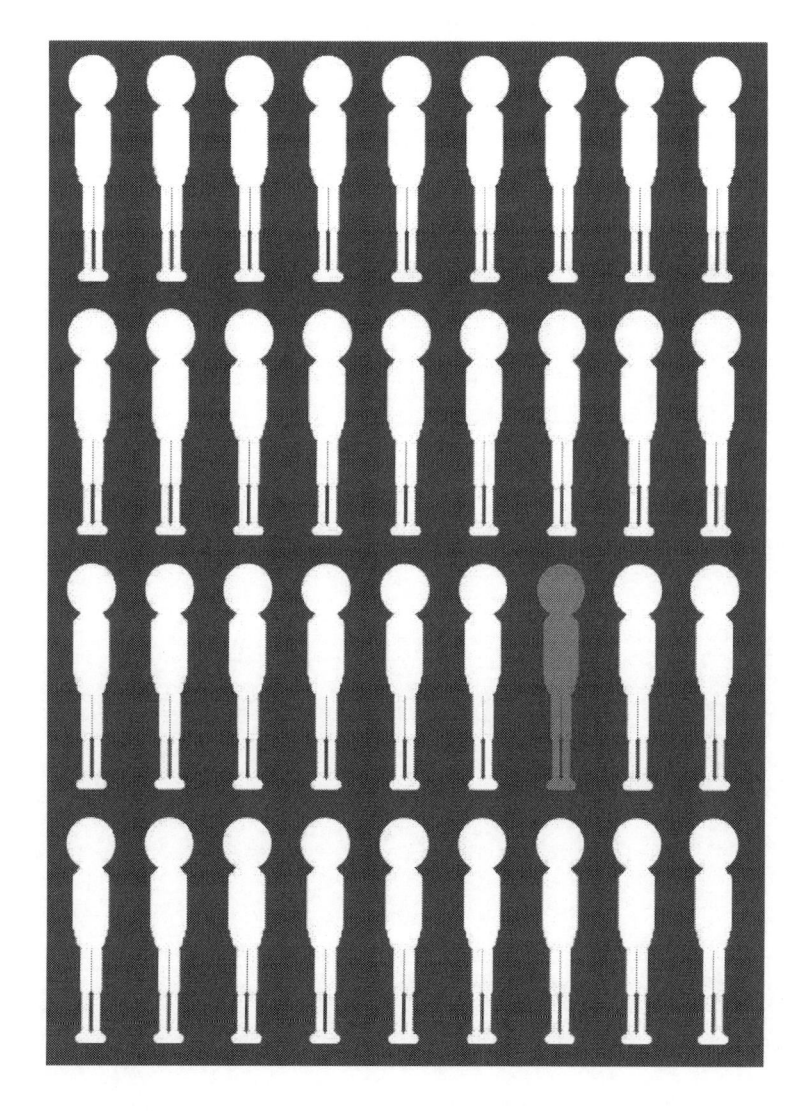

Picture by Mark Brereton, Temple of the Jedi Order

The Importance of Knowing Who You Are
By Who
Real Jedi Enclave

The Concept of Self-Knowledge

To know oneself is one of the greatest achievements a human being can hope to attain. It requires lots of time and plenty of patience but the first thing is to know what self-knowledge means.

What do you wear and why do you wear it?How do you speak and why do you say it?Who are your friends and how did you earn them?Where do you come from and how does it make you who you are?

Knowing oneself isn't about asking the question "Who am I?"You've been practicing your name since you were born.A name tells other people who you are, but it tells you nothing.It is less "who you are" and more "what you are, and why".

The most important thing that you can know in life,the greatest guiding principle for every decision you will make, is to know who you truly are. Not what others think you are,not what society or friends or even you want yourself to be,but who you truly are underneath the facade, the person you act like when nobody is watching.

Inner strength comes from this unknown and shadowy place. The confidence you seek to have with your life is born here.True power arrives from deep inside of you, but only when you've discovered what is there. A weapon will give you power, but only the power to harm. Information will give you power, but only the power to appear clever. Emotion will give you power, but only the power to lash out and touch the things out there.

There is nothing unnatural about wars and there is no shame in being clever and it is only human to reach out. But true power is not in these things. True power is in self-knowledge. It is in patience and time management. It is in courage and fear. It is in balance and idealism. It is in the refusal to give up or buckle to outside pressure.It is in the freedom to be who you are with no concern for what that means to others or to the world.

The wise warrior picks his battles and realizes he cannot fight all wars. The wise sage realizes his ignorance despite his abundance of knowledge.The wise Jedi knows that there is no trade-off for experience.Wisdom comes only from self-knowledge. What we know about others can help us know about ourselves but only you can know what makes you who you are.

Mental Strength and Personal Trust

Strength comes from knowing your limitations. To ignore limitation is to be very weak. Without limitation the body destroys itself, the mind degenerates, and the nerves become frazzled. Such a person can hardly be strong for oneself and if you cannot be strong for yourself then you will be limited in how you can be strong for others.

Trust is difficult to earn from others, but it is even more difficult to earn from yourself. People are defensive creatures, they strive to survive and thrive in this world of dangers and fear. No matter your qualifications, no matter how you promise, a person cannot truly trust you until you have proven that you are worth trusting in. They cannot trust until they know your soul. You, just the same, cannot trust yourself until that dark and shadowy abyss is known to you.

You will never be able to answer the question "Who am I?" with any degree of articulation. No amount of words could possibly encompass everything. So how will I know that I am known to myself? You ask. You will know. You will know when you make a decision that surprises you because you've finally decided to do what you want and not what is expected of you. You will know when people try to change you and you meet them with a pleasant smile and calm explanation of why that isn't going to happen.

The violent and angry person is not strong, they cannot trust themselves, and they most certainly do not know who they are. The one who is pretending to know themselves will flaunt and brag and argue and carry on. The one who is true is also humble and honest and comfortable in their own skin. There will be no need to talk a false game, to be theatrical or flashy, or to yell at those who do not know. Because the one who knows themselves can also see when others have yet to attain the same. And they understand, they are kind to them, they do not wish harm or bother to them.

They may become frustrated. They may be grumpy and sour and occasionally mean. But it is a frustration out of seeing what could be and what should be, but having to settle for what is. It is a grumpiness over the repeated misadventures of the soul, the countless times that they will have to trip over their own shoe laces before they learn to properly tie. The meanness comes in a lapse of judgement where the one who knows forgets that the other does not know. They see how they act and they forget that it is not who they are but it is who they are pretending to be. Sometimes the one who does not know forgets that they are not who they appear to be.

The Hazards of Being Lost'

The one who is wandering is only truly lost when they refuse to ask which way is west and which way is east. The one who is lost is only lost because they have not tried hard enough to be found. The one who is lost only remains lost when they refuse to believe that they have taken the wrong turn, or that they have lost track of where they are.

It is these people that are the most weak, the most vulnerable, the easiest to pray upon. The process of indoctrination begins with nullifying a person's awareness of what is true and what is false. An ambush of information and mis-information to confuse them and make them ask what is real. When they are finally broken, the indoctrinator substitutes his truth for theirs and they become one and the same. A unique individual becomes a puppet, a slave, cattle to another. One who does not know themselves does not know the truth from the lies, they are already confused and distraught in their confusion. How they jump with glee when the indoctrinator fills the gaps that they so desperately need to be filled. It is no matter whether the gaps are filled with concrete, or manure.

Without knowing who you are, you will believe anyone that tells you in the most convincing voice.

How can we know what is the right choice and what is the wrong choice when our internal compass is substituted for doctrine, and rules, and the influence of others? The ones who have learned great truths have never done so by adhering to the opinions of others. When no one else can see, you must find the light switch and turn it on. No matter how much you are told that the light switch does not exist or that it is evil or that the light cannot hold off the dark. You must believe that it can be done, but first you must believe in yourself, which comes from knowing who you are.

You cannot allow people to make you what you aren't. They may believe that it is for the best. They may believe that they are doing you a favor. But often this is like the blind leading the blind. They have not found out who they are to the extent that they know that all people are different. With different dreams. And different talents. The intolerant person has not yet found out who they are, thus they reject everyone else.

Wisdom

The path to wisdom is paved with self-knowledge and self-understanding. Wisdom is only attained when you can laugh with genuine gusto at your mistakes, and follow the path laid out before you rather than the one you'd rather have, and see others for who they are and not who you would rather they be. You must know who you are before you can know anything else. All other knowledge is just information -- some useful, and some not. Information comes from learning, but you may only truly learn something and attain mastery in it when you discover who it is that learns. And why.

The importance of knowing who you are is that all strength comes from it. You can gather all of the knowledge, do all of the training, act as a Jedi, and even serve others. You may do all of that before you have learned who you truly are.But you will never make dreams a reality, you will never discover truths, you will never see the world for the beautiful place that it is until you can follow those dreams, seek those truths with honest interest, and see without judgement.

A Jedi becomes a Master not when they have finished their training, not when they have been given rank or status by someone else, and not when they have done incredible things or served a certain number of hours. A Jedi becomes aMaster when being a Jedi is effortless. When it is who they are, through and through. Who they want to be and who they are finally converge and the struggle ends. They become a vessel for wisdom and kindness, a servant without even trying.

Beta's first lesson to Jedi Church
Beta Chambers
Aurora Borealis/Jedi Church(the Original)

Go to the Mirror:

In Aurora, The Padawan is reminded to take a moment at the Mirror, Often. Not to preen, adjust clothes and makeup, Not to fix the loose hair, or pop the latest zit.

No, We go to the Mirror, and call out our failings.

Later we write them down, all the failings we can think of, then we try with each one to find a Strength in it, or a counter to it, if it cannot be a strength.

Take a moment with the Mirror. Look at yourself, then look deep into yourself. Find your failings, from the simplest to the greatest, and know them. Write them down, then face them, and see if you can make a strength of them. If you cannot make a Strength of them, Devise a counter to them.

Force light your paths.

I will go first.
My Failings are:
- Arrogance
- Quick Temper
- Fear of my own fate, although such fate is unknown
- Lack of connection to Family
- Caffeine
- Sugar.

Yes, there are certainly more, but these are the ones I need to face.

- Arrogance = self confidence, but too much, with a little bit of brass to cover my simple fears. I must release the fears, and keep the confidence, and try to be a little less showy
- Quick Temper = Lack of calm. Maintain calm no matter the course, Guide the temper back into resolution, and energy

- Fear of my own fate = fear of the unexpected. Remember that the Unexpected is a nebulous thing, and is uncertain. at best. don't worry about what has not yet come.
- Lack of connection to family = family discordance, I must recognize that this is not just MY doing, and try to work WITH the others, and hope that they can work with me. If not, stay calm, and try again later.
- Caffeine = energy burst. Next leave, spend time adapting to going without caff, and find other energy supports (OJ and Chocolate Milk)
- Sugar = sweet tooth and dependence on poison. Gradually cut it back until it is no longer an issue.

None will be easy, but they are also only as hard as I make them to be.

The Art of Independence
Phortis Nespin
Temple of the Jedi Order

Self reliance

We all ask for help in our lives to learn and to understand. The problem with learning from each other is simple…How do you know either of you are right? The problem with learning from a book is that you have no idea if the author was bias or if the information contained within the reading is accurate. Dependence on another being is by far imperfect and can be laden with untruths, opinions, bias, and of course downright fabrication.

As I see self reliance, it is the ability to recognize that which you do not know, and find the answer for yourself. Each of us must be ready to find out the answer for themselves by going to the source. I did not know how to sew but I asked a person that I knew could sew because I have seen their work. That person was the source of my answer because they could teach me firsthand how to do it. I did not read a book about sewing or watch a video. I had someone with real world experience teach me.

Life cannot be lived by accepting someone else's word for truth. You may have an answer but you will never truly know if it is the truth until you find out for yourself. As the Holocron states…"You must dig your own well". It may be well and good to sit in a classroom and learn the basic rules of a given subject, but without practical application by you the learner, how will you know it to be true? It is Individual Insight or personal experience that makes the truth known to us.

Trust your feelings and trust that which you know as fact. The truth is the truth for all people. If you know the truth about a subject that you know as a verifiable fact, then that truth is absolute for everyone. Trust your feelings, if you hear something that does not "feel" right, search out the truth for yourself.

Self reliance is not just the ability to do something on our own, for that is just physical knowledge. It is the ability to think for yourself, find your own answers and believe in yourself. This is spiritual knowledge. The Force is not the truth, God is not the truth, and reality is not the truth. The truth is that which we can be absolutely sure of, and the Force, God, Reality, are that which cannot be known for sure.

So to this end we seek self reliance by combining all that we learn through books, videos, lectures, religions, and meditation, to understanding what we believe, what we know, and what our feelings tell us, and search for our own answers. This is why a Jedi can believe as a Christian Jedi, a Muslim Jedi, a Pagan Jedi, or a Buddhist Jedi. God, The Force, and Reality are as "One Unknown Truth".

Independence

There are two types of Independence, social independence and mental independence. It is important that we distinguish the difference so that we can concentrate on the more important of the two, mental independence. Social independence is the type that allows a person to be self reliant in the physical sense. You live in your own home, you buy your own food, and you work for yourself. You can "DO" whatever is required without the resources of other people. No matter how "independent" you think you are, there is always a need for assistance at some time or another. "No man is an island" and so independence is dependent on the percentage of time you can "DO" without others physical or monetary help.

True independence lies in the ability to think your own thoughts without the influence or subliminal ideology of others interfering with what you believe as truth. Our lives have been inundated with the beliefs of others dumped upon us since our birth. As children we believe what our parents believe. As teens we believe what our peers believe. As adults we believe what society wants us to believe. It is truly a independent mind that can see the influences foiled upon us and live within their own belief system.

Spiritual Self Reliance and Mental Independence are what I believe to be the goal of one who wishes to become enlightened to the "One Unknown Truth". As Jedi I believe we must strive to formulate our own understanding of the world around us and the world within ourselves.

I believe, "A Jedi who does not know himself, knows no one! "

Why can't I look in a mirror?: examining self-esteem
Gabriel Calderon
Chicago Jedi

Just yesterday I went to a seminar designed to help you live life to the fullest. While I did not like how they kept pushing me to register for a weekend (*read* pay lots of money), I could hear from people's testimonies how grateful they were. Part of what this program does is get you to examine yourself. specifically looking at those areas in your life that aren't going well, get to the root issue, and change it.

The area that came to mind was that of self-esteem. That area is a continual struggle for me. From what I have been told and read other blogs, I see it to be a very common issue for those who follow the Jedi path. So I kept thinking, turning it over in my head. When confronted by one of the moderators at the seminar, I was asked what would my life look like had I that confidence. My response was "I'd be awesome!" As I proclaimed that, I felt myself get lighter, be filled with energy, and much more focused.

So why can't we see that awesomeness in ourselves? ….fear and frustration.

I have chosen to walk the path of a Jedi. That in itself sets a high standard. I am to be fully aware of myself, my surroundings, and how I can best serve. The fact that I chose that path already speaks to my ability to attain that goal. I know that I can be better — and that thought is terrifying. We are so used to living a certain way that we have become comfortable in our complacency. We hide that spark of divinity within us wanting to burst out, that part saying "I AM AWESOME!" For with that recognition comes the calling to live it out. It would mean that I am more outgoing, willing to speak my mind, and telling the world that "yes, I am someone of value." We may think it takes an enormous amount of energy to be that active. Yet, it requires more energy to contain that divinity then letting it flourish.

But then there are those who have recognized their importance in the world. The interesting thing about being "awesome" is that you are awesome in all areas. (I am an awesome writer, an awesome speaker, an awesome teacher, an awesome friend, etc……) So we become aggravated not knowing where to even begin that portrayal of ourselves. It would seem more efficient to focus on one aspect and neglect the others. But that thought too only adds to the irritation because we know that it would be a disservice to our identity. Surprisingly, my mind wandered to an article I read where "willpower" is likened to a muscle that must be exercised. The more you practice it, the stronger it becomes. I had also just finished reading a chapter in a book my boss will soon have published on living into a role. The more we wear a mask, the more we identify with it – so we better put on one "better" than ourselves.

These two streams converged into my thinking the way to increase self-esteem, is to continue on the Jedi Path. It makes you strive to be better than you currently are. Eventually, you will reach a point where you will stop thinking about living as a Jedi and simply BE a Jedi. You will take down the obstacles of fear and frustration brick by brick until you realize that you are AWESOME.

From Rozen's White Journal
Rozen
Temple of the Jedi Force

I found a very interesting rabbit hole tonight that I think you may find interesting.

I was trying to more deeply immerse myself with the energy of the IM as usual, and lately I've been using bi-neural beats and deep relaxation to help in that department.

Quick backtrack: I came to an idea a few nights ago that spirit guides are pieces of the ego that are either fractured and in the process of integrating, or needing integration. It wasn't a great leap to realize an aspect of the IM could be a similar case. Keeping in mind that I used to deliberately fracture aspects of my psyche as a coping mechanism and problem-solving tool, this new perspective lead to the understanding that a small portion of the IM already exists as the 'Decider' aspect of myself.

Where the Thinker is the personified function of the brain, the Critic is the self-checker for social behavior, and the Observer is the personified function of memory. I think it is this Decider that actually causes the interaction between mind and body, as well as body to the world.

Small quibbles and more parcing of the Self, but this is actually leading up to something interesting.

What I was working on tonight was that I wanted to actually see the IM, not just experience it as a memory of voice and imagined layers of symbolism. All of those exist within the Inner Universe, and completely subject to my own misinterpretations. Those kinds of misinterpretations are costly on a karmic scale, and frankly, I'm getting tired of my Ego constantly getting in the way.

So I decided that with a certain tone on the bi-neural track I was listening to, I would reveal to myself the IM as it really is. The following is full of useless metaphor because I lack any other experience coming remotely close to this:

It is like opening your eyes, to discover you are a sponge. Porous, floating effortlessly in the energy of the Force. This is the body. The form of the sponge itself is hollow. Whenever I saw a thing, I would feel a thing. Whenever I saw something I desired, the Thinker would associate the object through the Observer (memory), and the Decider would respond with the appropriate chemical response. Underline: the Decider would decide to feel desire for the object based on memory. This empty sponge filament would then fill with the basic energy that causes the body to experience the desire.

This works exactly the same way with Reiki. When I chose to feel Reiki, it was this etheric membrane that filled up with Reiki that emanated from me. When I wanted to build my own Inner Universe, the membrane filled up full of complex weaves of memory, expectations, learned reactions, and so on, at the energetic level, causing the body to react and exist within this complex structure, like a temporary second mind.

I suddenly find myself in control of not just what I feel, but how I feel it. Not just with perspective, but down to every little bit of my energy.

There's so much more going on than that, but I'm going to sleep on it. Maybe I'll choose better descriptions in the morning.

Myth and Jediism
Merin Kyo Den
Temple of the Jedi Force

All religions no matter what they are have a Story to tell. These stories impart wisdom to the follower and show a path to the soul. That's what their there for. The story or "Myth" is what defines a religion. Now when I say myth it's not to say a religious story is true or false, to me that does not matter. What really matters is it true or false to YOU. These stories must be believed by the person who follows them. To believe the myth of your faith is to take it into your soul and make it part of your story, your myth if you will. You see it's that belief, that faith, that gives it the power to change us. without it how would it touch our souls? This does not mean to follow blindly, but to put your trust in the wisdom of the storyteller.

You may say that these stories cant be proven, but I ask you what is the value of faith if it can be proven as fact? You see, to me at least, faith is what changes the hearts of people, not scientific proof. Carl Jung wrote that the collective human psyche is inherently religious, I believe this to be true. We need the myth, as a race and as individuals. By our very nature we are religious. So you can say we need our myths. They tell us so much about ourselves, things we may never see without them. Everything we can be or aspire to is within our myths. From the greatest heights to the lowest depths of human nature, they contain all about us. These collective myths our the story of us. Our story.

We may not agree with the stories of other religions, and that's fine. Yet I think we need to look at them for what they do for there followers. Do they help them to learn about themselves? I think for the most part they do. To say to someone" Your religion is false. It's a lie" is missing the point. Telling someone that they are wrong in their beliefs does not in most cases steer the person to your point of view, but has the opposite effect. It puts them on to the defensive and closes them off, the opposite of what you tried to do! Instead, let me suggest this if I may. Embrace their myth as you embrace your own. Share myths instead of trying to correct mistakes. Do not judge the words, but judge the effect on the person.

A myth should be judged, in my opinion, on it's value to and effect on the individual and not on it's accuracy. To understand another we must first see things as they see it, and not by what we believe they see. If we learn to embrace all myth then we can begin to extract wisdom from all religion and all peoples. Remember that our minds, early on, our given to us by our parents and our society. When we look at another culture we look at it through the eyes of our own culture. This applies to all and not just one country or people. Right or wrong, lie or truth, this is relative to the mind we we're raised with.

Learning to embrace another's myths is to glimpse into the mind of their society. Further still learning to embrace all myths is to look inside the mind of all mankind. It's my opinion that if we all learned to embrace the myths of the religions of the world that would in itself begin a new myth to carry us into the future, our future. All of this should be embraced. It's my story, your story, the story of mankind that's being told after all by many different singers, but singing the same song. Maybe one day we will all learn to sing along in harmony. You with your myth, me with mine, but both together. Separate and still as one, Like a real harmony should be. So what about Jediism you may ask;

As Jedi what do we believe you may ask? In the inherent worth of every living thing, All life is worthy of respect, support, and caring just because it is alive. In working towards a culture that is relatively free of discrimination on the basis of gender, race, sexual orientation, national origin, degree of ability, age, etc. In the sanctity of all sentient life, In the importance of democracy within religious, political and other structures, In the separation of church and state; and the freedoms of speech, association, and expression. That the systems of truth in the field of morals, ethics, and religious belief that we have studied are not absolute, but part of a greater whole: they vary by culture, by religion, and over time. And in the importance of individual believers collectively determining influences and policies within their chosen faith group, and have the right to advocate for their change and evolution. These are just some of the beliefs at the very core of our faith.

A religious myth is not a yardstick with which to measure the world by, but a mirror to look at your true self. It's the yardstick you measure YOURSELF by. Jediism, as with all religions, is but a mirror to your soul. It's myths are meant to take you on an inward journey. Each story, each parable, reveals to us another aspect of the human soul. Much like the religions of today in their infancy, Jediism is still being defined by it's followers and struggling for acceptance in the mainstream world. When we look at this with just a glance, it's easy to discount this as just the whim and fancy of over dramatic Star Wars fans.

What we re going through is no different then what Islam or Christianity went through in their early years. Really in the end we have to ask ourselves what makes a religion valid in the first place. What gives any religion ownership of the truth. If you look deeper you will see that all religions tell the same story. The singer and the tune may be a little different, but it's all the same song. We as Jedi are not doing anything new. We are singing the same song as every religion before us, we just have new singers. In the end it's not really which one is true or false, that's not really what's important. What really matters is the effect, the change, it's brought about upon you. The absolute is not important, for it's the truth within YOUR soul that will bring forth fruit to enrich the world.

You see with religion, it really is the same story, told over and over. All of the major religions around today have borrowed from older religions that have come before them. The virgin birth is a god example. In Buddhism, just as in Christianity, we have a virgin birth story that seems to mirror the Christian one. As the story goes (or how I remember it....LOL) is that Maia, the mother of Siddhartha Buddha, was taken to a field and tended to by angles. They anointed her with oil and the a white elephant descended from heaven bearing a pink lotus in it's trunk. It then entered her womb and that is how the Buddha was conceived. Sound familiar? Also the Buddha was tempted with three sins of the world, Also borrowed by Christianity in my opinion. I could site more, but really the point is that if we learn to view religion as myth used to show an aspect of our nature to us, we can take and borrow wisdom from anywhere, even a movie. It's when we get caught up in the TRUTH of things that we run into trouble.

When we ascribe absolute truth to a myth then it can no longer effectively guide us the way it was meant to. Instead of making the inward journey that was intended the person ends up using the stories to judge the world around them, and not inside them. This is the danger of taking myth as an absolute. You close yourself off to all of the wisdom that may well be right before your eyes

Self Awareness and the Jedi Path
Charles McBride
Kharis Institute

Self awareness while one of the hardest qualities to test for within the animal kingdom is also one of the most fundamental concepts existent within the human experience. The core of self awareness is the ability of a being to be aware of it's own impulses, drives, emotions, and mental conditions. This state of being is one that while most people have some experience with the vast majority of the population is not fully proficient in. Often self awareness is seen as a concept connected to sentience and is considered only in the application of determination of sentience or in the ability to BE self aware. In this writing instead we will be examining self awareness as a state of being to be reached for, achieved, and it's key defining aspects as a core element of the Jedi Path.

In day to day life self awareness as an attainable state of being is of the utmost concern. Without self awareness we wander around blindly flailing a slave to both emotion and impulse. Self awareness while not necessarily altering our course tempers our direction and motivation with logic, rationality, forward thinking, and the ability to extrapolate complex outcomes in volatile situations. Further self awareness is important in society as it allows one to weigh their needs against the needs of others and determine without prejudice a proper application of time and energy toward a goal. For any who seek to better themselves spiritually, emotionally, and physically self awareness then becomes the cornerstone of their path and direction.

The Jedi path while having many external and internal components is rooted in the ability to understand the self and through that understanding hone and focus self and action toward a better goal and outcome in the world around us. This may be a very personal direction in which the world around us is our day to day lives or it may extend to the greater world such as service to others. In this self awareness is the unifying force between the concepts of Jedi that exist within various online and offline communities and in this it is the root of all Jedi development. In becoming self aware we become better able to determine not only the person we wish to become but also the person we truly are. We gain the ability to hone that person, change that person, and direct that person toward greater things.

The Jedi Path focuses often around The Jedi Code, referring to in this writing as the code which begins with "There is no emotion, there is peace."

This code though often interpreted in many ways is pivotal in understanding that one must look inward without bias seeking to understand and gain knowledge without the influences of rampant passions of the body nor emotions dwelling primarily in the mind and heart. In this decisions while made often due to emotions will not be made with the charge of emotion as the driving factor of intensity and ultimate resolution.

To give an example in the form of service the Jedi are often called to aid others in their day to day life. A being comprised of emotion without self analysis and understanding may give all they have even to self destruction to help another when a lesser sacrifice, or no sacrifice at all, is more warranted. Instead of giving the homeless man on the street a hot meal a being comprised only of emotion may in that moment provide him all of their home and belongings moving themselves into destitution in the action. In the next breath of regret a being comprised only of emotion may seek vengeance upon their former charge and kill them in a heat of passion. The fact that we rarely do things of this nature to such vehement intensity shows that a degree of self awareness exists. However a greater understanding of the self leads to knowing why it is you seek to help the homeless man, pass him on the street, or even drive him to the homeless shelter. In understanding the why of what you do you are better able to temper emotions in the heat of a moment.

In the recognition of the complexities of internal movement and decision we begin to understand our true selflessness as well as selfishness. In this we can then act to help others with a clear conscience knowing we were neither driven by guilt into the action of helping another nor moved solely by compassion without an understanding of their situation. It is this internal analysis that allows our good actions to be the best that they can and ensures that we do to the best of our ability the most we can to help others. Without self awareness we second guess not only actions but the roots of those actions. With no internal awareness each action is taken as a potential betrayal of our subconscious mind or emotional state.

To look into the world likewise we must also be able to look into ourselves. If we can not judge the world around us without some level of disconnection and distance then we gain no true measurement of the events unfolding around us. Every action becomes a personal insult, every reaction we make becomes an inevitable circumstance, events are seen as random, and ultimately we descend into chaos if we lack the ability to first look inward with awareness so we may then look outward without a colored lens placed upon our sight. If we can not see past our own emotional state, preconditioned prejudices, experiences, and internal dramas then we can not in good conscience act upon the world as forces of positive change within it. In this self awareness becomes even more essential in the path of the Jedi for without internal awareness we will perceive all actions only from our root position with no influence or understanding of the root position of those around us.

Jedi are counseled to seek knowledge, wisdom, understanding, and enlightenment through The Force. It is the very nature of The Path that we use The Force to gain a better grasp of the world around us. In this effort to gain better awareness of the world our feelings, premonitions, impulses, and perceptions are all the tools we have to truly tap into the Force. This makes it even more important that we understand our own thoughts and emotions as well as the roots they stem from. It is far too easy to turn the world into a black and white movie with The Force taking the sides of Good and evil. This is a great folly for a Jedi for in that they loose true awareness of The Force and instead become slaves to the ego and subconscious mind. Only through understanding the self, being aware of the self, focusing inward to see the influence of the self can we then gain a better understanding of the subtle influence of the Force and its movements. Further without the admittance of the self and the impact it has on our own interpretation of The Force we will never truly gain a guiding connection to it.

Self awareness is a honed state gained with practice and reminder. It is initiated in exercises of meditation, looking inward, and honestly seeing the whole of the self as well as its component parts. It is developed through action repetition. In the moment of a day in which we act without awareness we must as Jedi remind ourselves of the importance of being self aware, how we relate to the self, yet we must do so without harshness but with understanding. In The Code it is said "There is no emotion, there is peace." Regret as well as shame are also emotions and do nothing for the Jedi seeking to better the understanding of the world around them. Instead awareness is acceptance and the decision to change actions in the future. This requires patience, time, focus, and dedication to achieve and maintain to any degree of development.

From Rozen's Red Journal
Rozen_Mirax
Temple of the Jedi Force

I have been striving for self-improvement primarily over the last few weeks. My main goal was equanimity - to be able to see all people equally without attachment, aversion or judgement. Admittedly, it is REALLY difficult to always remember to respect the lesson and remember the goal, especially at work. I struggled, fought it, made mistakes.

Turns out my problem was that I wasn't aggressive enough in overturning the habit. Once I was able to start seeing and acting beyond people's ego as just a mask of their Inner Master, everything opened up. I started treating people equally, but here was the catch:

I could not use this perspective until I accepted that my own ego was just a shadow, a reaction of something living in the physical world. I detested that idea, that as the mediator between the Force and the physical, I was just a process. It is a very compassionless, loveless relationship.

Then again, my greatest karma is learning humility.

This is where I had so much difficulty relating to the new age movement, which is based in love. I totally get and respect that their lesson is in Compassion. Mine, however, is in Truth. When my IM asks me "What are you a Master of?" my answer is always Truth. I want it as the medium for everything I do, in speaking, in creating, in writing, in evolving. It is what I want to share with the world. When I follow the IM, every single lesson has brought me another step closer to being a clear voice for IT.

I can't tell you how lonely following this path has been for the last 20 years. It has always been my calling, and until coming here, I had never found anyone who I felt 'got it'.

So, in short, I guess what I am trying to convey is "always follow that little voice", even when it feels like it has you lost for a decade in a starless desert. The gift of being my True Self, attaining my Higher Purpose as a Jedi and as a human being has been the most enlivening and empowering experience I have ever had.

Trial Of Darkness
Michael Southerskies
Temple of the Jedi Order

Have any of you ever looked upon the dark side, within and without? Not just the dark side, mind you, but the unquestioning, evil thoughts that seep into the back of your mind? We've all been there, don't attempt to delude yourself otherwise. Temptation and impulsion rise up every now and again. You'll see them coming sometimes, and at others, they'll catch you off-guard.

In the Monomyth, the hero faces the Road of Trials, a "series of tests, tasks or ordeals that the person must take to begin the transformation", as well as Temptation. So too do we all in life. And our trials greatly vary, depending on who we are, or where we are.

Has your conviction ever been tested so? Have you ever looked upon the dark side and felt its embrace? Been tempted? Heard the whispers and liked their promises? In this sense, the dark is the cold. It's the creeping frost that you don't feel until it's too late. It's the sudden change in temperature we call a cold snap. The overnight plummet. The instantaneous fall.

The promise of wealth is common. Pleasure, in some shape or form. An easy way out of a problem, but at what cost? My own values? My ethics? My morals? Because often, that's the cost. Your self-respect. Your Self.

I worked at a liquor store in a fairly bad neighborhood. Every now and then I'd get the same offer: Deal drugs, trade stolen goods, sell to minors. And it all came with the same offer; "make a little more money". I turned them down, after a moment's hesitation. Then, temptation gave way for the rest of my thinking process. The moral, ethical and legal senses screamed out at me. And each time, I refused. Even the "little" offers that seemed so insignificant.

I stood against the darkness, the evils that lurk within my society. And I won a little victory there that day. I was in a position to ruin lives, to sell that which had been stolen by force, to sell poison to children. I refused to become part of what I hated. But when I gave it thought later on, I knew on the flip side, what I had refused. The money was tempting, for a moment. The power? I've seen the slaves addicts make of themselves, and they'd be beholden to me.

And so, I turned away from it. It wasn't worth my values or my standards. I looked upon the face of corrosion, and corruption. Its face was the Tempter made manifest. I looked at that face, and turned it down. And a victory was won. But I won't forget that moment where I weighed it up.

Where I thought to myself 'I could use some extra cash'. I felt the touch in that moment.

So too, the Jedi of the fiction have stood against darkness, within and without. It is a trial of willpower, of strength. A test of their wisdom, their courage and their conviction. Resisting the temptation of the dark side. And not all of them do. Look at Anakin Skywalker. Look at Isildur, from Lord of the Rings. They gazed too long into the abyss, and the abyss gazed back.

Evil and the Dark Side don't always whisper though. Sometimes they'll take you. Easily. In a snap. A momentary lapse in judgement or reason is all it takes. That one bout of profanity. One punch, or slap. A brief instant where you do something you'd say only a jerk would do. Inconsiderate, violent, abusive.

Like Rorschach in the Watchmen, who discovered something so fundamentally evil that it drove him over the edge in a single night. He went from street-walking vigilante who worked with a good man like the Nite Owl (II), to a grim parody of the loner antihero, amoral and nigh-sociopathic.

It just takes a moment. That one bad second. And bang. You'll regret it then, or you'll regret it later, but you'll go over the edge. You might just come back, but too late. You lost your control for a second there, and now someone or something around you is paying the price for your moment of weakness.

The child you yell at. The friend you abuse. The loved one that you injure. The stranger you're inconsiderate towards. The rival, or enemy, who just didn't deserve it today. These are all Dark moments. The lack of control.

I won't speak for everyone but I've been there. And I'm sure more than a few of you will have. Many of you who have, will regret it to this day. You'll have apologized profusely, made amends, grown from it. But the imprint is there, especially in those who did lasting damage. And the damage is done to you

Have you been there at the snap and resisted at the last second? Pulled back your raised hand, lowered your voice before it rose? I've been there, too. Recognized the signs and held myself back, as it were. Stopped myself unnecessarily escalating an already bad situation. And that's a victory, too. Not one you'd be lauded for, but a victory of principles, fundamentals and decency. And definitely one you can grow from if you know how to.

There I've listed two brushes with the darker side that we'll all experience in our day to day lives, without having to go look for it. It will find you. The point of this?

I want you to give it some thought. Don't just meditate, but contemplate. Introspect. Think about yourself. Think about your own experiences with these things. The quick snap, the slow corruption. The really dark side, that the Dark Aspect doesn't represent. The evil side.

Think about what you learned. Think about how you felt. About how you've grown since then. About your victories and your defeats. Reflect on what happened, how you reacted. Why you reacted that way. Make a note of it in your journal, or just mentally.

Chances are, you've been tried. It's just a matter of knowing, and willingness to learn. The defeats won't be proud moments. And the victories may just be our day to day lives. But that doesn't demean the experience. Learning from this experience is paramount, so that you may better stand against the darkness in the future and overcome the trials your life will throw at you.

May the Force serve you well.

"Chaos claims the unwary or the incomplete. A true man may flinch away its embrace, if he is stalwart, and he girds his soul with the armour of contempt."
~Inquisitor Gideon Ravenor, writings, Warhammer 40k: The Armour of Contempt

EXTERIOR

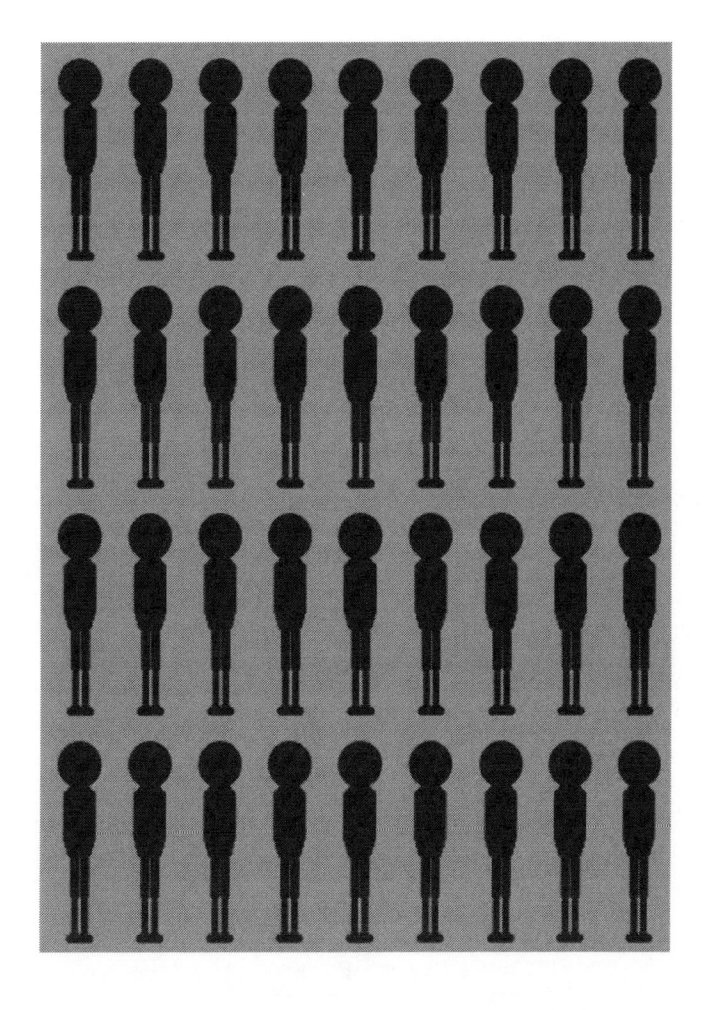

Picture by Mark Brereton, Temple of the Jedi Order

Emotional Integration
Ray Jenson
Jedi School

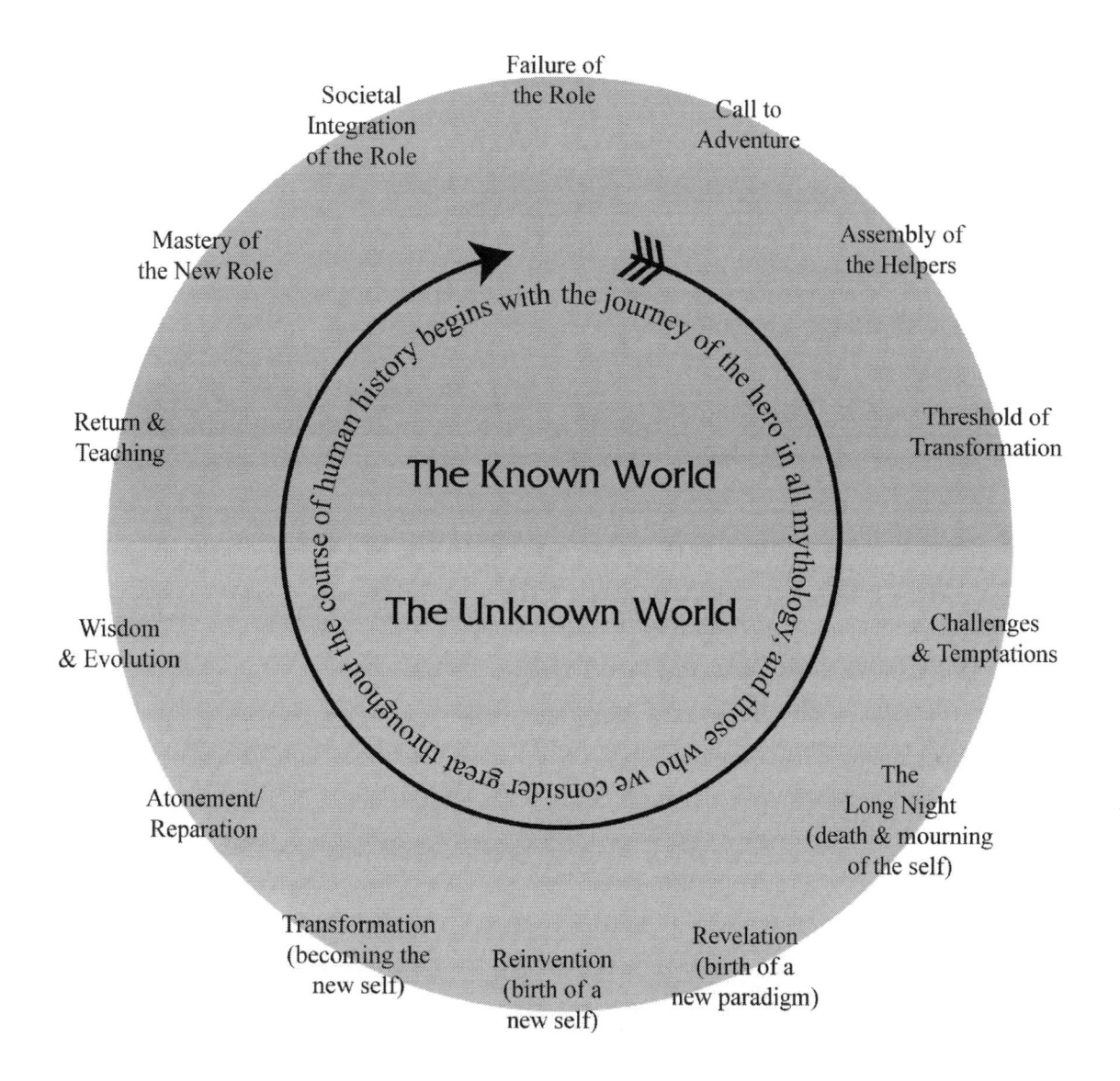

Diagram: A circular "hero's journey" diagram divided into The Known World (upper half) and The Unknown World (lower half), with text around the inner circle reading "history begins with the journey of the hero in all mythology, and those who we consider great throughout the course of human". Stages arranged clockwise around the circle:

- Failure of the Role
- Call to Adventure
- Assembly of the Helpers
- Threshold of Transformation
- Challenges & Temptations
- The Long Night (death & mourning of the self)
- Revelation (birth of a new paradigm)
- Reinvention (birth of a new self)
- Transformation (becoming the new self)
- Atonement/Reparation
- Wisdom & Evolution
- Return & Teaching
- Mastery of the New Role
- Societal Integration of the Role

The Jedi ways are based in service. So what service does a Jedi offer? Put very simply: a Jedi's duty is to overcome darkness. In that overcoming, we need to understand how darkness works, because one way that darkness works is to obscure the truth of things.

One of the first lessons we teach all of our students is emotional integration. At Jedi School, this is often referred to as "the only mandatory practice" and we believe (through our own observations) that about 80% of the ailments and issues in the world are because of emotional issues at their core. Clearing these up doesn't magically heal everything, but it prevents the harm from being ongoing.

To resolve issues through integration, there are 4 steps and 3 guidelines that we have arranged to the acronym <u>BIFOCAL</u>. We have found that those willing to go through the emotional integration process tend to have a much simpler time actually undergoing the process.

It's an ongoing process, because as human beings we are always generating emotions. These emotions can sometimes create noise, especially if we haven't dealt with them and they affect us strongly. At these times, our ability to listen to the Force wanes, and so it's difficult to stay true to ourselves and the role we chose in becoming a Jedi.

Results

Before we get into the actual steps of emotional integration, let's talk about the results. If you want to skip this boring stuff and go to the next heading, feel free.

Emotional integration has been taught around the world to approximately 100,000 people. And in our teaching, we have discovered that people who have severe schizophrenia, advanced Alzheimer's, and other biological conditions (structures in the brain created through DNA) which react poorly to stress, should avoid emotional integration. It advances these conditions, rather than preventing advancement, and that's counter to our aims.

None of these results is scientifically-validated. They are merely our own observations.

But those who are in the early stages of Alzheimer's and whose symptoms in schizophrenia are minor have had some really profoundly beautiful results, and a few have managed to reverse the progress of their symptoms. This doesn't eliminate the condition; it merely lessens the impact of these conditions on the individual, and allows for a greater level of productive living.

Those who have anxiety disorders such as PTSD and GAD will find that this technique is profoundly effective, as there are well over 1000 people with good results in both of these areas.

Those who have depression (especially anxiety-triggered depression) will find that they are blessed with the ability to use this technique to its full advantage very quickly. In fact, we've noticed that it seems to reverse long-term depression (dysthymia) in as little as 2 years.

In about 100,000 practitioners worldwide, nobody we know of has died from integration, directly. However, there has been one individual in Germany who had a heart condition and tried to do too much at once, and the resulting stress on his body caused a heart attack (myocardial infarction) due to the pre-existing condition. We specifically counsel people not to do too much, and to take it only to a particular level of intensity, which he refused to accept and so his death resulted from trying to resolve everything at once.

There is a point at which anything becomes harmful. We advise people not to torture themselves with their feelings for a long time, and this is why we recommend a 10-minute limit to integration.

A Few Definitions

In order to do integration, there has to be an understanding of a few terms that we throw around a lot.

- Ego: This is the part of us responsible for being reactionary. It's also the part of us responsible for survival. Rather than trying to eliminate or destroy the ego, we choose to train ourselves with it.
- Drama: This is any reaction which is stronger than is needed for the situation. It's appropriate to shout at someone who is acting like a moron if that helps the situation; it's inappropriate if its only purpose is to make ourselves feel better.
- Composure: The ability to resist overreaction.
- Severity: Consistent application of true principles (whatever they might be).

These definitions are our understanding. The concept is more important than which word we use.

The Process

The emotional integration process should be done daily, at the end of the day, for no longer than 10 minutes (and at least a full minute is recommended). We often feel exhausted at the end of the day, but somehow unable to sleep for a while. Emotional integration can help with the underlying emotional states that cause this, once we identify them. We will feel both ready to sleep and yet energized when we do this correctly.

With practice, emotional integration can become an automatic response to drama, allowing us to process our negative emotions so that they no longer have control. The negative emotions are still present; we simply don't feel compelled to act on them, and so are able to retain our composure.

Overview
Generally, the process is 4 steps, followed by 3 guidelines. The 4 steps are:
1. Breathe
2. Inhabit
3. Feel
4. Observe

These four steps are also followed with three additional guidelines:
5. Complete
6. Accept
7. Laugh

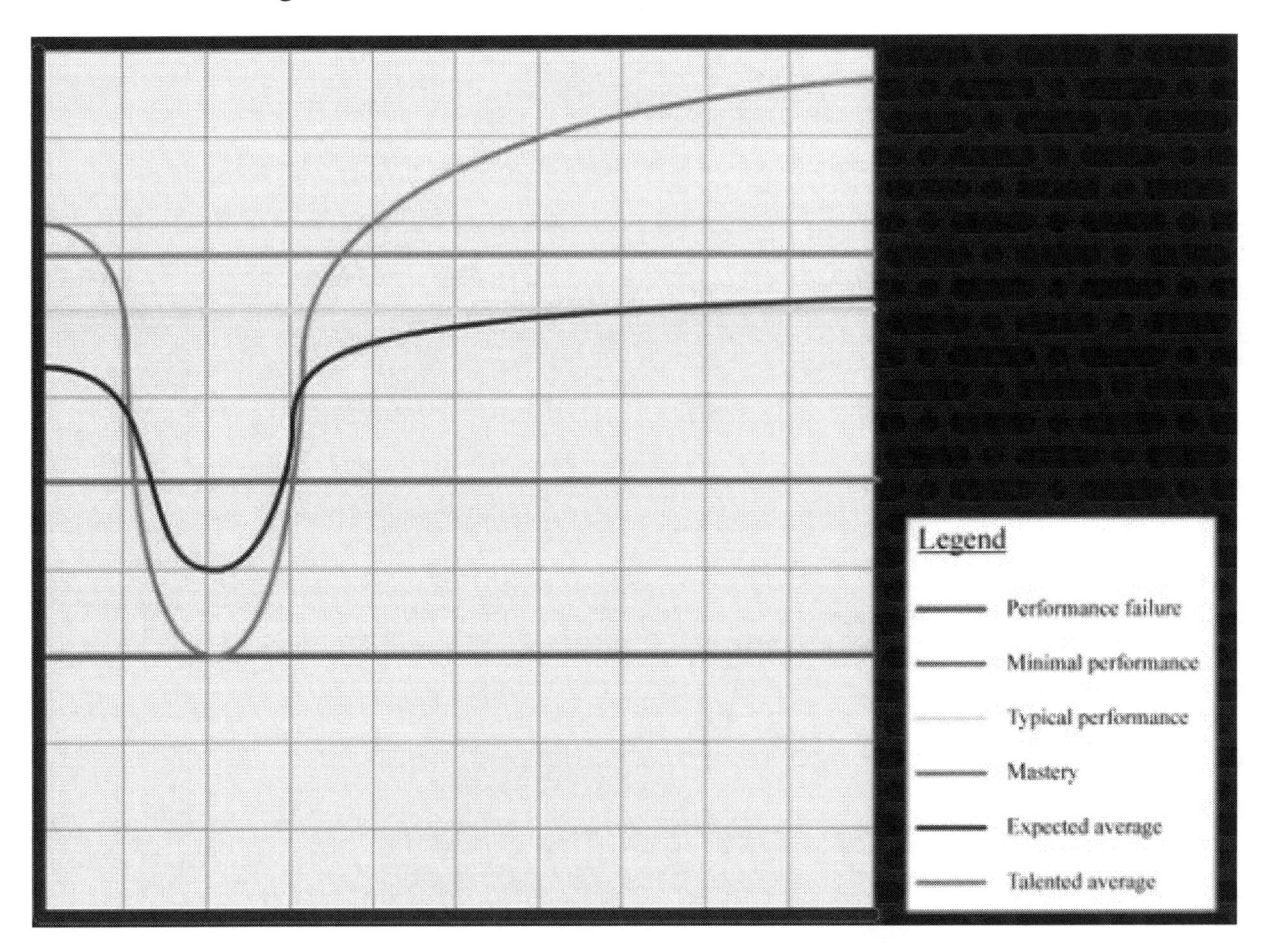

Fig. 1: The Performance Lull

All of these together are emotional integration. Failing any one of these, there may be good results for a while, after which there is a lull in performance. This "performance lull" is illustrated best with Figure 1.

The graph shows two averages: the expected average for most people, and the high-level average of a talented person. Like any skill, there are people who are very talented with emotional integration. Lots of people even do it naturally.

Talented people get very frustrated when it stops working, however, and so they believe that this failure means they really aren't that good in the first place. In general, this lull can last anywhere from mere hours to a year or more. But always, continuation of the practice will eventually overcome the lull, so long as there isn't inactivity.

There's a big difference between a temporary lull and a blockage, however. A blockage is due to our own resistance to the process, and our inability to see beyond ourselves and into an objective frame; or (conversely) being stuck in an objective mind-set and unable to see subjectively what is actually happening.

Blockages happen and are overcome by severity.

Performance lulls, on the other hand, are simply a normal part of the process. They happen from time to time. The only way to overcome them is...

severity.

Severity resolves both of these issues: one, because action must be taken; the other, because inaction must be avoided.

Emotional Triggering

Emotional triggering is what happens when we react to something. When we are reactionary, we have to wait for something to happen or we aren't really capable of taking action, since there's nothing else happening to guide us.

To be proactive, we have to learn to trigger our own emotions, and this is one of those things which is best left to a teacher in person. But in general, the concept is that we can actually pull up any feeling as if from a database, just reaching down within us and activating the feeling. Actors and politicians do this all the time. But to be fair, this is why we don't like politicians, and what makes us adore the actors.

But in the beginning, we can simply use an experience we had which affected us. We would also recommend smaller experiences first, since those need to be cleared before the larger issues can truly be dealt with.
Imagine a rock slide. In order to get to the boulders, the smaller rocks and pebbles have to be cleared away first. Then we can easily reach the boulders in order to break them down. We have to first comprehend that if we are to remove everything at once, the whole mountain would come crashing down,

Diaphragmatic Breathing

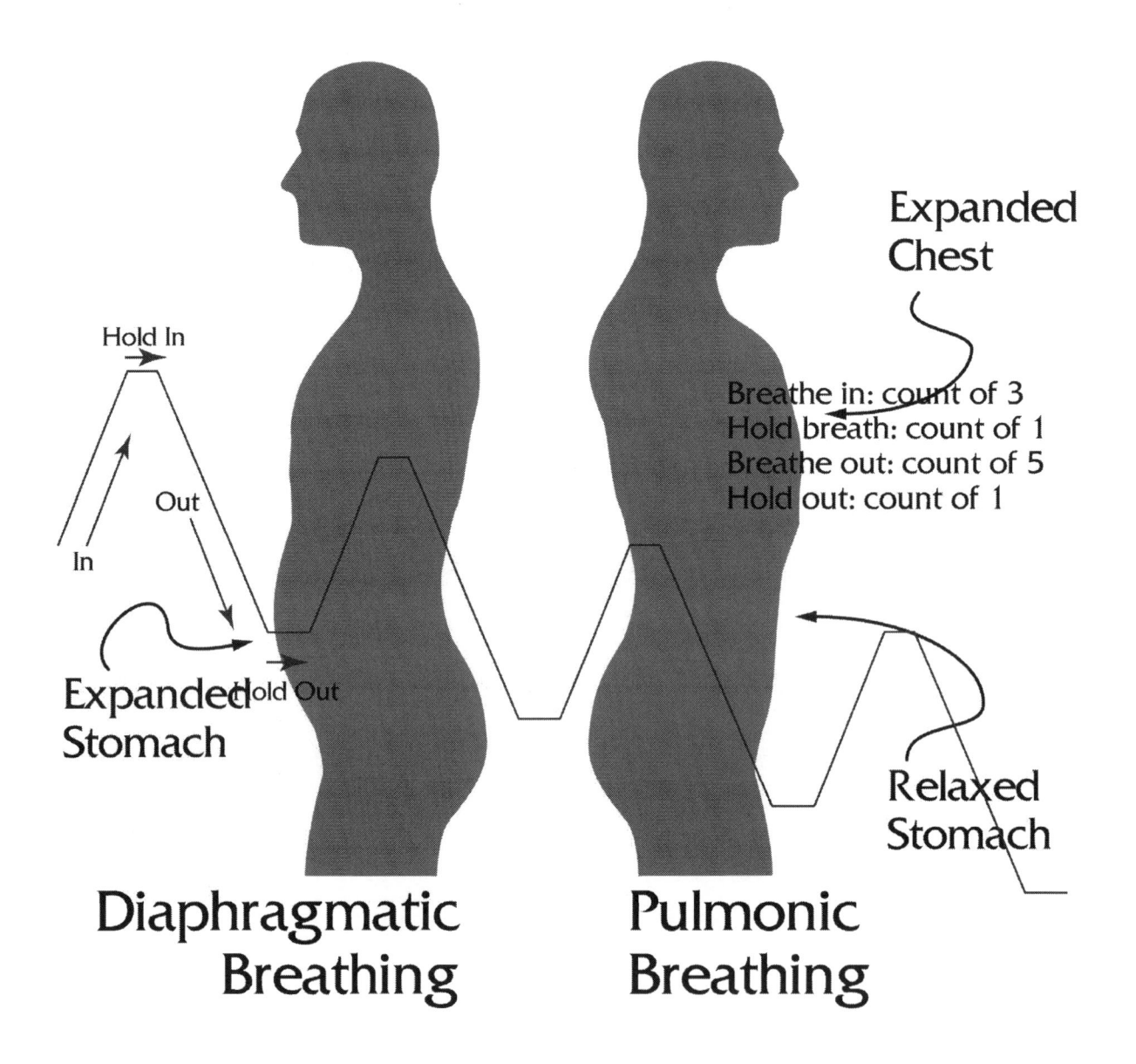

Hold In
In
Out
Hold Out
Expanded Stomach

Pulmonic Breathing

Expanded Chest
Breathe in: count of 3
Hold breath: count of 1
Breathe out: count of 5
Hold out: count of 1
Relaxed Stomach

and even if we survive, there will be scars that we're likely not to recover from.

So please: take your time. But be honest: have the integrity to say that when something is affecting you, you are affected.

Breathing

There are several things that people don't really understand about breathing. First, we do breathe as a function of being alive. We can't not breathe. But people try to mistake breathing deeply for breathing evenly. We breathe evenly when we relax. We breathe evenly when we meditate. And when we breathe from the diaphragm, we naturally bring in more oxygen. Breathing deeply isn't required. Breathing regularly with the diaphragm is.

When we're breathing with the diaphragm, the air flows more deeply into the lungs. And as the air flows in, your chest will naturally expand a little. The trick is to make your stomach do all the work. They teach this kind of breathing to singers and public speakers, as well as in meditation.

As you go through this process, the aim is to keep your breathing as even and regular as possible. But if it doesn't stay that way, it's fine: emotions can affect physiology when we react.

Inhabit

The concept of investment is one of really getting down into the experience of being yourself. It's been described as bringing the soul into the body, compacting and really fully investing in being you for a time. There is no technique: one simply does it with an act of apparent will, such as raising an arm. You will it to happen, and it happens.

Feeling

Feeling is paying attention to the emotions. It's nothing more than being aware of your emotional state. It takes practice (especially in men) to become aware of it, and sometimes that awareness takes us by surprise. Our aim isn't to dramatize or to overreact; our aim is to genuinely feel whatever is there, and remove its control over us. But in order to do that, we have to feel.

But rather than giving in to those feelings, we simply have to sit passively as the emotion runs its course. This is what we call *sitting in an emotion,* and it's an important part of our training. In fact, we have a chart about the emotions we feel, made through years of observation to teach us the nature of the ego, and its tendency to use the emotions to hide things from us Our ability to comprehend the above table will rely heavily on practice, and asking the right questions.

Observation

We want to create a condition called *separable awareness* in order to be able to both feel and observe at the same time. For this condition, let's first simulate it so that you know it's possible.

First, pay attention to the sounds around you right now. The motor of the air conditioning, refrigerator or generator buzzing. A dog barking in the distance. Traffic flowing by where you live. Birds chirping. Insects buzzing around. Listen to all of that. Be aware of what's happening. And be aware of how you feel inside. And be aware of your thoughts as they stream by. Second, pay attention to the fact that you are aware. Your awareness of all of those things didn't waver. You are still aware of all of it. But you are also

Table 1: Masks of the Ego

Category	Primal	Gestalt	Refined
Denials	Fear	Pride	Shame
Emotions	Abandonment	Rejection	Guilt
Assumptions	False Pride	Egocentrism	Overconfidence
Roles	Victim	Persecutor	Savior
Tools	Power	Control	Manipulation
Needs	Acquisition	Accumulation	Achievement
Attachments	Emotional	Physical	Mental

passively looking at your awareness from a secondary perspective. Try it! It works!

This condition—this state of being—is constant. We can do this any time we choose, whether or not we're doing integration. But in integration, separable awareness is a great tool to both be in the experience of an emotion fully, and yet to be able to passively observe its effects. Its efficiency in this allows us to really look at how the mechanisms of our emotions work.

If you aren't obtaining results, you may have to increase the intensity of your process. If you're under a lot of stress from doing this, consider decreasing. It should be just barely past what's comfortable for you.

And beyond that, it's simply observation. But what do we observe? And to what end? The aim is to uncover the true nature of whatever it is that we're feeling. We need to look at the actual nature of what it is that's affecting us. And that's why we use Figure 3 (included at the end of this lecture).

These four toxins (ignorance, hatred, greed and arrogance) are all interrelated, but they all have a definite function. They each have a source, a solution, and a result. And the process brings us all the way through each. We also offer a free PDF of the emotional integration process. Clicking the link will open it in a new tab.

The Guidelines

During the BIFO process, you should remember to completely disengage at the end of each session. Complete one session before moving along to another. And when you're done, give yourself a moment to calm down.

Also, you should accept the truth of whatever comes out of the process. Be willing to trust the results enough to allow them to work. Because it's the end result that matters most.

After the BIFO process, you should also engage in something positive. We suggest simple laughter, but we also offer the happy facing method which is a guided visualization. To laugh in the face of what is negative should be something everyone gets to enjoy from time to time.

But if you have the means, give yourself a treat that you enjoy: some visceral (e.g., physical) pleasure, like ice cream, chocolate, sex, or engaging in an indulgent habit. It should be something that helps you to unwind, whatever it is. Give yourself permission to do something you enjoy, for the sake of dealing with all that negativity.

Conclusion

The beauty of this system is that it really allows us to be exactly who we are, and to face down all the negative shit that affects us. It allows us to have permission to deal with the underlying causes of our own screw-ups, and to create frankly amazing changes in our own lives.

This is merely the first practice along the line of allowing us to align with the Force, to be an ally and to have it ally with us. We're not perfect creatures, we human beings, and so we should understand that what we see of the Force is merely a glimpse of what's possible.

The true nature of the Force isn't to control, or to be controlled, or to allow us to control; its true nature is to perform whatever will be of most benefit in service to others. With the Force we can influence many things in the world, albeit at a subtle level. And emotional integration allows us the ability to see what is actually our own influence, and what's not, and to revel in the light of truth, even when that truth is uncomfortable to some people. The path of light is a path of balance; not one of domination. When we are balanced in our emotions, we are like a diamond: unbreakable unless we want to be broken, with unparalleled clarity and flawless beauty within.

* The following three pages are pieces which accompany the lecture on emotional integration and was developed by Ray Jenson (Vishwa Jay) of Jedi School.

The Happy Facing Method

Let's begin by saying that this is a guided visualization. You should be seated comfortably. And then in your mind, visualize a smiley face.

See this smiley face in your heart, carrying a rubber stamp. And it stamps every cell of your bloodstream, every cell of your heart, and every cell it comes into contact with. But it's a magic rubber stamp, so it changes each cell into a smiley face. And each of those with a rubber stamp, and so on.

The sillier, the better. For example, imagine the rubber stamp making a big cartoonish "bloomp" sound as it strikes each cell, bumping into every cell with a "ploink", making some silly sound effect as its rubber-stamp magic wand spreads to every cell in your whole body.

Keep it up for a while. Some people can't help but laugh when that happens. And some people just feel really nice and warm. And some people feel nothing, but it's usually because they're not experienced at visualization.

This works by creating a self-replicating placebo effect. And knowing that doesn't diminish its effectiveness! It gets your physiology going just a little.

And we recommend it for use with emotional integration. But really, you can use this any time you want a quick pick-me-up in the positivity department.

Overcoming Darkness

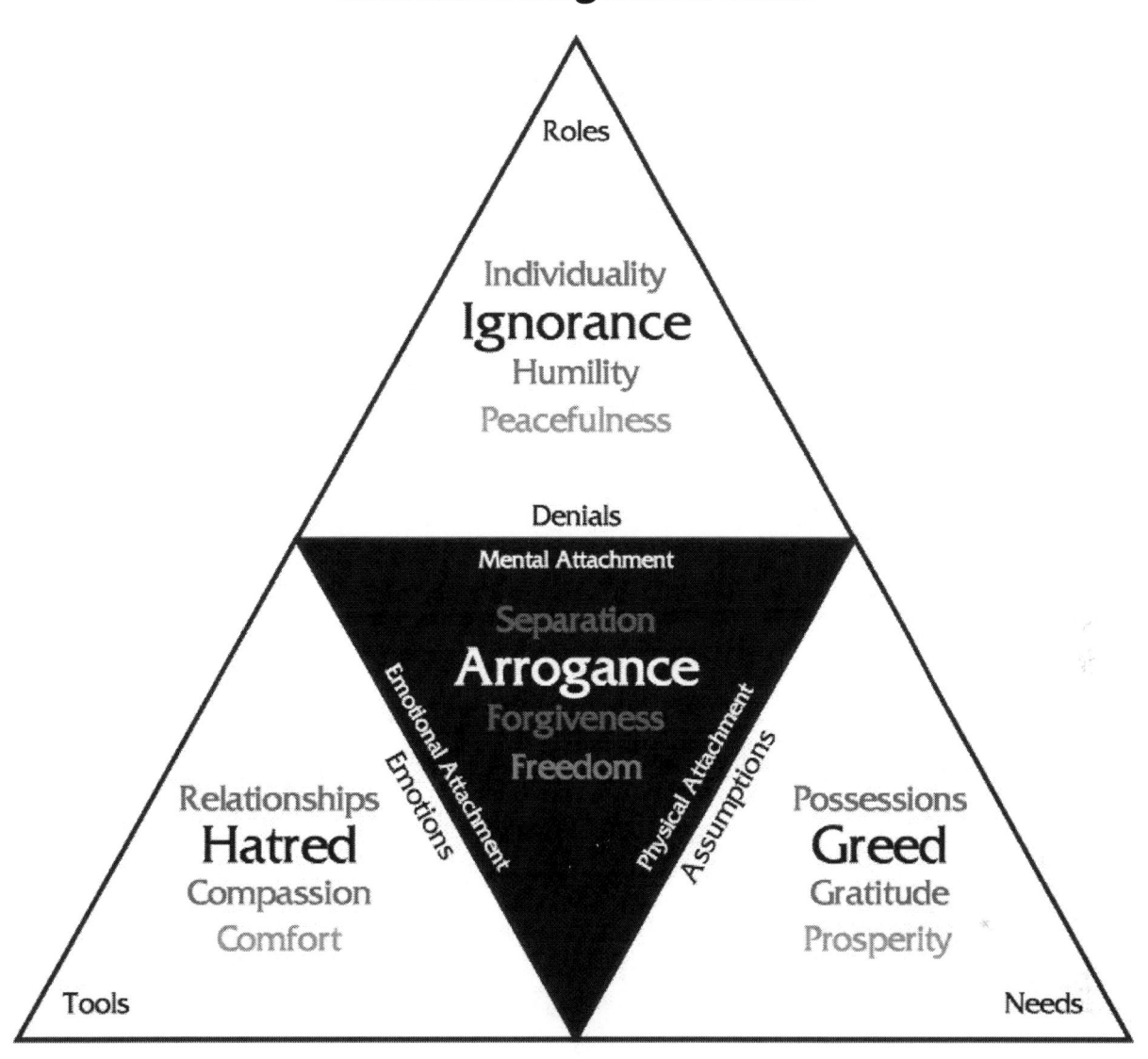

Roles

Individuality
Ignorance
Humility
Peacefulness

Denials
Mental Attachment
Separation
Arrogance
Forgiveness
Freedom

Emotional Attachment
Emotions

Physical Attachment
Assumptions

Relationships
Hatred
Compassion
Comfort

Possessions
Greed
Gratitude
Prosperity

Tools

Needs

Step 1: Issues (I=Internalizations; P=Projections)

Ignorance

Denials (I)   *Roles (P)*
Fear   Victim
Pride   Savior
Shame   Persecutor

Hatred

Emotions (I)   *Tools (P)*
Guilt   Power
Abandonment   Control
Rejection   Manipulation

Greed

Assumptions (I)   *Needs (P)*
Overconfidence   Acquisition
False Hopes   Achievement
Egocentrism   Accumulation

Arrogance
Attachments (I)
Mental Attachment
Emotional Attachment
Physical Attachment

Step 2: Sources
Ignorance: Individuality
Hatred: Relationships
Greed: Possessions
Arrogance: Separation

Step 3: Solutions
Ignorance: Humility
Hatred: Compassion
Greed: Gratitude
Arrogance: Forgiveness

Step 4: Results
Humility: Peacefulness
Compassion: Comfort
Gratitude: Prosperity
Forgiveness: Freedom

(All pictures for the Emotional Integration lecture set were created and provided by Ray Jenson)

Conquer Arrogance
::: Story Time: J.u.s.t Jedi Parables
Kitsu Tails
© The Keeper of J.u.st Jedi Holocrons

"The acceptance of others is not a guarantee. Like everyone else, a Jedi is accepted or not based on his behavior. The Jedi who believes that he is more important than others only demonstrates that his opinion is to be ignored."
—Dooku

"Did you hear about the stable raids?" Keryn asked one rainy evening, her tablet propped up in front of her as she laid on her stomach and kicked her feet lightly above her.

Alexis, her older sister sat down next to her with two mugs of coffee in hand "I heard they stole three of our horses, and slaughtered several animals in the process."

"That's because they did." Cody's smug voice chimed from the window "I was there. I saw. They came in when it started raining. Thought they could get away with it."

"Well. They took three of our horses...I'd say they succeeded" Keryn answered, sitting up to accept her mug of coffee.

Cody smiled proudly "Well they would have taken more if I wasn't there to scare them off."

"I heard you were there for disciplinary actions." Alexis teased "Mucking stables again, bro?"

The young teen bristled at the reminder but didn't let it bother him too much "Yea well, I came out with that ax Master Zachery keeps in the stable office. They were so scared."

"Scared of a twelve year old, wielding a ax far too heavy for him to carry." Alexis smirked "Must not of been all that terrifying. I bet a chicken could have scared them off."

"Alex!" Keryn chided with a frown

Cody made a face at his sister before puffing out his chest and sitting a little straighter "You weren't there. I was. I came around the corner and shouted that they get out and they ran."

Alexis rolled her eyes "With the horses."

"Yea but I saw their faces and helped Master Zachery file a theft complaint with the police. We will have our horses back soon." Cody answered smugly.

"Yea. Sure." Alexis answered, pushing herself back up onto her feet and gently nudging Keryns shoulder "Come on. I wanted to watch another episode before lights out." she said, before heading back to the girls dorms.

Keryn looked to her brother with a frown "I know that what you did was right, and you really helped to save our horses. Master Zachery was very proud of you. But there is no need to brag so much about it." Picking up her tablet and mug of coffee she followed her sister, glancing over her shoulder to see her brother's crestfallen frown and slumped shoulders. She felt bad for her brother but knew this was a hard lesson he had to learn eventually.

Arrogance is a hard foe to beat. When we gain Rank, find a Master to guide us, create our own methods and orders within the community...It is a fine line between sharing your achievements and being arrogant about them.

Quite often do we have new members join the community introducing themselves as "Masters" and profiling their certificates and abilities before even getting to know the new group they are joining. It is important to note that, while you may have earned achievements elsewhere, there is always room to learn and grow in new places. Never be afraid to allow yourself to be just the student, and offer your assistance when it is needed...and wanted.

The Cost of Comedy
Michael "Akkarin" Kitchen
Temple of the Jedi Order

What sort of person do you present to the world? This is a question we will grapple with every day of our lives, and both its answer and possible importance will differ for each of us. But while a great variety of subjects are talked about by Jedi it is rare that one sees, and perhaps this just reflects my own lack of awareness, a discussion about comedy. People will say jokes and link funny pictures definitely, but this Jedi does not remember, and again maybe this just reflects my own poor memory, a discussion about comedy for comedy's sake.

C, E Flat, and G walk into a bar.
The bartender says "Sorry, no minors".
Why would this matter? Well in part perhaps because the subject is not talked about so often and yet, for many of us perhaps, it will form a persistent if only occasional part of our lives and our social interactions. The question then becomes "does our choice of comedy reflect our Jedi sensibilities?" Well does yours? Does one think about the sorts of jokes they laugh at, or tell to others? Maybe one does, maybe one doesn't, but here are this Jedi's thoughts on the subject.

What's blue and smells like red paint?
Blue paint.
While recently re-watching the best Sci-Fi series of all time (Babylon 5 in case that description wasn't obvious), this Jedi was reminded of the magician/comedy duo Penn and Teller featuring in one of the later episodes as the comedy duo "Rebo and Zooty". When meeting someone of an alien race they introduce themselves with a joke and explain that *"Mimbari humour is based not on physical danger, embarrassment, rejection like human humour, but rather on the failure to obtain emotional or spiritual enlightenment"*.

Did you hear about the two guys that stole a calendar?
They each got six months.
So this brought some concern to my mind. Is human humour based on *'physical danger, embarrassment, rejection'*? And if so is this the sort of

humour we as a social society, and as Jedi, would like to encourage?

My Grandpa has the heart of a lion,
    and a lifetime ban from the zoo.

Fortunately I came across a TED Talk recently by Emily Levine *"A theory of everything"* which covers some interesting topics about the sort of humour she uses in her material. One such topic covered is the activity/passivity between a subject and an object. She mentions a book by Amy Richlin entitled "The Garden of Priapus" which details how Roman humour greatly mirrored Roman society, Roman society was arranged around the upper elite dominating the plebeians and similarly there is always the butt of a joke; things are funny when a passive person is being dominated by an active person.

Why can't you trust atoms?
    Because they make up everything!

So these two things, her talk and the best Sci-Fi show of all time, together got me thinking and made me question the sorts of things which I found funny and whether or not on closer inspection some "jokes" were truly worth the potential cost in the emotional well-being of their subjects. Now one can say "a joke is just a joke" so as long as one is enjoying the humour for humour's sake rather than focusing on the joke's context and subject(s) then is there really a problem? It may very well be the case that there isn't, but I'm not trying to advocate that jokes are regulated and censored, just that we pay a little more care to the kinds of jokes we say and the feelings of those who might be hurt as a result of them.

It's hard to explain puns to kleptomaniacs,
    because they always take things literally.

So what sorts of jokes might we want to take particular care about saying or laughing to?

What's orange and sounds like a parrot?
    A carrot.

We should be cautious about telling a joke which makes fun of someone. Any joke which makes fun of someone can often seem very funny for those telling and laughing to it, but for those on the receiving end it might very well end up becoming a source of emotional hardship particularly if made often or over a long period of time and especially if it is just one person or one group of people who have been singled out.

Did you hear about the man who got cooled to absolute zero?
He's OK now.

This Jedi is not an expert on comedy or joke telling, so there is not a comprehensive list which has been drawn up which details what jokes should be said and what jokes should not. Such authoritarian regulation of jokes isn't what we need in the world, every joke will have its place, its time, its correct context, but what every joke needs is someone with a responsible and appropriate frame of mind to tell it.

What do you get when you put root beer in a square glass?
Beer.

What we need is a cognitive and emotional awareness of joke telling, this is something we, as Jedi, can provide. We can provide this service when a peer makes fun of someone and we choose not to laugh. We can provide this service by not making jokes at other people's expense. We can provide service by offering people an alternative type of humour.

A horse walks into a bar,
the bartender asks "why the long face?"

What might this type of humour be? Well that's up to each Jedi to decide for themselves, but let's make it one which has been duly considered. And with that I leave you with this, "What happens when you cross a joke with a rhetorical question?"

TOLERANCE

Picture by Mark Brereton, Temple of the Jedi Order

Beyond Tolerance
Michael "Akkarin" Kitchen
Temple of the Jedi Order

Tolerance is an odd virtue to value oneself as having. Tolerance would seem on the surface to be a worthy and valuable trait, but once you begin digging you realize that actually tolerance isn't enough for a Jedi. Tolerance has the presence of being good while deep down breeding negativity and animosity. The question I wish you, dear reader, to consider is whether we should ever settle for "tolerating" something.

Tolerate: 'Allow the existence, occurrence, or practice of (something that one dislikes or disagrees with) without interference'.

Tolerating something means ultimately that, on some level, you disagree with that something. This bottom-line disagreement becomes a problem because it can give rise to resentment and tension in a relationship, whether that relationship is between you and a partner, an employee and an employer, or a dominant ethnic group and a minor ethnic group.

If you see something that you disapprove of you might think it polite not to confront the people doing it, deciding instead to tolerate their activities while you remain silently displeased. But what is not spoken can be just as detrimental mentally and spiritually as what is spoken, because the feelings of displeasure or annoyance or anger remain. These feelings bubble inside us like a resentment-fueled steam gauge until a valve suddenly blows and our efforts at "tolerating" these irritable practices/behaviors fail, erupting in a torrent of emotion.

These torrents of emotion could be "external" in the form of causing harm to another (most likely the person you were trying to "tolerate"), or they might be "internal" in the form of a mental breakdown. Perhaps this build-up of tension-steam will add to other pressures already being felt and something else will "snap", something unrelated to tolerance, the pressures of Life might get too much for someone if they feel overwhelmed. There are many different ways that this might happen and by no means are they all extreme and violent, but the result will leave you or another damaged mentally and spiritually, perhaps even physically in some extreme cases.

So if tolerance is not what we should be aiming for then what exactly would be a good alternative? What should a Jedi be striving for instead?

A Jedi should be striving for Acceptance. Acceptance is very similar to tolerance with one crucial difference, when one "accepts" something they do so without the dislike or the disdain. This can be achieved through empathetic understanding, and learning not to automatically consider the "other" as hostile.

A careful note must be made on the nature of the "acceptance" I am speaking of; acceptance must not be mistaken for resignation or apathy in this context. Acceptance is not simply saying "Oh well that's just the way things are, I accept the situation", the acceptance I speak of is very much about actively engaging with your environment by searching for connections that bring us closer together rather than farther apart. Similarly "acceptance" should not be mistaken for "agreement"; one does not have to agree with something to understand or study that something. Acceptance is not going to automatically fix every disagreement between parties, but what it is going to do is allow those parties to better empathize with each other rather than simply thinking that the "other" is "wrong" plain and simple. Thinking that they are just "wrong" is definitely not going to help fix disagreements between parties!

The human reaction is to focus on the differences between things, but acceptance requires the opposite, acceptance requires a focus on the similarities between things. If we learn to focus on the things we have in common rather than fixate on the things that are different and undesirable then our mind will begin letting go of the negativity of whatever it was we disagree with and we will feel less resentment.

Acceptance asks the same questions as Tolerance "Why aren't they the same as me?", "Why are they doing things differently than me?", "Why don't they want to do things the way I do them?" but acceptance recognizes each person as an equal individual on Joseph Campbell's "Hero's Journey". We are all individuals just trying to find our way in life. If someone else belongs to a different religion than you, prescribes to a different philosophy than you, or behaves different then you, acceptance requires that we do not simply dismiss these differences as somehow being hostile or offensive, you do not scoff at the person thinking that they cannot see the "superiority" of your position. As Jedi we value the cultivation of knowledge, particularly self-knowledge, and the proper application of knowledge in the form of wisdom. Self-knowledge is important in ensuring that we maintain our commitments to the various ideals of the Jedi path and this knowledge requires persistent and thorough introspection into our motives and reasons. By recognizing deep down that we are all just people trying to fulfill our human needs we begin asking ourselves what do other people find valuable in what they believe/do; doubtless other people have arrived at their conclusions with the same enthusiasm and conviction that we have arrived at ours. Even though other people have been moulded and shaped by their different cultures and different environments we are all more or less the same, we are all fundamentally Human. Because of this fundamental similarity we are required to examine these differences in belief and ideals by asking ourselves why we do not agree with them. Understanding why one does not agree requires introspection and this introspection into our own beliefs and ideals ensures that they are under constant scrutiny which helps keep us mentally and spiritually healthy.

Roman Krznaric, a philosopher and author, coined the term "outrospection" which is an important counterpart to "introspection". As introspection is the examination of one's thoughts, outrospection is the examination of another's thoughts. In the context of acceptance the examination of their thoughts is into their beliefs, their ideals and their reasons for both. When introspection is done in response to coming into contact with the beliefs of others outrospection is also needed. An object or idea can be defined as much by what it is as by what it is not. And once we begin to understand them as we understand ourselves we begin to empathize with them, we begin to accept them for who they are. This empathy helps remove the tension that can be brought about through disdain.

Tolerance is a type of control, a control of your emotional responses, and learning how to control your emotional responses is crucial if you wish to learn how to build a calm and composed character. Control requires that we keep the ego in check as best we can. Acceptance on the other hand is not a type of control; acceptance is a type of meditation, a conscious state of deep mental empathetic awareness about the similarities and connections between each of us. If we are all One within the Force then understanding that which we share will bring us closer to this realization and all the compassionate wisdom this entails.

As Jedi our lives are spent in service to others by our search for compassion and mutual understanding; accepting others by recognizing what connects us rather than what separates us is a valuable way of fulfilling our oaths of service. All this being said it is entirely reasonable to expect that one is not going to simply jump from not accepting something to all of a sudden accepting it wholeheartedly. We do not have to make a single jump, we can make several smaller steps and tolerance is a good first step in trying to get along! But as Jedi we should not stop there, we should take those other steps towards acceptance. A jump is desirable but unrealistic, we are not perfect, we are Jedi, and we are Human.

Inequity, Iniquity, and Justice
Senan
Temple of the Jedi Order

in•iq•ui•ty noun
1. immoral or grossly unfair behavior.

in•eq•ui•ty noun
1. lack of fairness or justice.

jus•tice noun
1. just behavior or treatment.

    To begin any conversation about justice, we must be honest with ourselves. Life is not fair. We, as human beings, are not equal. As members of the animal kingdom, we are certainly not equal. We, even as Jedi, are not equal. Some are born taller, faster, or stronger than others. Some are born into wealth while others are born into poverty. Despite our best efforts to be "equal", true equality is impossible. This does not have to be a bad thing.

    Allow me to share an example. A baby is born missing his right hand. His parents are tempted to scream "This isn't fair! What did we do to deserve this? Why must our child suffer?" The answer is not one that is easily accepted. It is because life isn't fair. But, must this child actually suffer?

    This baby was born as physically unequal to his peers. There is an inequity here. That is a fact of his life. What is also a fact of his life is that this inequity would result in iniquity from others. This was a lesson hard learned by this child.

    When he expressed an interest in sports, his father suggested soccer (he is American). It seemed like a reasonable choice considering the circumstances, but the boy wanted to play baseball. More than that, he wanted to be a pitcher. He was laughed at and he was mocked. He chose to look past the inequity, ignore the iniquity of others who discriminated against him, and he started to practice. And he practiced a lot.

    When it came time to play his first Little League game, he propped his glove on the stump where his right hand should be, took the pitcher's mound, and proceeded to throw a no-hitter. He went on to high school and played well enough to be named to the U.S. National Team. His career took him to Cuba where he defeated the heavily favored Cuban National Team in front of Fidel Castro, and then moved on to pitch for numerous Major League Baseball teams including the California Angels and New York Yankees. In 1993 while a Yankee, he pitched a no hitter versus the Cleveland Indians while throwing fast balls clocked at over 90 miles per hour.

When he retired, Jim Abbott wrote a book titled "Imperfect: An Improbable Life". In his book, he explained that accepting his imperfection and ignoring the negativity allowed him to find something he loved and go after it with all of his heart. Accepting the inequity and ignoring the iniquity of others allowed him to earn justice from people throughout his life. He was treated fairly by Major League Baseball and the teams that hired him. He was respected by his fellow competitors. He was considered an equal, despite the inequity.

As Jedi, we seek justice. It is our 2nd Maxim. Justice: To always seek the path of 'right'. Behaving justly in certain situations is often an elusive goal, but a Jedi must accept the inequities of life and diligently seek to eliminate iniquity in others. A Jedi should be knowledgeable in order to make informed decisions about any matter of "right" or "wrong". A Jedi should represent and defend those who are not capable of seeking justice on their own. A Jedi should not turn their back on iniquity or allow it to be disguised behind lies. A Jedi should appropriately weigh each side of an issue to determine the just response. Should said response require swift and forceful action, a Jedi must be fearless in its execution.
We are Jedi. We are instruments of peace. Peace can be achieved through the proper application of justice. We must not forget this.

The Force is Accepting and Tolerant
Merin Kyo Den
Temple of the Jedi Force

"Focus, too, can be constrictive and restrictive, limiting one's access to various perspectives and options. This is the point at which focus becomes obsession. At this point obsession constricts a person's point of view and it negates all of the advantages that focus awards us. This poses a significant threat to the Jedi. As Jedi it is our obligation and responsibility to leave ourselves open and receptive to the will of the Force. Beyond simply this we must further leave ourselves open to the opinions and perspectives of others. One of the great many complaints often heard of various religions is of their hatred and abhorrence of different religions, opinions, and points of view. This is the great trap of all faiths and as such we, as Jedi, must keep ourselves rom falling into it. To this end we must look to the Force. The Force is accepting and tolerant. It does not judge or condemn and, as such, neither should we. This acceptance on the part of the Jedi, despite our understanding, does not make us better or wiser than those who do not agree with us. This stance, further, does not grant the Jedi special access to the Force. The Jedi are common everyday people and we, like non-Jedi, simply strive to make our way in this world the best way that we know how. The focus of the Jedi is to further our understanding of the Force and to contribute to humanity. We must not let this focus grow so sharp, though, that we become narrow-minded and intolerant as so very many have done down through the ages. This obsession would insulate the Jedi from the prevues and criticisms of the secular world but it would also insulate us from the Force, cutting us off from the very thing that nourishes and protects us.

In summation, the challenge of the Jedi is to leave ourselves open to both the world and the Force. We must guard ourselves from allowing our perspectives to grow too narrow and our focus too tight. Perhaps the greatest Jedi lesson of all is acceptance and, in learning that lesson, we glow ever more brightly as conduits and reflections of the Force"

This is a great post by the way. I didn't write it, Brother Nassik did. Just look at that last sentence. "We must guard ourselves from allowing our perspectives to grow too narrow and our focus too tight." I could not agree more with that statement. And check this one " This is the great trap of all faiths and as such we, as Jedi, must keep ourselves from falling into it. To this end we must look to the Force. The Force is accepting and tolerant. It does not judge or condemn and, as such, neither should we."........Wonderful words, but are we doing that? Are we really accepting of our brothers and sisters? This is not something I can answer for you, the individual must do that. I can say this; If you are not tolerant of another's point of view or the beliefs they hold dear, then I would question if you are truly a Jedi If you are not sensitive to another's hurt then I would not question it, I would know you were not.. You as Jedi should bring peace to a situation, not use it as a soapbox. This is a part of your creed,. Do you know the creed? "I am a Jedi.

I shall never seek so much to be consoled as to console;

to be understood as to understand;

to be loved as to love;

for it is in giving that we receive;

it is in pardoning that we are pardoned;

and it is in dying that we are born to eternal life."

    Look at the first three lines. Is that what you do? Is that how you treat people that don't agree with your own point of view?

    Really read that folks. In that is what being a Jedi is. I tell you for certain, It's not when all is well and all agree that your true test comes, it's in the face of turmoil, in the face of intolerance, in the face of hate, that what we are tested. It's in our ability to promote love and peace that we pass such a test. I have heard talk of un-Jedi like behavior, I ask you this. Which is more un Jedi like, Not believing in force powers, or failing to promote peace and thereby letting fall the very foundation of your supposed faith? I again can't answer that for you, only you, through an honest search of your soul, can do that. I leave you all with this thought. If you hold a rose and touch it gently as it's on the bush, it will not wither and it's beauty will be admired from afar, but seek to pluck it from the vine and hold it firm in your hand it will soon wither and it's beauty be lost to all.

Acceptance
Alexandre Orion
Temple of the Jedi Order

> Grant me the serenity, to accept the *things I cannot change*,
> The courage to change the things I can
> And the wisdom to know the difference …

Many of us know this old prayer ; it is a remarkably solid piece of wisdom. Yet, as with all solid pieces of wisdom, it is subtle. It indicates a level of responsibility and mastery that requires careful cultivation.

Acceptance is often confused with an exaggerated passivity, with a nearly defeatist outlook on circumstances however they arise, with idly and stupidly putting up with whatever one is supposed to be "accepting". This is in truth neither acceptance nor is it humility : it is the other extreme of egotism, the "the Universe wants it this way" hallucination.

The Universe, the Force, what have you, doesn't 'want' anything in particular. There is desire, but any or all desires we ourselves as individuals may have are part of the universal desire, as well as all the fears associated with those desires compound in the collective tension that gives the Universe its equilibrium and the Force its balance. We have evolved in this way, as as with other evolutionary developments, it is not useless. And insofar as any individual contributes to the Nature of the whole, then also the whole determines the nature of the part.

Our nature is not simply that of the 'isolated Self', for we are indeed the 'organism-environment' to which Watts made reference. Much of the Self we have come to know is sculpted by and from our whole World – and I mean everything – which has ever surrounded us at any given moment. And this is as much biology as it is cultural or spiritual (each of these 'divisions' being *concepts*). We have come out of this World according to its development, our ancestors of every preceding species we've been have grown and matured in the measure of our capacity to act upon the environment in order to satisfy our needs. The three principal desires being *material* or those oriented to Self-conservation, *sexual* for 'self' – rather, the species – propagation or continuity, and *evolutionary*, that which gives rise to new forms, new psychological and physical capacities.

Among the new forms that have emerged in us the transformation, or perhaps the enlargement, of these three causes, the material and sexual impulses toward social and affective expressions. The evolutionary impulse continues even through these, becoming, as it were, the spiritual aspect. It is this which harmonizes the multiple and often conflicting desires wrought by the others.

And it is this harmony that is necessary for us to find fulfillment, it is the <u>essential desire</u>. (cf. Paul Deil) Without this, one or another elemental aspect of ourselves – individual or collective – would remain unsatisfied. One may not ignore affective needs for professional success, nor more mundane ones for intellectual or hypothetical ones. This engenders a warping of the psyche, resulting either in the perpetual, though negligent, search for fulfillment through personal empowerment. Thus, since the reconciliation of the essential desire is of an enormous investment (hardly congruent to the acceptance as we tend to understand it), we resist. And from this resistance, defects of character may arise which dissimulate the otherwise qualities of that character. For instance, behind *vanity* lies one's self-esteem ; behind *guilt*, one finds humility ; within *maudlin sentimentality*, one's capacity to Love is embedded and ; *accusation* disguises tolerance and compassion.

So, what we must consider with appreciation of acceptance is *how* are we accepting *what* ? Our entire evolution as a species has been through *acting* to modify our environment, to inter-*act* with it in order to bring about the satisfaction of our needs. Those needs have since been modified throughout the course of our development, but we still have the basic needs to which we must attend – both individually and collectively.

Therein resides the demand for *courage* and *wisdom*. If one can act to change things to favour the satisfaction of needs then one must. Of course, these needs must as well not be unethical ones, nor selfish in the sense that they cause un-due problems (and thus generate subsequent un-warranted needs) for others. For this, one must call upon wisdom : the fruit of focus and knowledge. Therefore, *acceptance* is <u>as much</u> recognizing the need to act, as much, perhaps even more, than simply accepting things the way they are. Accepting things the way they are, in their *"as-such"* as it were, is the starting point only, not the finality.

As has been emphasized in the many essays in which I have touched on the subject of *wô-wei,* 'non-action', this does not mean "doing nothing". Wô-wei stresses no 'inappropriate' action. When we can act to change something, this is also the way of the Force. Watercourses do indeed 'flow', they nourish that which is nearby and they alter landscapes – over time carving out large valleys and even canyons. It is often soft, does not insist much, but by its natural action does cause remarkable changes. Sometimes it is violent and causes huge changes very rapidly. It really all depends on the appropriate conditions.

Ergo – wisdom in any matter may tell us to stay our course. Be patient, be simple, be compassionate and accept to change the things that one has to do.

RESPONSIBILITY

Joshua Laskowski taking the Eagle Scout Board, Temple of the Jedi Order

Personal Responsibility and Accountability
Alethea "Setanaoko" Thompson
Force Academy

They are both a matter of owning up to what you do-good, bad or indifferent. It is important for a Jedi to take them seriously because you it earns you and the community as a whole respect and you can begin the process of learning where your faults are and where you need to improve.

Today I got half of the day off so as to make up for my working shifts this week. I find myself at a coffee shop on Kadena writing up this assignment because I just don't want to stay in my room all day. Since I've been here though, an Air Force officer has walked in, and I decided to ask him what his own personal take on Personal Responsibility and Accountability was. As it turns out, he had just as difficult of a time explaining his viewpoint as I am. Mostly because we both understand how we feel on the subject, but it is difficult to put down in words. But he helped me a lot when he spoke about how personal responsibility and accountability should be looked at from a professional standpoint. His conclusion, was that it sets an example for those around you.

He was referring to the fact that the US Military is considered "ambassadors" by our government. Any country we go to, we are what the local population looks at as the "American Example". So if we are terrible people, then the rest of America must be terrible people. If we are good people, then Americans must be good people.

One of the things that annoys me, is the ongoing issue that we-as the US Military Police Corps-have goes back as far as late 2003: Abu Ghraib. Although most of you know the story, I am going to give a quick brief on it, as I have come across military personnel who have never even HEARD of Abu Ghraib, let alone the scandal that took place there.

The 800th MP Brigade was discovered, tried in 2004 for treating detainees inhumanely. Some of the actions that were caught on camera (photographed) included detainees naked and piled up in a "human pyramid" with guards from the unit posing. Members of the unit who were found guilty were sentenced to spend time at Fort Leavenworth, Kansas.

While many of you don't see the on-going problems with it, Military Times has monitored some of the more outrageous things that have come from the madness. The last one I remember fairly well, because I ended up talking with everyone that came through the arms room about it. At the time I read it, I had already deployed, spent 14 months doing detainee operations and come back home. The article reads the following:

"Former Pfc. Lynndie England's recent apology for her role in abusing detainees at Abu Ghraib prison in Iraq was tempered by her scorn for the media, whom she blamed for sensationalizing "what happens in war."
In an interview with German magazine Stern, she said she felt "sorry and wrong" for actions such as holding a naked prisoner on a leash or pointing at the genitals of another as a cigarette dangled from her mouth. But, she said, those incidents turned into scandal only because the media broadcast leaked photos."

Being an MP myself, I personally feel that Lynndie is a disgrace to my corps. We as MPs are the example for the rest of the military. We are not perfect, but we should at least strive to meet the standard, and this unit just did not. You could argue that they may not have been taught Geneva Conventions. As it turns out, when this information started hitting the fan, I had already been to Basic Training at the exact same school they all attended. PFC Lynndie and her friends were taught the exact same thing I was-and we were taught about Geneva Conventions. In fact, the class stressed it. I attended school in June 2003, the inhumane acts (supposedly) began one month after I got back, in October 2003. Because of these individuals, MPs are not trusted by detainees, that coupled with the fact that the Iraqi Police aren't much better than the people who committed these actions against the detainees.

How does this relate to the Jedi Community? More than you may think. It shows the importance of our appearance to the rest of the world. If one of us messes up and does not own up to it-and instead blames his/her training/ trainers for not teaching them properly (such as the Abu Ghraib incident) that makes our community lose credibility-and as it stands, we are trying are hardest to gain ground on the credibility island.

I believe we should teach personal responsibility and accountability to our students. How? That is a good question. My best suggestion would be to give an example of what it can do (such as the story I outlined above) and then ask the student(s) to think about and share with the group (or with their master if it's a master/apprentice relationship) an example in their own life where taking responsibility for his/her action would have benefited them better. Inspire them to look at how their emotional state was effected, and how it effected their life at the time as well as that of others. By looking at the actual situation from a well-rounded prospective, we can better understand the importance of such a lesson.

Sermon on Responsibility
Mark Anjuu
Temple of the Jedi Order

My nephew recently started attending meetings of the Boys Brigade, which is similar to the Scouts but with more of an emphasis on Christian teachings. Even though a section of our family is Methodist, our immediate family is quite diverse in our beliefs – paganism, Jediism, atheism – and the driving force for this decision was to provide companionship, activities and discipline until he is old enough to join the Beavers, the youth section of the Scouting movement. As can be expected, members of the Boys Brigade spend time each meeting focusing on aspects of the Christian faith. A few days later, casual blasphemy from my sister (as a result of cutting her thumb while cooking) was met with a response from my nephew of "you shouldn't say that because God watches everything you do." When I asked him who he believed God was, the reply was "he's a person who watches what you do and doesn't like it when you're naughty". This got me thinking....

I understand that deep theological discussions may be too much for a 5-year-old to digest but in this instance, the notion of the Christian God in all its diversity had been reduced to the status of watchful admonisher whose sole role was to enforce "good behaviour" and punish the "bad". So many faiths build such a concept into their ideas of divinity along with rules and regulations deemed to emanate from such spiritual guidance. The Bible is packed full of metaphorical "do"s and "don't"s and even has its own handy reference table in the Ten Commandments; the Koran and Torah have similar notions; Buddhist principles encourage concepts of "right action", "right thought", "right speech", etc. But who enforces these rules?

It is certainly true that a great deal of religions impose on their believers the threat of punishment if transgressions are made. Sinners burning in Hell might be an obvious example of this but just as controlling is the "carrot on a stick" approach of rewarding good behaviour – do what we say and you will have everlasting peace in Heaven. Either way, it's a case of follow the rules and be rewarded, break them and face punishment. Generally in such cases there are entities in place to carry out such decrees, such as Satan and his demons flinging evil-doers into fiery pits while God and his angels fly the devout to a pious eternity.

In other faiths, such responsibility is borne by the individual – you reap the rewards of "good behaviour" and suffer the less palatable consequences of the "bad". In many neo-pagan traditions, this is summarised in the phrase "an' ye harm none, do what ye will". In other words, do what you like as long as it doesn't harm anyone. This simple phrase is complicated in practice – every action taken must be referenced to this and you are also included in the "harming anyone" notion; activities that cause you pain and suffering are also discouraged. But there is a certain ambiguity about this process that relies on the individual's moral compass. It is up to each of us to judge what is beneficial or detrimental to our own being and it is this deep internal reflection that is central to Jediism.

While TOTJO ascribes to a particular Doctrine and Creed, the contents may be seen as a "guide to life", or a set of instructions designed to allow each person to develop their moral sensibilities within a certain viewpoint and to ensure that every action taken is the most beneficial – to themselves, to others, and to the Force itself. How we enforce this guidance is up to us. Only you can know how well you are living up to these standards; while others may offer a perspective gained from a less personally-biased stance, you are the one dealing with your own thoughts and motivations.

There will be times when you have the ability to embody much of the teachings of Jediism but there will also be times when such behaviour is further from your experience. It is certainly useful to maintain personal standards because without such a goal, we lack the motivation to further our development. But when we admonish ourselves, it may be wise to consider the notion of harm again. Are you being too harsh on yourself? Are you not being hard enough? If you have failed to live up to your expectations how do you deal with this; would berating yourself excessively provide motivation to try better next time, or would it just cast you into a greater sense of failure, achieving nothing positive?

While those at the Temple – friends, colleagues, teachers, Masters – are here to help you and support your learning and development, the responsibility for maintaining discipline is ultimately your own. Be kind to your mistakes for they provide a useful lesson and such things are a part of what it means to be human. Strive to excel but try not to harm yourself, or others, in the process. Chasing after a positive standard can be more beneficial than being chased from a negative one. But whatever your motivations, however you feel guided to walk your path and to stay "on the straight and narrow", remember that you are an essential part of the Force and each and every one of us is divine. When we consider such a realisation, it becomes easier to "do the right thing" for ourselves and each other.

DISCIPLINE

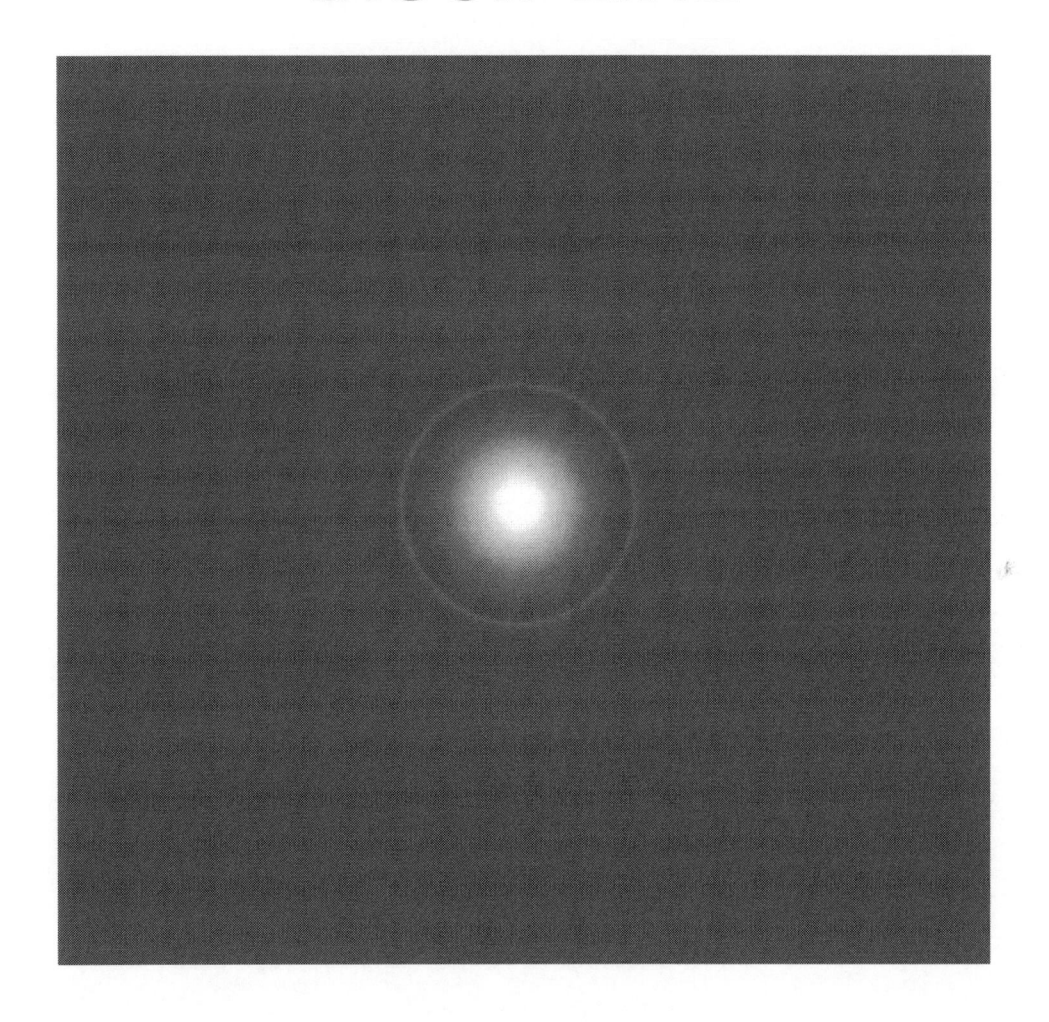

Picture by Mark Brereton, Temple of the Jedi Order

Self Control, Self Discipline
Talon Trevor MacDonald
Aurora Borealis Jedi

Per a previous conversation, Discipline, Self Discipline, and Self control.

Included extrapolations of lack of self control, and lack of Discipline.

Self control; Choosing not to do something you want to, regardless of how bad you want to. Not allowing yourself to do something you want to , knowing you shouldn't.

Examples; petty theft, like seeing someone leave money lying, and pocketing it. Snacking when your doctor says you shouldn't be. Getting drunk when you know full well it leads you to trouble. I, all examples, choosing not to do the misdeed.

Self Discipline; Training yourself to follow particular methods and means, setting patterns of habit to be followed, and making yourself to do what you do not want to do but know you should do anyways.

Examples; Martial Arts training, Long term dieting or exercise to get to better health, quitting smoking, quitting drug use. AND, learning to touch the Force .

See Self Control as Restraint of self, stopping an action before it happens. Things happen daily that likely should not be responded to, one way or another. A child sees candy on the ground, and having known his whole life that candy is good, picks up the dirty piece and pops it in his mouth. A Parent will tell the child not to do this, which is the control of a Parent, but when the child realizes that the action is unhealthy, and chooses not to do it, He has learned some self control.

By making this choice repeatedly, He has instilled in himself self discipline concerning candy lying on the ground.

Self Discipline; The Yellow Belt in Tae Kwon Do practices daily, punching the bag, Kicking the bag, performing Katas, and learning the forms, so to move up in the ranks. Her Knuckles hurt, Her feet grow sore, but she continues, persevering, and pushing herself to accept the discomfort, and train, and train some more. She has instilled in herself Self Discipline, doing something that she may not want to, but striving to do it anyways, to achieve a goal.

After she leaves the class, a neighborhood bully approaches her, and starts calling names. He does not attempt to strike at her, but persists on being rude and insulting, making fun of her in many inventive ways. She knows how to punch, and Kick, and knows that were she to do so, She would end his verbal attack in a single strike. But she chooses not to do this. As satisfying as it may feel to do it, It would be a breach of the very Tenets of the Martial art she is learning, Not to strike someone weaker than you, unless the threat is a true one.

Thus, She has learned Self Control.

Self Control and Self Discipline on Drugs and Alcohol.
Many people come to us thinking that muddling the mind helps then to see the Force, when in fact, muddling the mind damages your perceptions. You will see and sense things that simply aren't, and then argue with others about it, convinced it is "the way to go", as we have seen previously.

Alcohol, If used in Moderation, is actually beneficial to the circulatory system of the Body. Cannabis, if used appropriately, is also beneficial to the body. Misusing either can seriously damage the body, as well as muddle the perceptions of the user.

Self Discipline comes in here, when we must learn to only use such in moderation, and not allow such to control our lives. Self Control comes into play when we want that drink, or that "joint" very badly, but we choose to exercise control, and say no (this also applies to Tobacco).

I am usually fairly direct on this subject, to the celebration of some, and the chagrin of others. And factually, I seriously tick off some devotees to drugs.

But here is the deal, as good as it gets:

We are walking the Jedi Path. If you are to approach the Force, and have it become part of your life, You have to do it, Not some drug or gestalt. If you are unable to touch the Force on your own, using an intoxicant to imagine you are is only going to harm your perceptions in the future. Using Hallucinogens, Psychedelics, Primary depressants, Amphetamines, or opiates not only give you false impressions, They ale start destroying your mind and body when misused. A damaged mind will not clearly feel the Force, and a Damaged mind that may feel the Force will certainly be in no shape to handle such appropriately

Alcohol also has this same detriment. When over-imbibed, one becomes drunken, and thinks and feels things that aren't quite right.

How many men and women fell in love at the bar, and woke up to something from the "SAW" Movies in the morning? How many users of Marijuana feel that they are performing some super-heroic dance move, and when seeing the video, hide for a week due to embarrassment at just how foolish they looked.

I remember a group of people pulled over in Mid Michigan in the early 90s. The police unit followed them for nearly a half mile down the highway before hitting the lights. Upon being approached, The driver rolled down the window of his Chrysler Le Baron, and Marijuana smoke rolled out. The Officer asked him if he realized how fast he was going... The boy said "80?" The officer said "8"., and arrested the driver, along with the rest of the car-full, for intoxication, etc.

Then there is the bride's brother, at the wedding... He has had a few too many, and swears he is the best dancer around. He plows onto the dance floor, sloshing his drink so that is sprays over some children. The groom's family gets quite upset, as the children happened to be from that side. three minutes later, The Bride's brother, swearing he is a Ninja, is trying to take on the Groom's entire male bloodline. Thank the Force for excellent bouncers.

These are minor, but accurate examples of how clouded minds work. There are others, like the Auto dealer in Mid Ohio a couple years back, that thought he could drive like a Nascar star. he pushed the Mitsubishi up to nearly 130 MPH, missed the curve on the highway, and wound up killing the man he was trying to sell the car to. The blood test showed trace amounts of alcohol, likely from the night before, but a Lot of Marijuana, which later the man admitted smoking at lunch.

I could list examples for days. I have seen the case files, and written profiles on these and other similar societal issues, But lets just get to the point.

Be YOU, and not some imagined and unreal shadow of you, when it comes to the Jedi Path. If you cannot do it without some chemical making it "happen", Have you really done anything at all?

Self Discipline, Training yourself to reach the goal.

Self Control, maintaining the goal, by not giving in to the wants, the Temptations.

Self Discipline
::: Story Time: J.u.s.t Jedi Parables
© The Keeper of J.u.st Jedi Holocrons
Kitsu Tails

"Self-discipline was one of the key concepts of Jedi behavior, and Jedi Padawans were taught this from a very early age. The lessons started off similar to what might be taught to an ordinary student; however, as the student progressed, so did the complexity of the lessons." ~ Jedi Behaviors Exert from The Jedi Sourcebook.

"Welcome Younglings." The voice of a calm instructor greeted, bowing to the small group of new attending students of 'The Retreat Center.' The Retreat Center was a place for Jedi, young and old to come and learn the ways of the Force. Gatherings were held here. Workshops were common place, as well as many various classes and programs ranging from the calming and reflective Meditations to the Rigorous practices of self defense and physical training.

This class was the Initiates Studies for the younger generation of twelve to sixteen years starting their first steps on a life long Journey in the ways of the Force. Master Emrys is their guide and teacher for this semester. "Today we will be going over your expected schedules and getting you settled into your rooms. Pair up with your roommate and follow respectfully."

There was a soft mummering of students as they shifted about the room until a set of lines was formed in front of the Master. Many of the students were fidgeting and whispering excitedly to their room-mate, some were pushing others in play before catching the stern gaze of their Masters eyes and quickly falling into a giggling restraint. "This way." The Master instructed once satisfied that they were ready to continue.

The tour would start outside as the Retreat itself was much like a large campus with several buildings dedicated to the different subjects and needs of the community. Master Emrys showed her class of new students where the kitchens were located as well as the locker rooms. She also guided them around the village where the staff, teachers, and guests would sleep in the various huts provided. There were also gardens that students tended and fields where they conducted group events. Much to Cody's happiness there was also a training camp where students learned about being a Knight and how to train in both physical health and combat. He could even see his father out on the gun range teaching students about weapons safety which prompted the young boy to shout out and wave his hand excitedly before he was ushered on to the 'Center Building' a school building where all students started out as Initiates and dormmed in the provided rooms for the summer program.

"You will be expected to rise early in the morning. Dress appropriately. Participate in morning gym and attend your class's on time." Master Emrys explained to the students that filed into the conference room "Every Wednesday we hold conference here. This is Mandatory."

One of the students raised a hand "What happens if we are late?"

The Master turned her gaze on the young student. Tall for her age and smiling with that quirky smirk that suggested she planned to do just that several times if she could easily get away with it. "A Jedi knows Self Discipline, Alexis. While you are here, you are expected to learn this Behavior quickly or be escorted off the program your parents paid for. However, we are willing to give you a few chances to learn it and have several chores you will be expected to perform should you be late or disrespectful to the ground rules."

"Yes Master." Alexis answered back, giving the girl next to her a nudge and leaned down as the Master continued to explain the schedule "Did you see that building across from the Kitchens?"

"The Tavern?" Blue eyed Keryn asked softly "Yea, it also says only apprentices and up are allowed there."

Alexis brushed this small detail off "Oh common! It could be fun! I've always wanted to see what a Tavern is like."

"Shh!" Keryn hissed in response "I'm trying to hear the schedule. I hope they let us work on the farm with the horses!"

"Boooooring!" Cody snickered behind the two girls "I hope they let us try out some of the cools weapons they have! Then I can be a real Jedi Ninja!" as he spoke he rose his two hands mimicking sword cutting motions "Or maybe a cool trooper with a super gun, bang bang bang!" his sword hands rose as if holding a rifle and aiming three practiced shots between his older sister's eyes, a wide grin on lips.

"Shhh!!" Both girls hissed at their brother in unison, causing some of the other students nearby to giggle and snicker at the siblings.

"Younglings." The Masters voice cut in sternly "Last warning."

All the students fell silent. Heads turning back to the front to listen as the Master returned to her lectures. It didn't take long however for Cody to lose interest "Did you see dad out in the field today?" he asked, leaning between his two sisters with a grin.

Keryn sighed in frustration while Alexis grinned "He looks really cool out there!" she answered.

"Maybe he will let us try some of the tools out. You know? For real!" Cody's voice rose which quickly prompted warning shushes and hisses from other students.

It was too late however as the Master now stood over them "Unfortunately you three won't be able to try anything out until you learn to sit quiet and listen to instructions. Now. Please excuse yourselves and seek out Master Zachery in the Foyer. Perhaps some time in the stables will teach you Self Discipline."

With silent protests locked behind closed lips. The three siblings bowed their heads and quickly departed to do as requested.

Self Discipline is an art form that takes time and practice. When we are young, or excited, or experiencing new things it can be difficult to maintain that control over your own self interests. Like the three siblings in our story, sitting silent and respectful can be a tedious and even boring task. But in our anxiousness to move on to the more exciting things, we are prone to miss the small yet important details.

There are many methods and ways to practice Self Discipline. Meditation and/or Martial Art's are great ways to train your Mind, Body and Spirit to conduct itself in a socially acceptable behavior.

Some ways you can practice Self Discipline at home are as follows:
1. Perform a task, even if you are not in the mood to do it. Such as that pile of laundry you have procrastinated against all week.
2. Repeat these tasks, Self Discipline is gained through the repetition of set schedules.
3. Exercising helps to improve your physical health yes. But it is also a great method to awakening the spirit and mind so that you can better perform the tasks you choose.
4. Remain positive. If we are always looking at the bad of things... we are less likely to do them...even when we really need to do it. Find the good in all that you do and the task will become easier.

My Review of the Way of the Apprentice
Ziphin
Temple of the Jedi Force

The story Way of the apprentice has many different avenues that one could take in a review of the story. It could be about arrogance, or perhaps it's about the carnality of beings. Truth is the first time through the story I thought it was about how arrogant Anakin was and about the transformation of his arrogance, but as I thought more about the assignment there where things that just didn't fit. Anakin's arrogance; while a constant in the story starts to decreases towards the climactic end slightly. After I had come to this conclusion I thought of the carnality of beings and decided that maybe I didn't understand the story fully, so I decided to have a second go at it this time trying to analyze every action form both apprentice and Master. As both Master and apprentice clearly think differently they are forced apart by events that neither of them foresaw. What is interesting is that during their time of forced separation they both often times think of what the other might do, once more they are correct about what the other would do.

What I realized is that the story is about two main things. First is about submission of will. Anakin is confronted multiple times with situations that he thinks he knows how to solve yet he does not even consider that others may have a better answer. At one point he is forced to stop trying to be the alpha leader and is forced to allow some one more suited for the job do it. Secondly that as he spends times away from his master his masters teachings step in and guide him. He is in a way transformed by his Master's absence. This transformation forces Anakin to think as his Master does in order to achieve his goals.

In comparing this story with my training under Master Scythe I realized that Multiple times I have been separated for the teachings of my Master. Some of my separations lasted longer than others. I know that during my separation form my Master I found myself thinking back to my lessons regularly on purpose some of the time and unintentionally others. I unintentionally resorted to meditation training that Master Scythe has helped me through during my time at the fabrication shop without thought as my stress levels climb. My stress levels and focus have never been higher in all my life, but Like Anakin there were times where I had to force myself to do the things that my Master would have wanted me to do. As an example I realize that I determine my own focus and like Anakin I get an idea in my head some times that will not leave until they are completed, but while I know how to focus there are times that these ideas over ride everything else.

In searching for Issues with my training I can honestly say that I have not had full dedication in mind as I have allowed myself to get in the way. For instance I know that life happens but I think that my coming and going is more because I hadn't the dedication to my training that I should have. Which ironically my training would have helped me in many of the things that transpired during my time away. The place I work just adopted a program that is designed to help people communicate and collaborate more efficiently which strangely enough has a lot of the same concepts that submitting to a Master does. I have been to focused on my will like Anakin that I didn't really have my Heart in the game. I would have to say that the only true issue that I have with my training is me, also the fact that I have not learned more. I have meditated on this for about two hours on this now and I know that this is where i want to be and is what i want to be dedicated to.

FORTITUDE

Fortitude
Dineara
Institute for Jedi Realists Studies

I think my fortitude is decent. It could use strengthening, sure, but I am fairly strong when it comes to holding on to my principles, navigating through troubled seas or getting a task done. I am not one to be easily swayed without sufficient arguments and proof, but am flexible enough to give in when I realize I'm on the wrong side. Not following the mainstream, I am used to doing things in my own way despite criticism, mockery, wonder or efforts in trying to turn my head to the other direction. I simply won't budge unless there is a good reason for that, whether that reason comes from the inside or the outside. If I bring horoscopes to play, both my parents are Aries and I'm a rising Aries. That's fire and horns and stubbornness and sticking to one's ideals and concepts and all that. When you put contradicting views into play you can imagine the war it creates (especially if one of them is a passive aggressive depressed teenager!). I've learnt to hold my ground, and while it was through stubbornness back then I now can take the good part, the fortitude and resilience, and ditch the must-persist-for-the-sake-of-persisting part.

I have willpower, and I actually have to be a bit careful with that, since in certain environments (like school) my natural way of being will lead everybody to assume it's right and what I'm doing is out of pure wisdom, which it might or might not be. I know I'm smart but considering who I'm put against (people mostly five or more years younger) it's no big deal. It's a challenge for me to present my opinions in a way that will allow space for other thoughts – kids can be awfully receptive to influences and form quickly judgements that will strongly dictate the way they act with a certain person. I'm the smart one, I know everything, let's ask her, she knows. She says this, she has obviously thought it through, let's do as she says. This is not what I want, so I have to be mindful with my doings.

Then again if I'm put against a stronger friend or foe who has remarkable arguments my resolve can waver because they seem to know their stuff so well. In the end, though, no matter how good the argument might be, if it doesn't feel right I don't go with it. I simply can't go against myself in things that matter, that would feel like betraying me. I'm inclined to finding my own path in my own way, and following it in my own way – taking what works and leaving the rest. It allows me to practice objective criticism in situations like this. "I understand your point but it's not the right way for me."

So I'd say I have fortitude, but when it gets 'emotional' (for example with people I respect, like the Jedi community) I might not be so resilient, as I become unsure of my own thoughts and feelings. Then again it doesn't bother me one bit since my purpose here is to tear myself to pieces again and again and then put the pieces back together, leaving the faulty ones and putting new better pieces in. For example, I'm up for trying new things and especially here in the community do it very voluntarily, but if they don't work, then no matter who tries to assure that it's what I must do I won't go there. I'm open for new views and possibilities, but if something contradicts my values it takes a helluva lot of work to get me convinced. I'm not saying I'm immune to outer influences but there is this core of fortitude that is hard to penetrate. Also, if I fail to be resilient at something it's usually combined with the lack of discipline and rarely appears on its own.

I guess the best example of my resilience would be recovering from depression. Damn, that was hard, but I persisted, no matter how horrible it was at times.

The Trial of Courage
By Ziphin
Temple of the Jedi Force

I feel it is appropriate when talking about courage that the word be defined so that it is truly understood what we are talking about when it comes to courage. Courage is defined as the ability and willingness to confront fear, pain, danger, uncertainty, or intimidation.

We know that fear has one of three reactions inside people. The three reactions are fight, flight and freeze. Every person responds to fear in a different way and depending on the events and severity of fear it is virtually impossible to know how a person will respond to fear. As an example a person who is deathly afraid of spiders may freeze around a spider. That same person may be afraid of snakes but instead of freezing they back away slowly due to the flight response. And likewise that person might be afraid of big dogs buy refuses to back down when confronted by a dog. People are complex beings that are unpredictable some times.

In order to describe the thing that scared me the most it will require a bit of a back story, so here goes. I was living at a friend's house when I made some enemies. I reacted to a situation out of anger and without thinking about the consequences of my actions. I swore that I would carry my actions to the grave with me so that no one would ever know what I had done, but after a few weeks people started to forget about what had happened and I ran into a person who hated the person I had acted against just as much as me or so I thought. I'm not sure what came over me but I slipped my secret to this person. Almost one week to the day I'm sitting on my couch when there is a knock on the door. The person I had wronged was standing there with the person I had told as well as four skin heads. They invited me outside and I refused. I knew better than that, I would not go outside and get jumped in the middle of the street. So I told him that if he wanted to talk he would need to come inside where I thought I would be able to sit down and talk with him about the events that accrued. How stupid was I to think that he would want to talk…. Don't answer that. After I got jumped on my couch by two of them my roommate asked me to move out (same day). So I left to speak with another friend about what had happened.

To get to the point the person I had wronged sent a person to my next place of dwelling with a handgun. Rather it was for intimidation or to actually kill me I don't know, all I know is that my new roommate asked me to stay in side when they showed up. They told him to get out of the way or they would shoot him. That's when I truly felt fear. I knew this was for real and that I could die. In fear I told myself to run but when I noticed there was someone by the back door I decided that if this was really going to happen I would make it happen In a tight spot where I would have more control of the situation or so I hoped. I went to the closet in the back of the back bedroom waiting with a candle stick I picked up on my way down the hallway.

When they had searched the rest of the house it was time. The sliding door in the closet was open about 2 feet and I watched two of the people come in the room. I stepped back and raised the candle stick preparing for what I was sure would be my last stand. Call it luck or fate, or anything you want but the fact is that they looked directly at the closet door and neither one decided to look inside. They simply left. Four hours later that day while I was walking to my parents' house they did a drive by on the room I was staying in. no one got injured but none the less they were gunning for me (pun intended).

I overcame my fear that day only because I was faced with no other option. Flight was not an option for me but making it more difficult was. After wards I decided that I would never strike out in anger at another person ever again and to this day have lived up to that standard. I also promised myself that I would never be as helpless as I was that day ever again. I purchased a handgun and got my concealed weapons permit, And Then I trained with my firearm. Beyond that I started practicing martial arts so that in the event that I don't have my firearm I would be able to handle myself. I refuse to be a victim ever again and that is why I have adopted the saying Sic vis pacem para bellum, which means if you want peace prepare for war. Preparing for war is exactly what I've done, I don't condone violence but there are times where there is no other option. I pray that I never have to use any of the skills I've learned in preparing on another human being ever.

The Purpose of Adversity
Jackie Meyer
Institute for Jedi Realist Studies

I'm writing this as I'm going through quite the period of adversity. As I lay in bed and think about what I want to focus on in my sleep, I caught myself thinking, "Why does it take so much adversity before we make the necessary changes in our lives?" But the answer comes to me almost immediately. It's necessary because we make it so. I could to the right thing and eat properly, take my vitamins, and all of that. But, when I feel good, do I? Sometimes. Sometimes it takes some aching muscles to remind me. When that doesn't work, I end up getting a cold or worse, so that I'm forced to take better care of myself. In the end it would be much easier to just do the right thing the whole time!

My wife has far worse consequences to not doing the right thing. When she doesn't take her medication she has seizures. These seizures cause secondary injuries when she falls, and gives her muscles aches and pains from the seizure in general. In some cases she suffers from amnesia after, losing many years of her life until we work her back up to the present time. Now, there are many other issues that contribute to her trouble remembering to take her medication, but the example is still valid.

How many of us overspend our money and end up behind in our bills? We know how much money we have, and how much it costs to pay for things. Yet, many of us still end up choosing to see a movie or buy a book, overextending ourselves financially. Then we get that reminder as our bank account quickly approaches zero that we need to be more responsible with our money.

As we go through life, ignoring the little lessons, they will grow until we finally pay attention. Why? Because life is about growth. Our inner self, which is connected to the Force, sees life from a larger perspective. It knows that if we grow stagnant, which tends to happen when life goes well, then we aren't growing. So, it brings situations to us so we can learn and grow.

Now, we can avoid much of this adversity by learning lessons early. If we're not stubborn, fighting through small issues instead of taking the time to see what can be learned, they won't escelate into bigger issues. Also, when life is going well, take the time to look couragiously and deeply inside. What are your weaknesses? What issues are triggered from time to time? Try to be proactive and address these issues before they are an active problem. In this way, many of these issues can be resolved before reaching the point of adversity.

You see, all of our adversity is created by us, for us. If you want to avoid it, try to address your weaknesses before they are triggered. Also, remove the believe that adversity is required for growth. That belief will only bring more adversity to you. Instead, realize that you can grow, with or without adversity. But, when it does come, accept it as an opportunity for growth. Accept it, be thankful for it. Then the process of overcoming adversity won't be nearly as painful.

And finally, don't be afraid to ask for help from someone who you feel will have a different perspective on the situation. After all, sometimes the lesson is a simple as learning to ask for help.

INTEGRITY

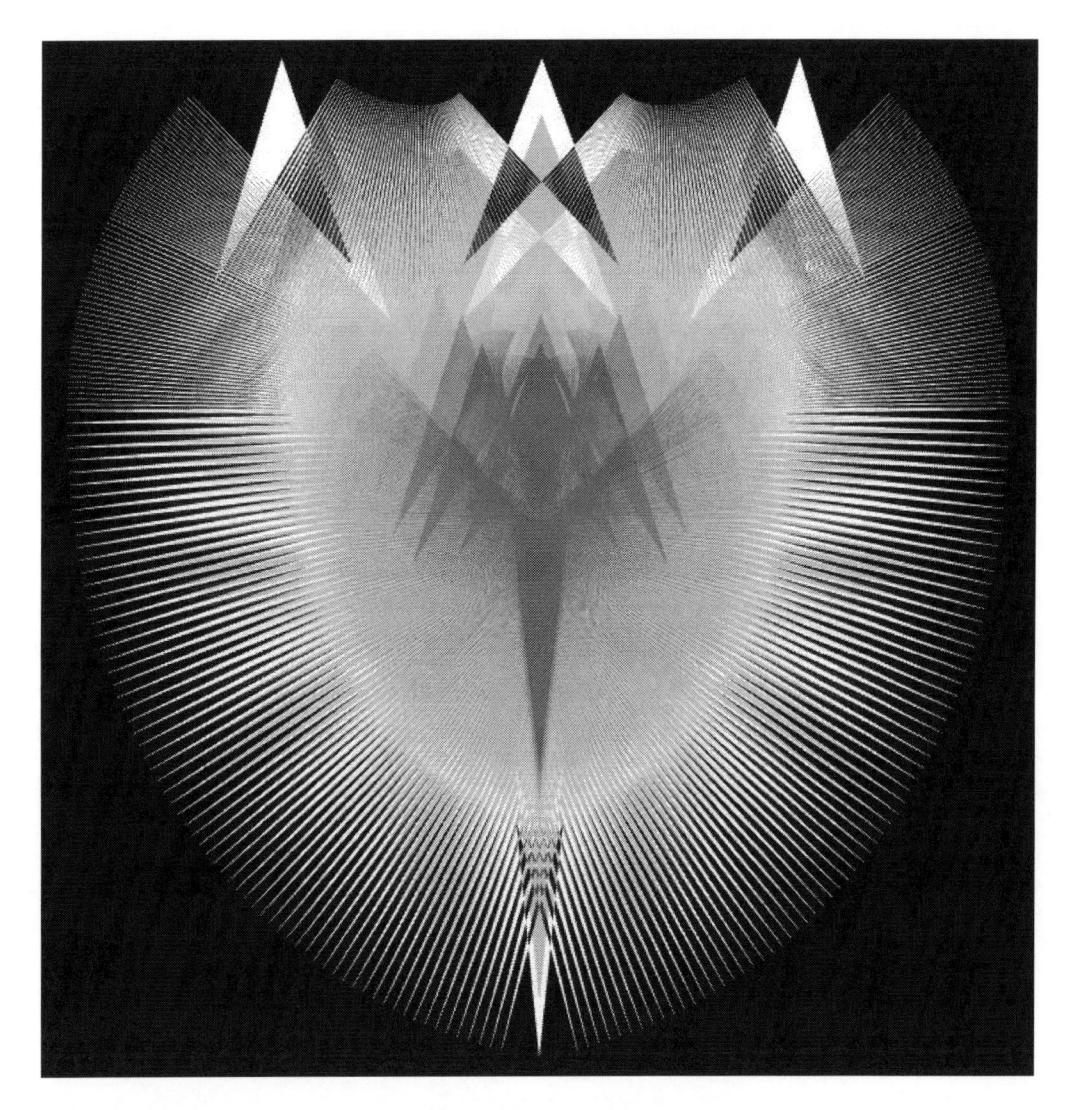

Picture by Mark Brereton, Temple of the Jedi Order

Integrity is not Old School
By Grayson Dark
Temple of the Jedi Force

Integrity is not old school, it applies today like it ever did."- Richard Norton

Martial art virtues include such things as courage, discipline, and character development. Part of living with what I call the Warrior's Edge is based on the role martial arts can have in helping a person develop character. And I do believe there is no more essential or defining aspect of a person than their character. But what is it?

To me, a person of character lives by personal ethical virtues like honor, reliability, trustworthiness, and kindness. A person who has good character is thought to be especially worthy, virtuous, or admirable in terms of moral qualities. Character is comprised of those principles and value that give your life direction, meaning, and depth. They constitute your inner sense of right and wrong. Character is concerned with doing the right thing. Honesty, courage, fairness, generosity, and integrity are essential attributes of good character. Showing respect to others is part of character. These are essentials for true martial artists and those who learn how to hurt, or even kill others.

I agree with how John Wooden described integrity: "Integrity is purity of intention. Integrity speaks for itself. Sincerity, honesty, and reliability are components that encourage and lead to integrity. We must never sacrifice our morals or values." And like physical strength, virtues grow through practice. Remember that, just like your martial techniques develop through the hard work on the mat, your virtues only become stronger and better through practice in your daily life.

Integrity is the consistency of our actions, values, and principles. It is not enough to read or recite a pledge that may hang on the wall of our place of training. Nor is it enough to just say that the martial arts help with character development. We must practice good character. This is more than just saying no to vices, but rather pursuing what is right and good. Remember what Gary Ryan Blair once said, "It is a lot easier to fight for principles than to live up to them." Practicing good ethics and character is hard. But for the true martial artist, the true warrior, and someone who wants to live powerfully with the Warrior's Edge, it is essential. Character is a must, and this includes integrity.

The issue of respect is often a difficult one to discuss. It's a term that is widely used for a myriad of circumstances. Consider how we are told to 'respect' a dangerous animal. In this case respect is nothing more than a reference to refraining from interfering with it, namely because it is dangerous. This is much different than holding something or someone in high esteem.

Respect?
Talon
Real Jedi Enclave

Then we must separate the respect for a person from their actions. I can respect someone's rights as a person and yet not respect them because they are dishonorable.

How do you show someone respect? This is cause of a lot of problems and any one of us that is interested in negotiation and diplomacy must understand. Not everyone has the exact same idea for how the need for respect should be fulfilled. Some people work extremely hard to become the best at what they do in order to "earn" respect. Some seek respect through demonstrating power, such as being a gang-member or violent criminal. Some focus internally and work on being a person that they themselves can respect. The issues of right and wrong don't necessarily have a place in this. It's merely an issue of culture and value.

What actions are disrespectful? Again, this tends to go back to the separation between the person and their actions. It is disrespectful to speak in negative terms about a person.

Saying things like 'You are a moron' disrespectful because it speaks to everything that the person is AND does.

However, saying 'X action was moronic' isn't disrespectful it's just a statement of fact or opinion. We all do moronic things in our lives but that doesn't necessarily mean that we are all morons.

This is a distinction that we all need to make, especially as Jedi because oft times we'll be told that certain actions are inappropriate, wrong and etc. We need this. It's like walking around all day with a piece of spinach stuck to our teeth. We can't see ourselves and so the spinach is hidden to us. We need something that allows us to see or understand things about ourselves that we can't see for ourselves. We need the mirror to see our reflection or we need someone to let us know so that we can change it.

I don't know about you, but I'd prefer someone take the time to let me know that there is spinach in my teeth rather than everyone keeping quiet for fear that I'd be offended by the message. Just the same, I'd prefer someone to take the time to tell me the flaws that they see in me because I don't know how I'm perceived and only through being told can I make changes.

I've been told that I'm very disrespectful because I challenge teachings and ideas -- but that's not how I see it. It is only those with something to hide or fear that resist being challenged. To be challenged ALWAYS gives you the opportunity to explain yourself and make things clear, to provide sound reason to solidify a position or to look deeper at the position and see where it may be based on unstable ground. There is no down side to that if we are truly Jedi. We shouldn't want to stand on unstable ground or use strategies that don't work. But again that's just my perspective. Others might wish to be seen through rose colored glasses and never challenged.

So where do you derive your respect from? What do you consider to be respectful treatment? Why?

ToTJO Live Service: Integrity
V-Tog
Temple of the Jedi Order

My school motto was 'Integrity'.

Just that. Nothing else.

I didn't know what it meant when I became a pupil there at the age of 11. But it was emblazoned across the school logo on my uniform and sports kits so people started to ask me what it meant. Once I found out, it became one of my favorite words and something of a personal motto too. I wanted integrity to be a label that I could wear truthfully and proudly.

It's a word that I haven't heard so much since moving on from that school. I'd forgotten how much meaning it held for me until the revised 16 Teachings came into being at TOTJO (and it's also one of the 21 Maxims). Teaching number 9 reads as follows:

"Jedi have integrity. We are authentic to what we believe and are open, honest and true to our purpose and our minds. We remove all masks to reveal ourselves as courageous and noble of heart. We do not hide from fear of damage to our image because we know that our image cannot be blemished from the words and actions of others."

In a broad sense, integrity is about being consistently true to oneself and one's principles. And it's often not as easy as we might think to do so. We can unwittingly be swayed – by our peers, by an event, by the whims of our Ego…

It's important to understand that there is a difference between a permanent shift in one's principles and a deviation from them. Integrity does not necessarily mean that one must hold the same principles throughout their entire life.

It's important to be who you are. If who you are is someone that you don't like very much, that's something that you can work to change. The first step to change is recognising and accepting yourself – hence, pretending to be someone you are not will not help and is more akin to just papering over the cracks, or, as described in the 9th Teaching – wearing a mask.

One of the problems with religion and doctrine is that it can inadvertently encourage people to wear these masks. You might read the doctrine and you think "Teaching number 15 says that Jedi have eternal life through the Force. I don't believe that – but in order to advance at TOTJO I'm going to have to pretend that I do."

No.

Here, you don't have to pretend. Jedi accept that not everyone shares the same values and principles and we don't aim to create a community of cardboard cut-outs.

In order for your training and your time here to be of meaningful value, you have to be open about who you are. Many of the 21 Maxims cannot be achieved without personal integrity – courage, faith, humility, fearlessness, nobility, honesty, pure motive, harmony…to name but a few.
That's not to say that you have to shout out all your innermost secrets, but that you must be honest with yourself and let your words and actions be rooted in that place of honesty.

We all make mistakes. You might not believe in hurting others, for example…but then you are provoked into insulting someone in a heated debate. If you believe that you went against your principles and the Jedi principles, what should you do in that situation? Carry on getting embroiled in the argument? Go away and try to forget all about it? Or hold your hands up, admit the mistake, and apologize?

Integrity can be hard work. There will always be times when it will seem to slip away from you. But, in the end that's your choice. If you want to regain it, to stay true to yourself, fight for it. Refuse to let it go, no matter how hard it tries. Sometimes, on the surface, doing the right thing – acting in accordance with your conscience and principles – can seem like the hardest thing in the world. But take everything else out of the equation, see yourself as you are, and sometimes you realize that it really doesn't need to be.

Provided that you are not causing unnecessary hurt – stand up for what you believe in, don't be scared to speak your mind, and don't compromise on being your true self.

Don't let yourself look back on life regretting the time that you spent trying to be someone else.

As Oscar Wilde once said:

"Be yourself; everyone else is already taken."

OBJECTIVITY

Picture by Mark Brereton, Temple of the Jedi Order

Compassion or Pragmatism?
Derek Thompson
Ashla Knights

I never saw a wild thing sorry for itself. A small bird will drop frozen dead from a bough without ever having felt sorry for itself. – D.H. Lawrence

My upstairs neighbor knocked on my door this evening while I was in the middle of preparing dinner and said that a baby bird had fallen out of the nest that had been constructed in one of the shrubs outside our apartment building. After a moment of hesitation; trying to decide on what to say and/or do, I stuttered a bit because I was a caught off guard and said okay. I opened a kitchen drawer and pulled out a pair of house gloves and went down stairs.

My neighbor…already outside, pointed at the baby bird which was hopping up and down frantically in the mulch due to a damaged left wing. I watched for a moment thinking that I had never touched a living bird before and trying to reconcile the pity and fear I was feeling for this creature because it was absolutely terrified. I told myself I had to commit to action mainly because the neighbor was watching me, but also I had to do something for it, so I stalled for an additional moment to put on the gloves and then I walked parallel to the bird's path. I actually had to steel myself before I reached down to scoop up the bird and not entirely because I was a bit squeamish, but mainly because I was feeling what this creature was feeling. It saw me coming and frantically hopped away from me and I didn't want scare it any more then it already was, so I backed off a bit. Then I tried again and again before I actually got the bird in my hands and three thoughts danced in my mind as I walked with the bird toward the nest:

(1) I actually have a bird in my hands and this feels strange.
(2) I hope I'm not holding it too tight.
(3) I think I'm going to have to throw these gloves away.

I got to the nest and placed the bird back in it but the bird was so terrified that it hopped out the nest and landed back in the mulch. I looked down and the bird was breathing so hard and fast that I could feel the bird's terror and fatigue. My neighbor spoke what I was thinking which was to let it be for a bit to which I was most thankful because this poor thing was actually breaking my heart. She said to me that should would figure something out and then our downstairs neighbor came out and told us that the mother and the other hatch-lings left it behind when it fell out of the nest and broke it's wing.

    For a split second I was stunned…asking myself how a mother could leave one of it's own behind and then I realized I was assigning human notions of compassion and empathy to creatures that have none. Yet, as I walked up the stairs back to my apartment I thought, that can't be right because every animal in nature has compassion and empathy so it is not that they do not have any, they simply have different constructs at work. If they didn't, they wouldn't care for their young at all. The bird's wing was broken and I believe that this is like a horse breaking it's leg…it's never the same. I opened the door and walked into my apartment and thought, "the mother actually did what had to be done. She left a child behind because in her world she knew there was nothing more she could do for it and there are other hatch-lings to consider." She did something practical, she in affect…pulled the plug. She let go of one of her own that was technically already dead.

Was she being pragmatic or compassionate? Or, was she being pragmatically compassionate?

Advanced Conflict Resolution
Paladin Vandor Draconis
Force Academy

As was pointed out in my lecture on Conflict resolution, it is important for a light jedi to be able to handle such a situation. There are two forms of this. Mental and physical.

For the physical portion of this, you all are welcome to join me in my Hanshi's dojo.

For our needs here at the FA, a focus on the Mental aspect is what is important. Verbal abuse…drama…reading those things we would just rather not read.

Up to this point, we have talked about tools to de-escalate another in order to resolve an issue outside of conflict.

But now, we are talking about how to handle ourselves in a conflict situation.

I wish to note one thing before I continue… unlike the last lecture, these techniques are reliant on ones own ability to stay grounded in their reasoning. If one cannot stay grounded and rational, these techniques will backfire on you.

When it is determined that another will not de-escalate or that we see we will not, there is a process to follow:

1. Remember your initial reasoning.
2. Question it.
3. Explore minutea.
4. Multiple approaches
5. Have multiple intentions
6. Remember, there is no winner, only levels of loosing

Remember your initial reasoning
More often then naught, those who go into conflict seldomly will remember what led to the situation at hand. It is important to remember this reasoning for all conflicts start out from a reasoned state. Remembering it will help anchor a person to the ability to reason.

Question It
Understand, if conflict has started, your opposition has stopped

questioning your reason. You must and you must do it in a way where you feel comfortable you could disrepute your own reasoning. You have to be willing to be wrong and looking to prove it to yourself. If after this you can't... 3,4,5 now become possible. Prior to taking this step, they are not.

Steps 1 and 2 should be taken before every rebuttal.

Explore Minutea
One of the greatest points of Movie History which talks to this was in Star Trek IV. Near the end the group comes to see god, god asks for a ride out and Kirk responds...'Why does god need a ship?'
Look at what is presented, focus on small items and explore them with another. This does three things:

1. Opens up a new avenue of learning for you.
2. Forces your opponent off topic into a new forum.
3. Confuses your opponent. Makes them think.

The greatest thing you can do as a jedi is re-introduce thought.

Multiple Approaches
As a conflict drags on, reason slips further away. Which if allowed will focus a person solely on the one thing... to be right. Through the exploration of the Minutea, we can then start opening up more then one approach to the issue. Using this method, we start to take advantage of the others need to maintain a single approach within the conflict. Exponentially exposing them to the need to think and increasing the possibility that through the increase of confusion... you can literally confuse their intent to themselves, throwing one out of conflict completely.

Multiple intentions
Conflict normally starts with a single thought. Two bulls colliding as it were. By developing more then one intention, we give ourselves the ability to think more then two dimensionally. Giving us the ability to jump from one intent to another.
Remember, there is no winner, only levels of loosing
A lot of times, we go into conflict with some grandiose design of conquering an opponent, etc. If a light jedi can see themselves in this light...

they have lost. One should not go into conflict with the idea something good can come out of it… it seldomly does. When conflict is entered, it is because all else has failed and we should do so begrudgingly. We go into conflict not to win… but to minimize the losses. Those who would think such is a victory, clearly are misusing the tools presented here.

As you can see, this entails changing ones perspective of conflict as well as altering the environment of the conflict. It entails the best qualities of a Jedi, information gathering and expanding our own mind as well as anothers.

In this fashion, a Jedi is given a unique opportunity to help another. To learn from another. But most of all… to learn themselves.

Jumping to Conclusions
V-Tog
Temple of the Jedi Order

One night last May, my town was buzzing with the news that a terraced house in the town had blown up as a result of a gas explosion. Pictures of the house showed...well the house no longer existed. The houses on either side were still standing, but between them was simply a hole, and a pile of debris. The next morning I was interested to see that a man in the town had been arrested under the Explosive Substances Act 1883 and a garage, and over 100 homes in the surrounding area, had been evacuated and cordoned off as Explosive Disposal teams investigated further. Of course, you can probably already see where this is going. Conspiracy theories immediately went through the roof. Everyone seemed very keen to link the two events, despite the Police stating that they did not believe there was any link. And with both gas explosions and explosive related evacuations being such rare occurrences in sleepy towns like mine, it was not altogether surprising.

Now I am not using these events to suggest that anyone here is a conspiracy theorist. But it does serve to remind us of the way in which we humans all too often have a tendency to jump to conclusions and work on assumptions.

As Jedi, and as people living in society, we will sometimes be called on to make decisions and judgements based on the facts presented to us. It is part of our duty as guardians of peace and justice to mediate, or investigate, when necessary. Perhaps sometimes we may even be placed in the difficult position of having to decide whether someone has done something wrong, or determine who is at fault for something. Such things sometimes have retribution or punishment of some kind attached to them, and as such it is imperative that we are able to come to the right conclusion with a clear conscience.

So how does this tie in to the explosion related events? Seeing people so quickly assuming that two events must be linked reminds us of the pitfalls of doing so. Jumping to conclusions in this way can lead us to make a wrong decision, or even if no decision is made at that stage, it may influence any decision that we do make. Likewise, freely voicing such thoughts may influence the thoughts and decisions of others.

Within the Temple's 16 basic teachings of the Jedi, it states that "Jedi are guardians of peace and justice. We believe in finding peaceful solutions to problems, gifted as we are we remain negotiators of the utmost ability. We never negotiate out of fear, but never fear to negotiate. We embrace justice, protecting and preserving the fundamental rights of all living creatures."

To me, amongst the fundamental rights of all living creatures is the right to be judged on unbiased fact and evidence, rather than guesswork. A guardian of justice understands and respects that justice must be preserved and given through a meticulous investigation of what we know to be true, or false. Justice founded in assumptions is not justice.

The 16 basic teachings also include the following:

"As Jedi, we trust and use our feelings. We are intuitive, more so than others and with this heightened intuition we become more spiritually evolved as our minds become more harmonious with the Force and it's influences." Should we therefore discard or ignore this teaching?

There is nothing wrong with listening to instincts and intuition. They can be useful tools, and in many walks of Jedi life they are very important. However, in situations of judgement we may have a feeling that we are right about something. But although it is not necessary, or perhaps not even advisable, to discard such thoughts, it is important to ascertain that we have all the facts. We cannot base such important things as judging right and wrong on feelings, no matter how convinced we are of their accuracy. In essence; listen to your feelings but do not act rashly on them. Perhaps you can use them to inform your investigation. But perhaps approaching them from the standpoint of 'Can I find evidence to show that I am WRONG about this?' would be preferable to setting out to prove them.

So, where does that leave us? Sometimes things happen that remind us of how easy it is to jump to conclusions. In examples such the happenings of my town last May, it is often due to the way in which people get so easily carried away with 'jumping on the bandwagon'. Many of us enjoy the mental challenge of trying to spot links between things. But these links must be carefully thought through. Making links simply for the sake of making links is probably unadvisable. Making links because of intuition and instinct is sometimes unavoidable, but should always be approached with caution and an unbiased mind. If you ever feel the temptation to use assumption to make an important decision, whether that be an decision with major consequences or simply a decision in your own mind, just stop and think, 'Have I really examined all of the facts available to me? Am I acting as a Jedi should – as a true Guardian of Justice?'

Objectivity / Subjectivity
Kol Drake
Institute for Jedi Realist Studies

The Merrian-Webster Dictionary online lists one of the definitions for Objective as:
* expressing or dealing with facts or conditions as perceived without distortion by personal feelings, prejudices, or interpretations <an objective history of the war> <an objective judgment>

Tapping that same source, Subjective has many more possible meanings and here I have to grab two to explain the 'opposing stance' to Objective:

* relating to or being experience or knowledge as conditioned by personal mental characteristics or states

* to a particular individual <subjective judgments> modified or affected by personal views, experience, or background <a subjective account of the incident>

In most forums addressing an analysis of the creeds and codes, one might come away thinking, "A Jedi should be Objective in all their dealings with others". Some might read that as acting 'detached from emotion or emotional intent'. One could also argue if we face life objectively, we do not think or feel in the moment because we revert to our stored data to deal with our lives. We would be acting as computers programmed to operate functionally and efficiently. Of course, as time goes on, we gain new information and so we update our hard drive and software. With this model, we are not much different than a computer.

Herein, I play a bit of devil's advocate (Sith's advocate?) and venture to suggest that being subjective in our dealings with the outside world might be as important as holding to an 'objective calm'. The subjective self is what gives us our human qualities and capacities; not our physical body or the outside forces that serve as our computer programmers.

"Outside forces that serve to program us" – Consider, we swim in an overload of 'input' from 24 hour transmitted opinion claiming it is 'just reporting the fair and balanced truth', innumerable 24/7 twitter feeds describing every moment of the day. Many people today seem to rely upon pop culture, the latest YouTube feeds, Twitter, or Facebook to make decisions in their life. By relying upon these external forces, people are not utilizing their own subjective experience, potentially becoming detached from their own wants and desires and, instead, being hypnotized into following the mass market consensus of 'what and how you should be and behave'.

> "The unexamined life is not worth living"
> – Socrates

If we do not take the time to explore our values, feeling, beliefs, and emotions, the direction of existence will be molded and shaped by the external world alone. When we busy ourselves with work, with social media, and with continual activity to avoid confronting who and what we are, there is a strong likelihood that we will be living a dissatisfied existence. Apathy develops because of the absence of subjective awareness. Subjectivity has the ability to unlock doors and expose the depth of one's being.

It takes time to cultivate the Self, but that process must start somewhere. Growing up, becoming the Jedi decision maker in regards to your lives, requires the development of a reasonably stable set of definitions of who and what you are and what the world is. While we gain input from many sources such as parents, siblings, relatives, friends, teachers, and the media, each of us alone weaves our own unique design for existence. The subjective self must illuminate in response to the challenges reality presents on a daily basis. The answer for 'daily living' is in each of us.

The subjectivity of each of us is the seedling of our uniqueness and individuality. Jedi are not clones. Jedi are not programmed to act and react identically in each situation. Nor are we all Vulcan-like in our ability to be totally and utterly objective when asked to judge or react to a situation. Objectivity alone is not always ideal. The lack of subjective awareness can cause an inability to see the possibility of choice. Choice comes from being aware of the possibilities that exist when responsibility is taken for the direction our lives are taking. There is no doubt that environment and observed behaviors can contribute to our worldview. However, we have the power either to accept or reject what we see. We may not be able to control our circumstance, but we can control how we respond to it.

We, as Jedi, are all trying to make sense of the world in a new way. This can lead to confusion. However, it seems many are looking for external answers to what is an internal process. If we listen to the Force, different options will manifest. This can be tough. As a generalization, we were all never taught to listen to our Self – to be guided by our inner voice. Instead, we were all told (repeatedly) to listen to parents (your own and others), teachers, organization leaders (scouts, etc.), professors, bosses, the church, the government, science, faux news, etc. Almost any outer source of instruction in how to live your life. We are lucky to have any individuality at all after 20 plus years of that kind of 'molding', let alone being able to then 'turn inward' to examine Self comfortably.

Actively communicating feelings is important, but not as important as knowing that a subjective self has the potential to exist. Taking direction from the inner voice can summon new ideas and possibilities. We are most alive when we are open to all the many facets of our inner desires, emotions, the flow of ideas, body sensations, relationships, reasoning, forethought, concern for others, sense of our values, and all else within us.

There is emotion; yet you can still have peace

- me 😀

We must work to integrate all the aspects of our being so that we can live a more fruitful existence which is grounded in authenticity. We must be centered in our experiencing. Taking the objective stance while still keeping the subjective avenues open or we risk being so insular to the world and people that we can no longer relate to anyone or thing at all.

Identity based on what we have done, how we are viewed, what others think of us, is past-bound identity. It can lead to staleness and repetitiousness in living. Heck, trying to conform to 'labels' assigned by others is a sure way to doubting self (and Self) and downright depressing when you are shoved into a square hole when you have such multi-sided potential. Embracing Self (and the Force) allows one to be alive in the moment and free to change and evolve with the flow of our lives and Life. Thus, the more awareness, the more consciousness we have. The more we are conscious, the more we are living authentically. The more authentically we live, the more vitality we have. The more we are in tune with the Force.

WISDOM

The Essence of Wisdom
Alexandre Orion
Temple of the Jedi Order

I would speak to you this evening on the third and most elusive of the Three Tenets : Wisdom. Please keep in mind that I know absolutely nothing about it. As it were, it is directly from the heart of foolishness that I write a Sermon on Wisdom.

Wisdom cannot really be a goal, that is, one really cannot seek to 'become wise'. One may of course display some wisdom from time to time. For some, it is frequent – for some others far less so. Strangely enough, Wisdom often comes across as absurdity, as contrary or contradictory to what we are sure we 'know'. It tends to rise out of what our focus has left out. It eludes our grasp.

Wisdom is a lonesome thing, for it avoids the 'common sense' of the crowd. What everybody thinks and what everyone knows is as far from Wisdom as remembrances of yesterday are from the hopes for tomorrow. Wisdom isn't 'knowing' anything in particular. It isn't true Wisdom to be able to parrot parables and proverbs. It is nothing one can hold onto like a position or a title or a status.

One often looks to the lofty heights toward a light of Wisdom, but notices nothing in one's own shadow before one's own feet. In other words, contemplating the 'vault of heaven' is much more likely to cause one to stumble and fall over something than to render Wisdom. In fact, one may very likely find more glimmers of Wisdom during a walk in the garden than in the Library.

One can go around and around it and never find a way in … It doesn't come with references or in a well-annotated bibliography. It isn't obtained by quoting philosophers or poets word for word. It is as a train ticket that has been punched – it can get you where you're going once, but then it becomes rubbish.

It is as common as grass, but we can't feel it everywhere because we think we 'know' what we're looking for. 'Ordinary' doesn't seem the right shape. 'Extraordinary' seems too bizarre. Reflected in still waters and teardrops, its Image dries away with the out-breath.

Wisdom rarely shouts ; neither does it accompany 'always' nor 'never'. It cannot be known, thus it comes more readily to the un-clever. It makes its home in the present, and neither protects the 'old ways' nor presses toward 'progress'.

Ergo :

> When one comes to the Knowledge that 'one does not know' – And can Focus on the Moment (rather than concentrating on cause and effect) –
> One resides in Wisdom and no longer needs to 'have' it.

Foolishness, yet Wisdom
Michael "Akkarin" Kitchen
Temple of the Jedi Order

Foolishness and wisdom are a dichotomy of human nature, but what makes an action foolish and another action wise? This can be a difficult to discern, but one can take steps in the right direction through deliberation and careful study.

But first what exactly is Wisdom? Well there have been many attempts to try and come up with a coherent and sensible description of what we mean by Wisdom. A brief understanding of Wisdom and its history as a trait of human character can be read about on the Stanford Encyclopedia of Philosophy[1]:

- Wisdom is a form of rationality.
- We would say one was wise if they were: knowledgeable about a range of fact-based subjects
- Had a variety of justified beliefs on how to live rationally (morally/practically/factually)
- Were committed to living by these justified beliefs
- Had very few unjustified beliefs and is sensitive to one's limitations

Wisdom therefore can be seen as the successful adherence to the above principles, while foolishness can be seen as the unsuccessful adherence to the above principles.

Jedi are both foolish and wise; this is inescapable, because we are not perfect, nor do we have all the right answers, as Jedi though we should feel compelled to do our best. Our best in any particular situation requires integrity to our values, our principles, our justified beliefs.

Wisdom betrays sight of deeper truths and relationships in reality than we are normally aware enough to pick up on. Wisdom requires a profound understanding that looks beyond what is immediately obvious at first glance. Not everything requires such deep investigation of course, but anything beyond the immediately practical should be investigated with due patience and care.

Often it is possible for one to find foolishness masquerading as wisdom, this is because wisdom's sometimes elusive nature makes it easy for

---

1. [1] http://plato.stanford.edu/entries/wisdom/ - See "Wisdom as Rationality", last accessed 16/Oct/2014

one to accidentally feign. There are some guidelines that one can follow to ensure not only that what they are witnessing is wise, but also that the actions they themselves are doing are also wise.

One who is wise knows that they cannot "know". Given this, Jedi should be careful of anyone who proclaims their belief to be "**the** answer", such people often elevate their own authority in such matters, which ultimately betrays a lack of due outrospection of others.

Similarly one should never mistake "seriousness" for wisdom. Quite often seriousness is portrayed as wisdom, but wisdom is much more closely related to "sincerity". If one were behaving in a ridiculous manner by messing around and not taking things so seriously, doing what one thought was fun, one might colloquially be called a "fool", but in fact so long as one were aware of what they were doing and the reason for it then they might be a lot wiser than some. These "fools" see the inherent humour of living in such a crazy beautiful world, but only having so long to appreciate it, while those who are "serious" can quite easily elevate the importance of trivial Conventional Truths.

One must take care that when something looks wise it is not quietly foolishness in disguise. Wisdom overlooks nothing and doesn't "stick" to anything, bearing this in mind one must conduct one's own thorough investigations into each particular example.

Wisdom is changing, wisdom is fluid, from this flows its strength. As the world changes so does the wisdom we use to understand it, as we change so does the wisdom we use to understand ourselves, as others change so does the wisdom we use to understand our relationships to them.

Wisdom is not simply "knowing" something, wisdom is also about "applying" that something. If the situation in which a thing is to be applied changes, then we need to adapt ourselves to understand these new circumstances. Wisdom is constantly evolving.

A Jedi's actions should be tempered with wisdom, but wisdom is not a cheap commodity. One should not take wisdom for granted and one should treat wisdom with care when thinking to apply it.

Wisdom in Action
Talon Trevor MacDonald
Aurora Borealis

I, and others like me, represent those that have been faced with the choice to kill, or be killed, and in some cases kill, or allow innocents to suffer or be killed. Because of this, I have numerous real examples of Why killing is not always murder.

Something to consider: How many are here, simply because they believe the Jedi in the Movies to be "Cool", and want to bear the name, but had no clue of the responsibility of bearing such a name?

I turned Naturally to this path, after a lifetime of service in the Military, College, work in Law Enforcement as a "profiler" and Forensic Anthropologist. I have, on many situations been required to use weapons in defense of myself and others, and Yes, I have used such weapons offensively, which is what happens in war, or when removing threats to others.

As Jedi, I accept that I must walk a clean and clear path.

I understand that I may be required to place myself in the way of harm, to protect the weak, and innocent.

I work, to make sure my skills and wisdom are up to the task of keeping me alive, so that I may keep Others alive and unharmed.

I learn, daily, so that my wisdom is always capable of helping me choose the right way to go in such situations.

I am familiar with the laws of my city, state, and country, so that I may exercise my duties accordingly, whenever possible and whenever appropriate.

In public, I maintain politeness, and pleasant discourse, so that when I am needed, people will not view me as the threat. In private, I deal directly with my own doubts and fears, so that they are not present when I am around those I have elected to protect, and sometimes lead.

Every minute of every day, I am an Ambassador of the path I have chosen to live and represent. I, thusly, must act appropriately in the representation of that path, and the others in that path. Part of this is understanding and effectively living up to my responsibilities, that I have chosen to take unto myself, by accepting the title: "Jedi"

Wisdom through Insight
Sinistra
Temple of the Jedi Force

Last Saturday, I took part in a project called "The world is a better place with you". This monthly event is organized by a Hungarian spiritual singer, Bella Bagdi and is about spreading positive thinking, building up connection and communication with people we are living in the world. My friend invited me to it, who was also invited by her boyfriend.

The place we went to, was a small house, looked kinda worn and old from outside, but inside its energies and atmosphere was more than awesome. My friend said she hadn't felt it so much at any places in her life. (I did so, but very long time ago.)

There was no litany added to the start, after everyone introduced themselves a bit, we immediately went to "in medias res" mode and started with little assignments. Each of us had to choose a pair who we complete the assignments given by the leader of the group. Pairs changed from assignment to assignment, and at first I chose an older man, who was a really good choice because of his humble, yet enormous intelligence. That man is awesome and I immediately felt it as the leader assigned me to choose a pair. The tasks were mainly about telling our experiences, about important things happening to us, about charity and kindness and about events which remained in us or affected us in a great way. Both members of the pairs got 3-3 minutes to do this, though the conversations became two-sided as it does in a natural way. We didn't mind it at all, also that we often went off-topic and continued discussing about spiritual, scientifically, etc. topics.

When the tasks were done, the leader gave us a presentation, which was about our monthly topic, this time, helping and charity. (Every months have different topics, November's topic was, for example, the importance of maintaining and nurturing our love relationships.) At the end of the program, we had to choose a permanent partner (I believe, it changes monthly) who we keep the contact with and of course, I chose the wise, "Jedi-like" man. It turned out that he is a healer who gives sound and resonance therapy with tibetan singing bowls. He said that the first occasion would be free so we agreed to call him and talk about an appointment.

My experience was about people that they can be loose and open-minded enough if they want so and take the effort. The program was closed with a huge group-hug and small other hugs, along with telling our experiences and how we felt during the event. It was not perfect, of course, but we all felt awesome for sure.

AGGRESSION

Picture by Mary Coleman, Heartland Jedi

Conflict and Training Through Conflict
Paladin Vandor Draconis
Force Academy

There is no emotion, there is peace. -Jedi Code

This is one of the lines of our Jedi code. When we all first came here and went reading through the lectures given here, we all came to this, looked at it, and pondered it as well as some of the other lines within the code. When I first read it, I wondered to myself if this was conditional for it seems logical as human beings that we will from time to time experience emotions which will govern our actions.

In this lecture, we are going to take this idea to its limits, at least to the limits of what the FA can provide us. And as the title suggests, it is conflict. But unlike what the title suggests, which some might have read as saying one can gain peace by conflict. But rather maintaining peace as conflict continues. Conflict as a light jedi is avoided like the plague. It is a common belief that there are always methods of avoiding this and for many here, this is a reality.

I do not deny this and I for one am extremely happy for them.

But the reality of our site and our lives in general is that conflict can happen at the drop of a dime. We as human beings are blessed with imaginations, these imaginations can help us to leap beyond logic and allow us to create in ways that benefit life for all. However, nothing comes without a price. Many times, our perceptions differ. And depending on how much you believe in a subject, and depending on what you have learned in life as being acceptable or not, will dictate how far you are willing to go.

This is the primary reason that conflict or confrontation is frowned upon by the light as it is the most notorious time when emotions will govern our actions which would have us do things we may regret. This is where the code applies. It reminds us that the more we control our emotions, the more likely we are to answer a given situation as positively as we can. But also, this is a time when the true reason the jedi exists can be used to its best outcome. For the more you can learn of a subject, the more you can talk intelligently to a subject and avoid an emotional response.

The reality of a confrontation is that it uses the same path that anything else in our lives do, the exception though is to avoid the desire within us to create an emotional response and that normally such a situation tends to add a level of urgency to it.

When challenged as individuals we all have the following to rely on:

>Our personal code
>The tools we have created for ourselves
>Outlets for information

I talked previously in a past post about this personal code which we all have. This gives us sort of a boundary or parameters that we as individuals follow.

The tools we have are those tools which we as individuals utilize on a day to day basis, but in this case we focus on the tools we have created for ourselves to assist us in human interaction. In my case I have been in the military, worked in corrections, juvenile detention, and in the Health care fields, so I can bring a fair amount of human interaction to a conflict for the majority of these areas are noted for conflict-oriented environments and I have been taught the tools to be able to handle these areas.

And finally, outlets of information. There are always people we can ask for information. Other perspectives can help us to see what we did not see before.

But how do we use these tools in a conflict? There are two common mistakes a person can make during a conflict. First, a person can just assume they are right, which has the possibility of leading to a prolonged conflict due to the fact that where the conflict might have started as a seeking of knowledge, it soon warps into a need to prove one self as right. The second mistake is that we stop asking questions and just assume our information is right. In some cases, these are seen as the same thing. I separate them because when we think in terms of our individual self being right or wrong. We are thinking in terms of the versus mentality. When we talk about information being right or wrong, we are working more in the realm of the light jedi. Assuming our data is right can be rather problematic for a jedi for when such assumptions are made, we are also stating that no further data is accurate. Which means we stop learning.

In a conflict situation, the need to learn is paramount. Time is of the essence and the ability to learn or unlearn a thing can be the very thing needed to resolve a dispute effectively.

When in a conflict, the light Jedi keeps their emotions in check and focus their minds to learn in order to cope within a conflicting environment. As with everything, the object is to still affect positively as many people as you can. In the case of a conflict, to resolve it as amicably as one can. But without keeping ones cool and being able to learn can help one to get to that resolution more rapidly.

In handling conflict, it is important to note the nature of conflict. Typically as one moves from the open debate frame of mind to the conflict frame of mind, there is a visible closing of the mind within the individual. So when one has reached the conflict point, they normally are as close minded as they can be.

Another aspect of conflict is that very seldomly is conflict engaged in that can result in an amicable solution. Both parties have normally came to the point that they need to be right, that it is an impossibility for common ground. Conflict can only bring about resolution through the submission of one or the other.

Conflict quite often is engaged in solely for the purpose of doing such and often without the first dispute in mind. Very often, those confronting one another are so focused on victory that they will even forget what brought them to conflict in the first place.

Keeping these in mind. The Jedi goes into conflict knowing that their choices are to stay out of conflict mode in order to solve an issue amicably or to engage with the intent of forcing submission. The second clearly not being the choice position.

Some of the tools that can be brought into play are listed below:

Intervention
The light jedi can inject an idea which can throw the people out of conflict and make them reasonable again. Interventions are a standard tactic used by psychologists in therapies to help in anger management.

The Wall
When one goes into conflict, their intention is to cause another harm, be it mentally or physically. A Jedi can present themselves as a wall which cannot be hurt by such. In the case of verbal, understanding a person is not at their normal capacity, we can present ourselves for verbal abuse in a way that it does not affect us. In the physical instance, we can do the same, allowing another to beat upon us until they are tired.

Neither is for just anyone. One must be mentally focused on who they are and what they intend to be, and are able to be, which is a mental wall to verbal abuse. To be a wall to physical abuse one must be conditioned and be of certain character to withstand such as well as a mental state which would help them to refrain from returning violence onto the other person.

Diffusion
The Jedi can diffuse a situation in order to de-escalate another to return them to a more reasonable state of mind.
Consolation
Can be used to give the other person the impression that you are trying to see their side.
Bandwagon principal
Where you try to help the other person to see that you both share common ground.
Reversal
Where instead of arguing a point, concede the point and support their perspective in order to de-escalate them.

All of these tools are used to create parameters so that learning can continue.

One of the common misconceptions of conflict is that it is the end of reason and therefore the end of learning.

If this were accurate, then we have no business calling ourselves Light Jedi. I say this because our judgment, peace making ability, and even our own knowledge base, all rely on having opposing viewpoints. For a light jedi, a conflict situation is presented by one who believes in their perspective so much that they are willing to escalate to conflict. For a light jedi, the why is important. Hence where our focus of learning should be.

Overcome Aggression
Yoshio
Institute for Jedi Realist Studies

How would you describe the difference between aggression (Aggression, Angriff) and assertion (Durchsetzung, Behauptung)? Do not limit yourself to the physical, think about how these words and thus experiences differ energetically. Please provide an example. Do you struggle with aggression, either now or in the past? Are there perhaps specific situations which cause you to become aggressive?

For me aggression goes hand in hand with the use of force, be it physical or mental, to achieve what one wants to see achieved and this more often than not against the will of the opposition.
On the other hand assertion means for me to make one's point clear, stand up for one's own rights and being able to reach an agreement which is in the best interest of both sides.

With this "definition" for me aggression feels energetically as a forceful confrontation which is not targeting for an agreement or a win-win-situation but only for getting one's own interest through. On the other hand assertion feels for me as using one's abilities, knowledge and whatever is at hand to make one's own point clear and reach a stage in which both parties can agree on a conclusion without feeling fleeced or damnified. Hope this is understandable!?

As for the rest of these questions I feel it is legal to say that I hardly had been aggressive, neither in the past nor now. This might be due to being an introvert or because of the way I was raised but anyway obviously there are some points which would trigger me and hold the chance to put me in an aggressive stage. But my aggression hardly would find its expression in a physical form other than a regulated competition. It is more likely that, should I become aggressive, that I would forget about my behaviour and speech and it is likely that I will use improper language.

For example, when I ride my car, especially on the German motorways – we don't have any speed limits here – and I ride on the left lane – which is the one for the ones who want to go fast – and then need to deal with someone who is going slowly on this lane. First I will be polite and try to make the driver aware of that it is not the lane for slow drivers. But if this one doesn't show understanding or if a situation like this happens too often during one ride, it is likely that my emotions are running high and then I will think off or even say things like: idiot, stupid driver, tramp or similar and sometimes even worse things.

But, as I said and maybe likely due to my martial arts training, physical aggression I know only in competitions and in a controlled way in martial arts training but since after the brotherly fights with my younger brother, I have never ever felt the need of making use of physical aggression.

RECKLESSNESS

Recklessness (Rücksichtslosigkeit, Sorglosigkeit, Draufgängertum)
Yoshio
Institute for Jedi Realist Studies

Have you been reckless in an area of your life? Based off what you've already read in this course, what are some ways you can overcome recklessness?

All these words, this terms I can only answer based on my German spoken background and the understanding I therefore have for them. I hope that, because of that, nothing is lost in translation!?
Anyway, I guess every one of us had been reckless in his life sometime. Especially as kids we don't know "every" thing and therefore we often might feel the need to try something even when or sometimes especially because our parents said we should not do it. But, as those times are content of the past for me, I have no clear memory of them anymore. Although there is one situation which, obviously, will always stay in my mind. When we had been kids, we liked to race around the block with our bicycles. As it had been traffic calmed area or living area this hasn't been per se dangerous. What made it dangerous, at least for me, had been my strong desire to be the best, the fastest. At that time we all had bicycles with a back pedal brake, except for my brother who had a kind of racing bicycle. This bicycle, obviously, had more gears and therefore one could go much faster than with our other bicycles. So I asked him to lend me his one. The problem started with me crossing the finish line. I, having been the quickest, wanted to imitate the sportsman and therefore raised my arms into the air, forgetting that this bicycle hasn't had a back pedal brake. My only focus and my whole mindset had been on being the fastest, to win this race, neglecting and forgetting about anything else. This resulted in me hitting the wall more or less with full speed which caused a major damage on my brother's bicycle and a mild concussion on my side.

Nowadays I know better than that and although I, obviously, still would like to win and be the best, I would pay more attentions to the circumstances and the things which would have an effect on me. This is for me then also how one can overcome recklessness by getting as much information and knowledge as possible and needed to be able to rate a certain situation correctly.

Jedi and Drugs
Alethea Thompson
Force Academy

DISCLAIMER: *This discussion is in regards to illegal use of drugs and drug abuse. It is not meant to take anything away from the doctors that are legally sanctioned to prescribe medicine approved by the FDA (or similar organization of your country).*

Every couple of months the question gets asked somewhere in the Jedi Community "What is the Jedi's take on drugs?". Some orders take a firm stance against illegal drugs and drug abuse, while others do not make a specific affirmation and let the congregation talk over it. Those of you that know me, probably know that I am rather proud to say that I spent a year as a Drug Abuse Resistance Education (D.A.R.E.) officer teaching 5th graders about drugs and how they affect your life- all in the hopes that they will heed my words and say "no" every time. So it should be a no-brainer what my stance is on whether or not a Jedi should get involved with illegal substances or drug abuse. What you might not know, is why.

Throughout history drugs have been demonized or exalted by people on various ends of the spectrum. Arguments about why certain drugs that are said to "not be all that harmful" were made illegal in the first place have been spun to demonstrate why we shouldn't let "the man" get us down. Those that support drugs to enhance the spiritual experience will tell you that in moderation and with the proper supervision you should be fine. Although I can see all sides of the spectrum in these discussions, my argument has nothing to do with the mainstream debate. I will not condemn a shaman that uses drugs, I simply do not agree with them. I will not condemn someone that does drugs, but I will not hire them until they were completely clean and proved they would not make a relapse. I will be there to help them overcome their addiction if I had the time to become their friend. I will not allow them to do drugs in front of me. I would not turn them in to the authorities unless they did something reckless while under the influence.

Recklessness is at the heart of my argument against drugs. Between the fiction and our real life Jedi, we all seem to agree that a Jedi should work on overcoming recklessness. Drugs are reckless, and you'll understand better why I say this as this piece goes on, first let's define what each of the types of drugs are and what effect they have on you. Most of these will probably know, some you may have experienced directly, or watched others go through.

Narcotics: A narcotic is any substance that takes the edge off of your senses, and can causes someone to become drowsy in higher dosages, there is even the possibility you will slip into a coma. In the medical community doctors try to limit how often you take narcotics because of the damage if could cause someone.

The first time that I watched what a narcotic did to people was awful. His name was Marques Long, and he was a fellow classmate. Not even a year after we graduated High School, I found myself attending his funeral to support a number of friends. The story was pretty terrible, a friend of his had played a prank on him and his girlfriend telling them that her father had called the police to go after them for kidnapping. The problem was that the possibility was quite plausible based on his knowledge of the girlfriend's family. So in all of her brilliance, she talked him into carrying on in a Romeo & Juliet story, with the poison of Heroin. Juliet lived past the event and frantically reached out to the police to try and save Marques- but it was too late. The first time he took Heroin, a drug he said he would never take, was his last.

Hallucinogens: These are drugs that alter perception, for some it might come in the form of seeing things that are not there, messing with your emotions, you might not be able to comprehend space and time. Hallucinogens are not used by mainstream medicine, but is under review by some for treating people on a 12 step program, and other possible methods of treating emotionally based medical diagnosis (such as bipolar or obsessive compulsive disorder).

The night Marques died, I had friends calling me frantically while I was working a Steak 'n' Shake drive thru. It was difficult, but I managed to sneak the calls long enough to discover they would all be at the local Waffle House when I got off work that night. I got there and it was a bit of a nightmare, everyone was taking hits off of a blunt, there were probably two of us total that were not trying to get high. We moved in on the group that had gathered and proceeded to talk with each of them, helping them work through their issues, and even talked with each other, because Erin had been close to Marques too. Although they each shared in their experiences to grieve over some weed, it wasn't the same as voicing their frustrations with Marques and his girlfriend. We stayed there all night, and worked on getting each of them home without incident, by calling cabs, driving them home ourselves, working with the Waffle House staff to ensure that no one did anything stupid. The staff, having become friends with Marques, were more than happy to help out.

Marijuana might be popular, but it is not the only run in with a hallucinogen I have had. The other was in Iraq. Just imagine for a moment that you have someone who always has your back, they are your gunner, your driver, or simply just another member of your team, then you go up to the door of their housing unit and realize there's a problem. No one is coming to the door, but you are confident the two people you saw go into the room about an hour ago have not left the unit. Suspecting something horrible has happened, you call the medics and the on base housing office, periodically you knock on the door to try and see if someone will answer. When the door is finally opened, to your horror there are air cans spread across the floor, and two bodies, one looks slightly responsive, the other…Quickly the medics rush in and assess the situation, they take the one that was responsive out and get him to medical, while you and the other people on the scene have to carry the body out.

I got there while they pulled the two out, adding to the chaos at that moment would not have been a good thing, so I continued to move on and let the first responders handle it, while tugging my friends away. This battle buddy that I had barely known apparently had been inhaling canned air for awhile now, to take the edge off of what he was experiencing every time he left the wire. It was the only thing they could do that made them feel alive again. And it took it's toll on everyone. Later that night, the unit called everyone for an emergency meeting. The command wanted answers, we were all given a blanket counseling statement that made it clear we were not to engage in illegal drug usage, and that they wanted people who knew what was going on to come forward. Being amongst the few Military Police there, we were asked to officiate everyone's statement instead of having their direct line leaders do so. As I got around, people expressed how hard it was to lose someone, they were not only losing morale, but some wondered if someone else was quietly doing the same thing- would they lose another battle buddy that is suppose to have their back? The more people that were lost, the more dangerous it would get for them to go out on patrol in the combat zone. The unit got through the incident, but it should not have happened. And no service member (military, cop, emergency services) putting their lives on the line or having the lives of others in their hands should have to fear that the person next to them might not be at their best due to drug usage.

Stimulants: Stimulants can be helpful in medicine, as they increase alertness either mentally or physically. In the medical community the can be used to treat AD(H)D, narcolepsy, obesity and a number of other good uses. But they can cause a lot of problems when they are not properly administered or they are abused in general.

In the community we have a member that overcame his meth addiction, and has even helped others overcome their addiction to the substance. He bore physical scars from using meth, but the final straw was dying in an ER. He realized that he never wanted to go through that again, and made the decision to overcome the addiction.

Depressants: Being ready brings me to my own experience with a drug. Depressants are the substances that bring your body functions down while you are using them. They take a toll on your ability to react, and to think straight, they can play with your emotions, whether they are good or not.

The drug I took isn't illegal. And in fact, I didn't purposely abuse it. I just didn't have a tolerance for it. In my life I had made the effort to never do illegal drugs, I waited until I turned 21 to drink, I have never smoked, nothing of those natures. Shortly after I turned 21 I had a grand total of maybe 6 drinks over the course of a couple of months. While in Iraq, I didn't drink a drop, got back home and found myself a month or two later in a break up, so I went out and had two drinks not realizing just how low my tolerance was. By that time I was slurring my speech, so I cut myself off. My friend took me out to a beach where we talked, and suddenly in all of my stupor, I got a call. The person I had on the phone was in a bind, he had gone to a party, was underage and suddenly realized that he needed to work through some things, as well as try and figure out how he was going to get home because he didn't want his father to find out. My friend needed me right at that moment, and I was drunk. I managed, it took everything out of me, but I managed to communicate with him. I concentrated hard to understand his words, and made more effort than I should have needed to enunciate my words so that he could understand what I was saying.

All of the experiences I had prior to this event started becoming more real to me. Before that night, I didn't do drugs because it was illegal, and I didn't want to get caught, and I didn't like the idea of having health problems. But on a night in 2007, the reason changed to a Jedi reason, rather than a selfish reason: Because I'm no good to anyone if I'm not on my best game. To allow myself to be in a condition where I cannot take charge if I see someone hurt, or cannot speak when someone needs counsel or when I'm witnessing a crime is reckless. It is also reckless of me to elevate someone to the status of knight that is irresponsible with controlled substances.

You never know when you're going to be needed. I didn't think that one random night, in a very rare incident, that someone would need me, but it happened, and the situation could strike any other time. Since that night, I've found myself in situations where I could have enjoyed drinking, but as it would turn out it was the best decision for me to stay sober. Think about that next time you want to ask the question: Is it okay for a Jedi to do drugs? What possible ramifications might occur?

ATTACHMENTS

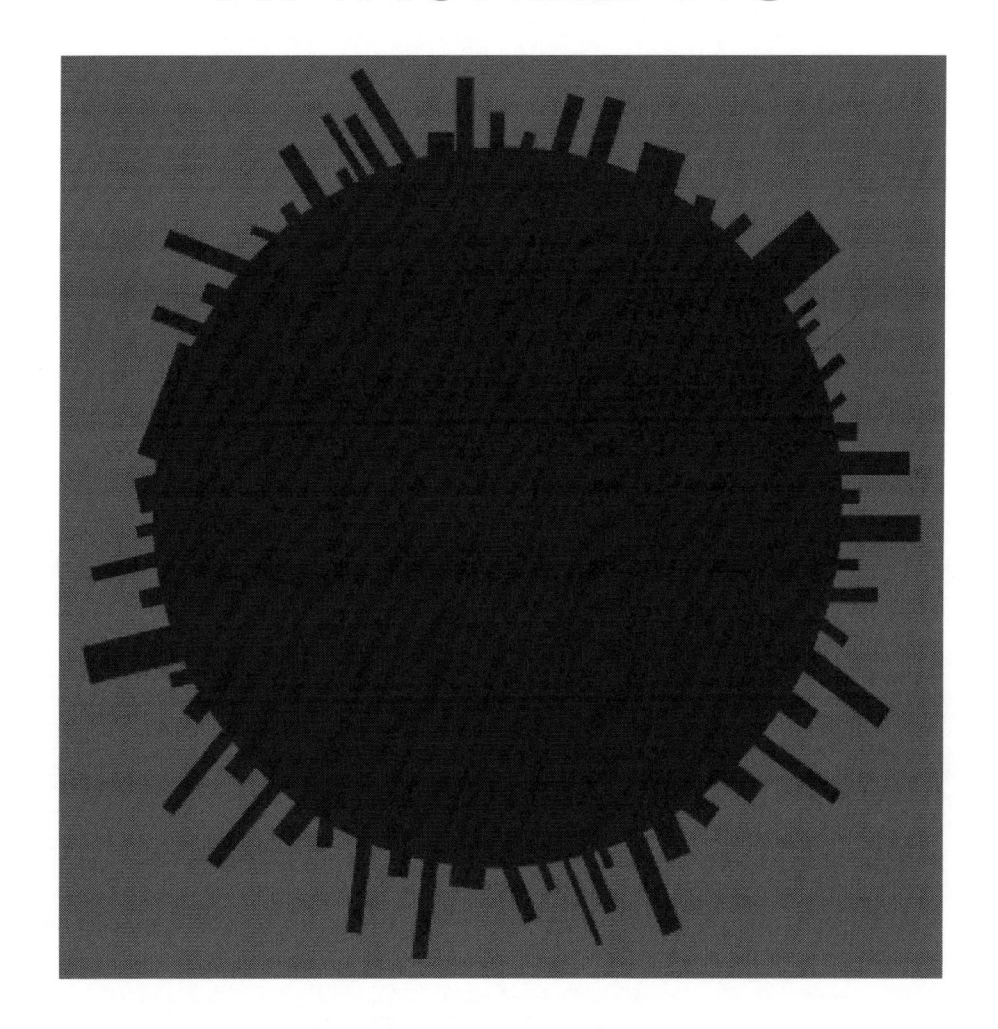

Picture by Mark Brereton, Temple of the Jedi Order

Letting Go: Living a Life Without Attachment
Christopher L. Bird
Jedi Path Academy/California Jedi

"Attachment is forbidden. Possession is forbidden. Compassion, which I would define as unconditional love, is central to a Jedi's life, so you might say we're encouraged to love." -- Anakin Skywalker[1]

"Train yourself to let go of everything you fear to lose." -- Yoda[2]

"You're [Jedi are] allowed to love people, but you're not allowed to posses them." -- George Lucas[3]

In a Clone Wars Writers' Meeting in 2010, George Lucas gave a short talk about how he envisioned the Force, saying the core of the Force, the Light Side and the Dark Side, one was selfless and the other was selfish. It was this core of selfishness that leads to the Dark Side. According to Lucas, if one is selfish, that leads to greed. The wanting of things, for the Sith usually wanting power. Obtaining things leads to momentary pleasure, but it is fleeting. In order to keep the pleasure, one must obtain further things. This ramps up and soon you begin to fear losing it. Not for the possession itself -- but the pain of not having it. This fear leads to anger, and anger leads to hate, and hate leads to suffering, usually the suffering of the person with selfishness.

Having things one fears to let go of is having an attachment. Now attachments are not necessarily physical things, but can be merely the desire. Now desire for physical things are not the only attachment, but the cautionary tale of Anakin Skywalker teaches us, a powerful attachment can be wanting things to be different than they actually are. This is not to say one should be content with injustice, poverty, hunger and other ills. One should work with what means they have for beneficial social change. The attachment I am speaking of is desiring changes that are beyond one's power to do anything about, such as events that happened in the past, or hanging on to things past their time.

Now, I do not know if it is possible to live completely without attachment or if this is a desirable thing. Where I am in my training is trying to let go of all unnecessary attachment. I need the basic things of life, and technological conveniences allow me to do things I would not otherwise be able to do. I do not think the Jedi Path is an ascetic one, nor is it a life of extravagance. Somewhere in the middle is the right way, I think. To me it is permissible to have such comforts as long as one is not afraid to let go of them, if it becomes necessary to do so.

Now the first step of being able to let go of attachments, is to be able to recognize the attachments you have in your life. This takes meditation and self-reflection. In this, we can find the guidance of Master Yoda, to let go of everything we fear to lose. While we examine our mental attitudes, do we find something that we feel we cannot live without? something that would be painful to lose? a desire that is causing us emotional pain? These are some of the ways to recognize attachments. While Lucas has said attachment leads to fear, which leads to anger, hate, and suffering, the Buddha simply said that attachment leads to suffering. I think Lucas identified one of the paths that leads there.

So how does one begin to let go of attachment? I think the answer can be found in the Jedi Pillars of Strength: The Force, Knowledge, and Self-Discipline. By using the Force we manifest the attitudes of the archetypal Jedi, in this case, the core of the Light Side according to Lucas, selflessness. As we encourage within ourselves the attitude of selflessness we find joy in giving, and in letting go. The second pillar, Knowledge, we use the knowledge from our self-examination to identify our attachments, and this leads us to the third pillar, Self-Discipline.

It is through self-discipline we actually do the work of letting go of our attachments. We must bring our will to bear to shape our very mind and thought processes. Make no mistake, this is training, and it is difficult. But like a muscle that is exercised your self-discipline will get stronger over time. There are no shortcuts with this.

There is not one technique to bring your self-discipline to bear in shaping your mind and personality. What works for one person will not work for another, and vice versa. That being said, no one can do it for you. A therapist can guide you in such exercises, bit it will be you doing the work.

Letting go of attachments is training that is never finished, as we create new ones all the time. In this a Jedi should be ever vigilant. But when one finds they are able to let go of attachments the also let go of the temporary pleasure of having things (or having things be the way they like) and enters into a hard won, but much more satisfying joy.

Footnotes:
[1]Star Wars Episode II: Attack of the Clones by George Lucas and Jonathan Hales
[2]Star Wars Episode III: Revenge of the Sith by George Lucas
[3]George Lucas - On the Force - 2010

Attachment
Anirac Morgan
Temple of the Jedi Force

Most likely the Jedi assignment I'd have the most trouble with. I attach strongly, rather than easily. Meaning I haven't gotten attached to a lot of people through life, nor things for that matter. I have only one good long-time (as in more than 5 years) friend IRL, and connect very loosely with colleagues and people I have gone to school with. I have friends online, but I would only consider one of these ... how to put it... a good friend. (Yes, Michael, this is you). That's not to say I haven't had more friends, I simply haven't felt it hard to leave them behind as I have moved forward. With some we outgrew each other, with others I moved away or changed school/job and didn't bother keeping in touch. Not sure why, but I moved a lot as a kid, and I lost friends early. Also being bullied I grew up thinking the only people who I could count on was my siblings and my mother. Today I have that one solid good friend IRL who I have known since high school, and we speak every 2nd or 3rd month, due to her living far away. I have no issue going months without speaking to her, and this is "normal" for our friendship. When we speak again it's like no time has passed at all. When something bad happens, she calls me. I don't that often call her, even when bad things happen, but that's because for those times I lean on family, she has little family to speak of who she can trust and really talk with.

When thinking attachment, I am thinking things or people who it would hurt me greatly to be without. And although I would be sad to lose my friends, I don't feel attached to them in that same way, even if that may sound a bit bad. I feel that when they move on, when they're no longer a part of my life, I'll let them go, like I have let go of friends in the past. Guess I just have a lot of experience in losing/letting go of friends, unlike my girlfriend, who has had the same friends since she was a kid, and who would hurt a lot if she lost them.

However, while I haven't formed attachments with a lot of other people, the attachment to my family is very, very strong. During the worst of my depression I really wanted to end my life, and the only reason I didn't do so was because I knew it would cause irreparable hurt to my siblings, even if that was what I desperately wanted to do. I researched suicide methods for hours and hours, and it was all that was on my mind for days at the time, but eventually I saw that no matter how hard things got I wouldn't ever be able to hurt them like that. My therapist felt that my upbringing had caused a co-dependency with me towards family, that my role as guardian sibling had caused me to not develop a proper individual identity, that I was too into the role of sister and daughter, and less capable of handling being myself and live my life, so she advised me to move to a different city as she felt getting some distance would be healthy for my mental health. So, yes, I am sort of the type to either attach completely, or not at all. Not meaning I don't care for other people, because I do. I have a lot of empathy, also for strangers, but I don't easily connect to the point where I need to have them in my life.

I have had to put a lot of thought into this, the subject of attachment, as my mother's health has worsened. What will I do when I lose her? How will I react? Will I lose my siblings as well? Will they end up in foster care? How will I handle that? I know my family is a very vital part of me, and I am not sure what I'd do without them.

I would say once upon a time it definitely held me back. Yet it was also the only thing that could save my life. My attachment kept me alive, and yet it also kept me from progressing, because it was too intense an attachment. After all these years this isn't such a problem anymore. I can go through my days, not overly worried about what goes on at home. There's now a healthy "me" bubble, and a healthy "them" bubble, inter-crossing in some parts, the way I feel it should. However, if I actually lost them.... I haven't come to the point where I'd be able to let them go. My attachment to the siblings does enrich my life, because my love for them tends to overshadow things like stress or worries. When I've had a rough week, going home feels like finally reaching the surface after holding your breath under-water. Like I can finally breathe. Watching my siblings play, eating popcorn and enjoying a film with them on Sunday morning... Those small moments of peaceful joy. Those moments are infinitely valuable to me. They are a solace and a comfort that I hang on to, but not all the time. I tend to my life and my duties most of the time, and then when I come home one weekend a month I pour my energies into having a great time with them.

Regarding items and possessions... I don't have a whole lot of stuff, and less still that I'd worry about losing. The computer is important, but I could easily switch it out with another one. Its value is that it's a tool to get in touch with others, and to play games with my siblings so that we can spend time together even if we're not even in the same city. So, it's a matter of what I get from it, which is social interaction. Other than that I would be sad if I lost the family albums. I've been collecting photos and memories of my siblings for years, since I was only 12 years old. There's a lot of history and memories in those boxes. Good times. Happy moments. I wouldn't do well with losing those, and I think it's more important to me because I have a terrible memory. I don't remember things well, my long time memory isn't all that good, and I tend to remember a lot of the bad stuff that happened. So, having actual physical memories of positive things, it's important to me. Some books I wouldn't want to lose. Mostly though because they gather dust in my bookshelf, lol, and that's an important thing to have, something that gathers dust. No, seriously, I do like my books. If the apartment burned down I'd probably have to go out and get some replacements, lest I have an empty shelf with no imaginary worlds in.

Basically, my attachments are about the people in my life who are important to me. Take the apartment I don't own, take the car I don't have, take whatever possessions you wanna take, I couldn't care less. They're just things, of very little importance. People though, my family... That's the only thing I'm really afraid to lose. The only attachment that could severely hurt me. And I am afraid that it will, because at some point I know it will. I won't have my mother forever, and with five siblings chances are something will happen to one of them. So, at some point, I will lose someone I love, and that thought scares the crap out of me.

Oh, well, that's my weakness, I suppose. Good thing I am just a learner. I have time. And the day when that time runs out... We'll see.

Attachment
Memnoich
Institute for Jedi Realist Studies

    We all know that the Jedi frowned upon personal relationships and attachments. After going through what I have for the past 4 months, I can understand why. You see, I'm finishing up a divorce, my divorce, one that came out of nowhere. So I now feel I have a unique understanding, and comprehension of that idea. I hope no one ever has to go through a divorce to understand, so maybe my experience can lend some insight to others.
You see, 4 months ago my wife came to me talking about how she's not sure she married me for the right reasons, but couldn't give me any reason's for the sudden changes in her, and from there our marriage started going downhill. She started doing things and behaving completely different then I or anybody had known her to act over the last 4 years. This put me in a position to lose my trust in her, because of which I did some things that I'm not proud I did, I started snooping and spying on her. I became obsessed with knowing what she was doing and with whom. My life got put on hold during all of this, all that mattered was fixing our marriage and getting her to come back. Looking back on it now, I'm not sure all of it was about losing her, but mostly about losing the marriage, the relationship, the fear of being alone. I never went too far, but I did end up spending a lot of money, and justifying to myself some of the things I was doing. I did, and still feel, jealousy over her, but it was more, in the blink of an eye, love became obsession, caring became jealousy, I became so dependent on her that I lost my own sense of self, I lost myself to the feelings, and to the pursuit of her, nothing else mattered. This is the perils of Attachment, this is a pitfall to watch out for, and I missed, I fell.

    To try and describe it for you is difficult, we have all lost a loved one, and we have all had someone we know die. That is easier to deal with, then to have that loved one, just leave. To try and help you understand the feelings, think of someone you love dearly, someone very close to you. Now try to imagine the future as you see it, with them as a part of it. Now try and imagine that same future without them in it, try to imagine how you would feel if they walked up to you and said, I want nothing to do with you anymore, no explanation, just that, then they walk away. That was where I was at. My wife and I had so many plans, so many things we wanted to do together, the thought had never occurred to me that she wouldn't be there in my life 20 years from now, let alone 6 months, and now I was suddenly having to deal with the idea, she would not be a part of my life, her family would not be a part of my life, in just a few short months. I put my heart, and my soul, all of my love into this marriage, and now it was being thrown away. The Family I had grown to love in its own way was now no longer mine, and I was no longer part of it.

I am now trying to rebuild myself; I am trying to find all the parts of me that got lost in the rage, and jealousy, and obsession, but most of all the depression. I lost myself in those emotions; I gave in to them, and did and said things that I'm not proud of.

So yes, attachment can lead to the dark side of oneself. It can allow you to justify things that you wouldn't normally do. It can lead you to losing all sense of self, and become something you never wanted or thought you could be. On the flip-side, having a relationship with detachment is impossible; it would never work without some kind of attachment. I think that's why the Jedi did allow some forms of relationships, and even marriage. It was allowed to those that knew of the danger, could see the danger, and was believed to be able to control the emotions that would come from that attachment. I'm not saying avoid relationships, as everyone deserves to feel love. What I'm saying is be aware of the dangers of attachment, the danger of focusing so much of your life on another that you lose the sense of self that makes you who you are.

Love Without Attachment: A Jedi view on Romance and Intimacy
Christopher L. Bird
Jedi Path Academy/California Jedi

There are many misconceptions about the intersection of romantic love and the role it plays in the lives of those that subscribe to a Jedi Path. These misconceptions spring from unfamiliarity of Jedi Philosophy and teaching, misconceptions of the Jedi Code, and misconceptions about what love is, and misconceptions on what leads to a healthy romantic relationship.
The guiding principle for Jedi when it comes to romance is that of non-attachment. The attitude is usually summed up as being able to let go of anything we fear to lose. Being able to give up a romantic relationship, to many beings seems anathema to their perception of commitment and fidelity.

A Jedi can be as committed to another (or many) as any other, but the motivation for that commitment can either be a healthy or an unhealthy one. What is the determining factor? Consider this quote, from George Lucas, during a story meeting for The Clone Wars television series:

"You're [Jedi are] allowed to love people, but you're not allowed to posses them."

This is the first thing that one must recognize when one loves and enters into a relationship as a A Jedi, is that people are not possessions. A person cannot belong to you the same way that your lightsaber prop replica or blu-ray collection can. To treat another being as such, is to deny them their own agency and autonomy. Treating another person as a possession, leads to attachment, or to put it in another way, a fear of loss.

If one treats another person as a thing to be a possessed, then selfishness can become a motivating factor in a relationship, and result in feelings of jealousy, which is a shadow of greed. Again this is rooted in a fear of loss, and a loss of the pleasing feelings of having this relationship. This is not so much the fear of a loss of a relationship, as much as it is avoidance of the pain of not having one. This fear leads to anger, and anger leads to hate, and hate leads to suffering, usually the suffering of the person with selfishness.

So what, if not attachment, does a Jedi rely upon to bond one to those they love, and enter into a relationship with others? Instead of attachment, a loving Jedi relationship is based on **CHOICE**.

An ideal relationship would bring all sorts of positive benefits to those participating in the relationship. If each party takes an attitude of selflessness, and it is reciprocated freely, then this is very easy to come by. A true measure of love, is not how happy another makes you, but how vital another's happiness is TO you. When a relationship is in this state, it is no great effort to exercise the choice to continue the relationship. A healthy relationship, is akin to the relationship between the midi-chlorians and all life-forms in the Galaxy Far Far Away, a symbiosis. Life-forms, living together for mutual benefit.

It is this mutual benefit that is fully keeping with the ideals of the Jedi. When this balance is not present, why would one wish to choose to be in such a relationship? I would posit, that it is a mark of a strong relationship that one is free to leave it at any time. To demonstrate why this is so, let's look at the contrast.

If a relationship was not resulting in mutual benefit, or was a patently unhappy or abusive in nature, and one felt as if they did not have a choice to leave, what would we call this?

This is not to say, that the Jedi attitude is drop any relationship that does not meet ideal expectations, and joyfully walk away whistling a happy tune. The choice to stay in a relationship, and applying <u>knowledge, self-discipline, and the Force</u> towards improving any shortcomings, or even making good things better, is more in keeping with Jedi attitudes, than to cut and run at the first sign of trouble. But what IS important, is that everyone in a relationship has a **CHOICE** to do this. It is my humble opinion that a relationship based on a self-determined choice will be more fulfilling than any relationship based on the obligations placed upon one by others.

Once we free our minds from the misconceptions that people are possessions, and take into account that love is not a finite resource bounds to concepts of division or economy, it leads to some interesting questions, some of which may be:

Does loving one individual in any way have any bearing on the capability to love any other individual, or many other individuals?
Does another's love for others, in any way have any bearing on if they can love me?

If I feel that love for another is expressed in the desire for their happiness, how should I feel about things outside of myself that also lead to their happiness?

I have found my own answers to these questions, and their

implications. You may come to completely different conclusions than I have, yet maybe you will come up with the same that I have, or maybe you will improve upon them. In the end, the choice is yours to make.

Overcome Attachments
Yoshio
Institute for Jedi Realist Studies

Where do your attachments lie?

It is a bit tricky to answer as I don't feel like I have many attachments. Maybe again this is part of being an introvert person or maybe because of how I was raised or because of what I did experience or most likely a combination of all that. Anyway, I'm fully with the example given in the lesson, as I'm now married, me too I would feel terribly sorry and sad should my wife die before me. But I also know that after a while of grieving, I will be able to carry on and live my life. To some this might sound hard but to me and where I'm now I don't see death anymore as the ultimate end of everything. For me it is another part of our "life" or maybe better said process during which we will transform from our earthly, physical form into something different.

This topic would not be limited to my wife, obviously, but to my whole family, meaning my mother and father, my brother and his family and all the others I hold dear. But having already experienced the death of two of my grandfathers and one grandmother and the death of one friend, I know that those times are hard times, filled with sorrow and grieving, but after a while those days passed and one will remember all the good things which shared with those who had gone before us.

Besides that there are obviously a couple of things in my possession which I like, especially those things I made myself like my radio controlled models. But also here there is no real addiction to them whereat I would claim that I couldn't live without them.
Obviously there are things which make life comfortable and more enjoyable but when thinking back, most of them I haven't had in the beginning and didn't miss.

For me the danger is found in when we start to take things as given and always there for one. When we lose the ability to see the value those things hold for us or in the other extreme when the value of them become all we can see, we start to run in the risk to get addicted by them and for me attachment and addiction are very close to each other.

PROWESS

Body, Mind & Spirit
Octagon
Temple of the Jedi Force

Spirit gives strength to the mind and body. Mind controls the body and can summon the spirit. Body is the foundation and home to Spirit and Mind.

Each Jedi leans towards one of the three. Body Jedi focus on the physical, exercise, martial arts, weapons, clothing, diet. Mind Jedi focus on the mental, history, memories, lore, technical aspects of Jediism as well as related rules and regulations. Spiritual Jedi focus on inspirational aspects of being a Jedi, meditation, dream interpretation, communication with spirit guides and their inner Master.

The Force gives energy to the body, focus to the mind, and inspiration to the spirit. A Jedi should not only master the aspect that they are most in tune with but eventually the others as well.

I believe all paths lead to the same road so mastery of any of the one will take you to the next until balance in the Force is achieved.

Growth is essential to a Jedi in these areas or a Jedi will find themselves stuck in a loop of dealing with the same situations and conditions in life this year just as they did last year. Growth is change. If our outlook on life doesn't change then neither did we.

DEFENSE ART

Photograph by Nathan Thompson

The Art of Defense
Alethea "Setanaoko" Thompson
Force Academy

"The evening comes, and with it the painted face and semi-nudity, courtesy of a Viking weapon-blessing ceremony led by Andy. In full view of the neighbours, I'm making toasts, drinking disturbing amounts of Jedi backwash and seeking divine approval for a £1 Muji gel pen." - Andrew Dickens, Shortlist Article Yoda Retreat

And there we had it. In one short weekend Shortlist Journalist Andrew Dickens had come to understand a concept which I and some great Jedi names such as Brother John Phelan, Vandor Draconis and Doug Turner have been trying to drive home for years: A Jedi does not need martial arts to defend others, there are other creative means. Although many hold to the belief that in order to call yourself a Jedi you need to be well versed in a martial art, there are those of us that would rather see our members pursue something that matches their talents in the defense arena. I am one of those people, I can certainly see the value in being a martial artist, it cultivates discipline, gives you an ability to defend others and is excellent for keeping your body in shape. However, I feel too many people rely heavily on their martial arts only to discover later on that it is not as "street worthy" as their sensei may have touted in class. I also recognize that there are people out there which medically cannot do martial arts, but have the ability to be physically fit without it. However, this is about "defense arts"; "physical art" is in a later chapter.

During the ceremony Andrew talks about in his article, he announced that he had once saved lives because of his journalism, and that was why he chose his weapon of choice for this ceremony to be a pen, amidst my own staff, a piece of broken glass, physical representations of "soul swords" (from a meditation technique developed by Charles McBride) and other random objects which could be used for physical combat. Andrew's choice of weapon, in my opinion, was the most valuable of all those present. Because it highlighted the a long history of writers that have defended people without ever physically attacking their assailants. Though writing and physical combat are not the only ways to defend others. There are a number of different methods to cultivate the guardian aspect of being a Jedi. It is my hope that through this lecture, you can begin to expand your ideas so that you can use your own talents to defend and protect others from others or even themselves. The following are a couple of ideas that I can come up with:

Art: There have been a number of artists which combat racism through their art. Whether it is depicting abhorrent actions of people being racist, demonstrating kindness or participating in a film aimed to teach the value of overcoming stereotypes, art can be used to teach valuable ethics by communicating to people which communicate and learn best through art than other avenues. An example of a work of art which has inspired our community to become great men and women is the Star Wars franchise, which conveys the teachings of Joseph Campbell's Hero's Journey in a fun innovative way. As a result, a great number of us have stepped up to the plate to live the hero's journey and help our fellow man in the process.

Psychology: As someone that wanted to pursue psychology as a career before I realized the amount of red tape a psychologist has to trek through, and a former military police soldier, this is an area close to my heart. We know today that everything we do can be linked to the development of our psyche, and it is through psychology that we are able to understand how others tick. Some of you may have watched shows such as Criminal Minds, although it is not an exact science, real life profiling and the latest interrogative techniques have become helpful in closing a case. But this isn't the only thing that psychology is good at achieving. Psychologists can also aide in awareness campaigns on subjects such as bullying and drug abuse.Everyone has their own skills and interests, and that is where discovering the right "defense art" begins for you. It may be combative in nature, so you might pick up a martial art, or it could be something more passive such as photography or film. It could be that you find your calling as a lawyer or a law-maker to defend others rights. Some of you are already pursuing such a skill, but for those of you who have yet to make the decision, here's a place to start:

List your skills and talents. Be honest with yourself, oftentimes we like to believe we have a talent in something which we really do not (I like to pretend I can sing, but I know I would never make it in the business, not even as a freelance), this will help you better understand what you might enjoy doing.

Next list your hobbies. The last step is to see if you can't find ways to combine both lists and use it to improve the lives of people in your community (whether online or offline).

Response to Defense Art By Alethea
Reacher
Force Academy

Ally,

Thank you for writing on this topic. I am not sure whether or not to post this here, but I wanted to give it a little traction. So here we are. Please move this to my journal if that is a more appropriate venue for it. And sorry for the inconvenience... 😄

I'm reminded of one of my all-time favorite book quotes as I read what you wrote about Andrew Dickens' experience.

I wanted you to see what real courage is, instead of getting the idea that courage is a man with a gun in his hand. It's when you know you're licked before you begin but you begin anyway and you see it through no matter what. You rarely win, but sometimes you do. -Harper Lee's Atticus Finch

For those of us who have not yet read To Kill A Mockingbird, Atticus Finch makes his children attend to the needs of a spiteful old woman in a wheelchair after they destroy her flower bed. They hate every minute of it and make sure their father knows it. When she dies, only then do they begin to understand their father's lesson. The woman was a morphine addict, and vowed to get clean of the drug before she passed. The Finch children were unwittingly part of that plan, and Atticus wanted his kids to benefit from watching a monumentally courageous undertaking. Her temperament was sour, her physical appearance disgusting and unkempt, she was feeble - unable to be of use to anybody. Her weapon of choice was the only thing she had left: Her will. What was she defending? The dignity of the human spirit. The belief that we are capable of transcending our base selves and become MORE. This is the calling we all share as Jedi: using what we have to affect positive change in the world. The world is an ever-ambiguous place full of complications and the fog of uncertainty - but broken down to prime camps, there are really only two. One that sees the world and centers itself on what is, the other sees the world and works to make it a vision of what it should be.

You discussed martial arts...let me mention that for a moment. Art is the pursuit of truth...the experience of the sublime. We of the west love our constructs, our systems, our clear lines of understanding and numbers. A martial art, in a real sense, uses the medium of human movement and combat to advance the practitioner's understanding of 'truth'. Endstates don't really matter in the true martial art experience. In many cases it is a truer expression of a person's personal philosophy. There are many other mediums to do the same. Applied martial combat science is something entirely different. I don't think this is anything new to anyone here. Unfortunately the words we use sometimes fail to fully elucidate the meanings we intend for them. Martial Arts and The Art of War are examples of difference in nuance. Yes, there is an 'art' to war in a very really sense which hovers more closely in the realm of the 'martial art' meaning, but that is in reference to the truth found in navigating unquantifiable variables found in a war zone.

In his article, Andrew writes about the Viking blessing on his pen. I see that as ritual recognition and appreciation for his chosen medium of discovering truth. His art certainly means quite a bit to him and he is one of the lucky ones who gets paid to do it. The woman in <u>To Kill A Mockingbird</u> had little left but her own will. In the end, this is the only thing all of us have. Andrew has found a medium to realize his will in writing. For some, it's the medical profession. For others, social work, security, or computer technology. Then again, not all professions are a chosen medium. Just as valid are those who put their time in at work and go home to start their true calling. Painting, singing, model air-plane building, video gaming...all are ways to purse and express. I cannot argue that society places the same value on a brain surgeon as a video gamer...but either one...even if they are one in the same person, is equally valid in the pursuit of an experience of the sublime.

The Art of Defense
Paladin Vandor Draconis
Force Academy

The Art of Defense

Given my epiphany last night, my mind has focused a lot on defense as a lesson. The core foundation of being able to confront an opponent is the ability to preserve oneself in such an engagement. And I find it amazing how this simple concept is overlooked.

For no matter who you are, no matter if you have ever been in an altercation or not. It is a thought which will go through your mind.

Facing someone who looks, "Seedy".

Being in an "Unknown Place".

The list goes on.

So as I prepare mentally for upcoming events, I thought I would share my thoughts on the subject.

When I find myself entering into a possible situation where I might have to engage another, my mind goes through a series of steps to prepare for it, these are those steps.

Step 1 Avoidance:
- The first step of any altercation is to avoid it if possible.
- Look for avenues of escape.
- Look for possible allies.
- Look for places where one could slip away unseen.

The first thought of anyone wishing to defend themselves should always be to not have to defend themselves in the first place. All factors must be weighed as to why such a defense would be required. Are there others around that I might have to defend also comes to mind.

Of note, this is not the pushing of the panic button to get away at all cost. The fact is, one should never let it come to this. But a reasonable, conscious effort to minimize the possibility of an altercation.

Always look for an escape, the escape route is the best option to have on hand. So if it is needed, one can exit and get away. This can be as simple as finding a door, getting to a form of transportation which will get you away from the place. Etc.

Looking for allies is the next best. Attackers are less likely to attack where there are witnesses, so gravitating towards a larger body of people is a good thing, not to mention if you find a large enough group of people, can provide one with a way of escaping.

Looking for places where one could slip away unseen is the final possibility of avoiding an altercation.

Slip around a corner, under a table, behind a door. Anything which would conceal you from a possible attackers vision.

The thing which must be pointed out here is that one should not consider it shameful to do the above. If an altercation does break out, someone is getting hurt. When weighted against this reality… it is completely reasonable for one to avoid such.

Step 2: Persuasion
- The next step to avoid a confrontation is to persuade the possible opponent to not attack.
- Trying to find out the other persons issue, Taking responsibility regardless of who is to blame, apologizing, self deprecation.

Once again, the ultimate desire is to avoid such an altercation. So the primary focus needs to be trying to ascertain the other persons issue. What caused them to become angry? Granted, this might not always be available. But it is apart of the knowledge search one needs to perform.

Taking responsibility for the situation regardless of who is responsible may help to diffuse the issue. Ultimately, one who is willing to fight for their position has already decided it is your fault, so jumping to this position can help to diffuse it.

Apologizing is another powerful tool. People who wish to engage in an altercation normally require emotional support to engage in such. Which is to say, they need to constantly be upset in order to over-ride the societal norm of fighting being a bad thing. Taking responsibility and apologizing start the process of removing this emotional platform.

Self deprecation is another tool at our disposal. Humor, pointing out negative things about oneself have the ability to even further remove anothers ability to hurt one. Even the most insistent of attackers will think twice about attacking an opponent who appears incapable of their own defense.

Step 3: Information gathering

This is called step 3, but it technically should have started as soon as

the possible altercation was recognized. Where steps 1 and 2 are hoped to stop a fight… another thing they also might do… and are more likely to work, is to buy time for information gathering.
Identify environmental weapons at your disposal. Analyzing a person, gathering data on them, consider what attacks could come from the opponent, which ones would be most likely to work for you. Identify possible weaknesses.

Environmental weapons are anything available. From the bottle of lotion in the shelf to the keys in your pocket, to the tissue in your purse, to the volume of your voice. Even the breathe you exhale… if its bad enough at the time. Consider if something is moveable or not, throwable or not. Blunt, edged, etc so you know what is available for use against an attacker.
The bottle of lotion can be used as a bludgeoning tool or you can put the lotion on your fingers so that when you poke them in the eye, it causes inability to see or even irritation.

Keys interlaced within your fingers make your fist more dangerous as the keys become piercing weapons.

Yes, even the tissue paper you use to blow your nose… can be used to temporarily blind someone simply by smacking it on a sweaty forehead, or by licking it to give it moisture then hitting it against their forehead… for added effect… blow your nose in it first… then smack it in their face. Walls are wonderful tools for ramming someone up against, benches for obstructions, you name it, anything is useful. All one has to do is to decide to use it. Analyzing a person, gathering data, consider their weapons.

Are they larger? Are they smaller? More wirey? Stronger? Do they have a limp? Any movement which would suggest a favoring of one side? Facial expression? Tone of voice? Movement?

Once you have gathered all you can about them, I then determine their most likely tools. Upper body development suggests punches/grappling, a bounce to their step suggests reliance on kicks. Heavier will rely on rapid attacks to eliminate opposition. Slighter opponents will rely on improved endurance and agility.

Then determining what weapons you bring forth. What will work, what will not given what you have seen of the person. Do they show an affinity for fighting instruction or the brawler type?

Possible weaknesses are important to identify and keep in mind. They provide focus for the possible fight ahead. At this point, the weaknesses determined are hypothetical, so to be tried out if need be.

The steps to this point are all for their intended purpose, but they provide for something else as well… which is the next thing I will talk about.

Step 4: Mental preparation

I do not remember the percentage of fights are already resolved before the first punch, but it is around 70%. A lot of the reason for this is due to the mental preparedness of the participants. Those who are willing to attack an individual, if they are doing it for the sake of attack, are doing it with the idea of NOT having a person fight back. Their mental preparation is to scare an opponent into submission so they can then take advantage of the attacker. So for one who is preparing to be attacked, mental preparation is just as important.

The first 3 steps start this process… focusing the mind on the altercation ahead and NOT on those things which would trigger the flight response… the what ifs. The reality of an altercation is that if you defend yourself or not, you can never speak to the mindset of your opponent. So cannot say if you act meek that they will leave you alone (I know, this is a contradiction from before… humor me), that is the response they hope for. So it is in the best interest of one being attacked to set their mind to defending their selves, being confident in them selves that they will do their best to defend themselves. In my case, it becomes a self fulfilling prophecy, that if an altercation starts, the finish is just a matter of time with me being the one who comes out unscathed. I do not let thoughts of doubt enter my mind for they are useless in an altercation.

Step 5: Turning on the switch, the initiation of hostilities.

If steps 1 and 2 have failed, there is one last thing one can do to avoid an attack. If one has done all 4 steps sufficiently, switching from the steps taken in 1 and 2 and moving on to the preparations done in 3 and 4 create a situation which is capable of shocking an opponent into a different mindset… and being readily defeated.

Kind of like turning an On/Off switch to the On position. That instant of going from completely meek and submissive to borderline psychotic and un-assailable can be a scary concept. Everyone has heard of the 5ft 2in very thin woman that everyone is afraid of… "She is scary" is the words spoken of her… this is the very tool such a woman uses to go from small thin, meek woman, to mega beast and scare the daylights out of others.

The key is spelled out in the above 4 steps. If an altercation is inevitable, steps 1 and 2, if done to their fullest will lull one into a false sense of over confidence. Then if 3 and 4 are done to such a level that when one switches from one to the other, the alteration is so rapid and so dramatic, that one can instantly be cowed into submission.

Step 6: Altercation in progress

In the early part of an altercation, I will always play with my opponent… this is the process of actually investigating my opponents perceived weaknesses and looking for new ones. At this point, energy conservation and defensive maneuvers are of the utmost of importance. This is the time to test out everything. Do they have a weak sternum is normally one of my first objectives. For larger opponents, the knees. Thinner opponents, the forearms or shins.

Also, looking for weaknesses in their attempts to hurt you. Do they over extend themselves? Do they have a pattern to their fighting? Favor one type of attack? Do they expose body parts?

When weaknesses are found, apply your personal strengths against those while staying away from their strengths.

Mentally, remain confident and thinking about the initial perceived weaknesses… improving upon them as they are proven or rejecting them when disproven. Keeping the mind actively finding an opening or a weakness will help one to maintain a focus on the altercation. At this point, any doubt in ones ability is futile. So getting one to doubt their own ability is a boon in an opponent. So talking is an effective tool. Not necessarily taunting, but using a firm, resolved, and loud voice as one continues will help to lessen your opponents resolve. Just remembering, that this is their desire as well.

At this point, the less you are able to focus on defense and allowing the body to defend itself, the more able you are to defeat an opponent. This is where the martial artist really has the advantage. The training of the body to react to an opponents' movements so one does not have to think about doing such.

Step 7: Escalation of the altercation

The ultimate goal in any altercation is to end it with the minimum amount of damage being caused to either. So one should in the initial part try to exercise escapes if possible.

If such is not possible, then an escalation of the hostilities is appropriate. The focus then becomes to damage the opponent in the least possible while not being damaged yourself. The playing phase I spoke of can eventually prove the futility of an altercation to an opponent, convincing them to stop.

If not able to do this, then the damage starts to be increased to cause actual pain. Pain is an excellent motivator to convince one that such actions are pointless. If this can be done while showing that you yourself are not being damaged… conclusions readily come about that continuing is a bad idea.

Finally, if in an altercation, an opponent is determined to go on. Then one is left with no other choice but to then act in ways to incapacitate an opponent. Shattering joints, breaking bones. Both are capable of ending an altercation if the proper bones are broke. Fingers and wrists are not as effective as destroying the elbow. The knee is more effective and readily broke then the toes or ankle.

Step 8: Termination

This is always the goal, to get the fight over as soon as possible. The longer a fight goes on, the more likely one is to be hurt. Also, the longer a fight, the less likely an avenue of escape will be plausible. Thereby, the riskiest strategy is one which requires the wearing down of an opponent. Not to say it is not plausible. Just one has to rely more on the strategy of the opponent using up too much energy then on their own.

A final note… death.

Causing death in another should never be required. The human body is quite fragile enough without having this consideration in mind.
The reasons for causing one death are outside of an altercation in my mind. That being if their death will save the lives of others. Cold, hard exchange of numbers and at that, if one regardless of the above can only stop such with anothers death.

Thankfully, the reasons for causing such are extremely rare (excluding those in combat zones of course). So thinking of such should be the furthest from ones mind in my mind.

PHYSICAL ART

Photograph by Nathan Thompson

Airsoft as an Integrative Practice
Amelia Long
Institute for Jedi Realist Studies

So...as I sat down and wrote out my Personal Learning Plan for IJRS, I realized that there was not really all that much that I had done with my life (thus far) to turn into an Integrative Practice. I only needed 50 hours, and while I could count a ton of things that I had done during my childhood and/or during High School or College, I wanted to start over fresh.
I wanted to use things that I was doing CURRENTLY as a way to improve myself and add hours towards becoming a Novice.

Well, the more I sat down and thought about it, the more I looked over the part where it in the Introduction where anything could be used as integrative practice as long as there was evidence to back it up. That's when I realized that I could already have ten hours worth of practice in if I applied all the things I had learned while getting involved/playing Airsoft (thus this blog entry now).

So give me a minute while I do my usual and take the long way around things so that I may demonstrate how Airsoft can be used as an Integrative Practice for Jedi.

But first, let me just refresh you on what Airsoft is:
----Airsoft is a sport similar to Paintball, only, instead of big plastic beads full of paint, Airsoft players are using guns that shoot .6mm plastic BBs that weigh .20gramms 😐

Guns look more realistic than paint ball guns, players generally dress in either SWAT uniforms or some sort of military BDU...guns can be metal or plastic and will be either powered by a battery or gas-powered through Red gas or Green gas.

Why did I pick up Airsoft?

I have never been the real-physical type. The only time I was ever physically fit was when I lost over 80 pounds one summer so that I could start training to be a Marine. THAT was about the only time that I can ever remember being truly active other than when I was a really young child.

So why would someone like me pick up on something like Airsoft? Well, there were multiple reasons for that one.

The first reason was due to the fact that my co-workers were ALWAYS talking about it. There were 3 m3n in particular that I sit with every day, hear them talk every day, AND we occasionally hang out after work. It was these 3 people that really got me through my time alone after Taz left for Basic training. But, day-after-day I would sit there and hear them talk about what guns they had just bought, I would hear them talk about gas vs. electric guns, and/or what camo was better to wear on the field and etc.

Without knowing it, I was slowly becoming something of an Airsoft expert just by listening to them every single day as they blabbed about competitions, matches, and skirmishes that were coming up in the summer. Finally I had heard enough, I was tired of being left out, and it was time that I did something risky and something different with my life...so I told them to count me in. I wanted to play Airsoft.

Secondly...I began playing Airsoft because, after Taz got back from Basic and started AIT...ever since I saw her marching across the field...I knew that I was jealous of her. Why? I was jealous of her because she was a soldier and I was not. Back then, it was not a known fact that I had (at one point) been dreaming of being a Marine.

In fact, the only people who knew that I had been talking to a recruiter in High School were my Mother and my Best Friend, Kirsten. But, as I mentioned in previous assignment posts, there were bumps in the road, I let myself lose to a fight against depression, and I gave up that dream because I became fat, lazy, and really sad. I went to college instead, thinking I would do what my parents wanted and become a psychologist. But, that too came back to smack me in the face when I ended up being $15,000 in debt my very first year and realized that college was not for me. then i met Taz, she was going to be a soldier, and I buried my dream of being in the military even deeper because now I had a relationship to focus on.

I knew then (and still know now) that if I were to join the military it would only ruin this beautiful relationship that I now have. With her being in one branch and I the other...and even if I were to join the same branch as her, chances would be that we would not end up in the same place as each other, we would not have the same MOS, we would see even less of each other than we already do...and by now I'm sure you get the point.

Either way, I was (and still am) jealous of Taz because she achieved what I never could. So...when I heard my very good friend Byron (an Army Veteran) talking about Airsoft...I knew it was for me. Airsoft is not simple...it's based around re-enactments of war...it's based around military operations and objectives. you have to be fit, you have to know hand signals, code words, the pneumatic alphabet, and the chain of command. It's one of the only sports that even gets close to what the military actually does as far as its exercises for training recruits, and thus, I jumped at the opportunity to play.

But now we can get into the evidence of why I want to use Airsoft as an integrative practice:

The Physical Benefits:

Airsoft in itself is a very physically-demanding sport. Since it's based on military operations and military training, there are certain requirements to play (you can actually play without having these requirements down, but it's not a good idea, just FYI). You have to be quick on your feet and able to run a distance of at least half a mile. This is necessary because when the enemy comes charging, you need to be able to draw back.
Objectives do no wait on you, so taking your time to get somewhere is not an option. The place where I play my games at is 12-acres alone, so, you have to be able to get around, and quickly.

The next thing is…you have to be able to do military movements. Nothing really complicated…but Buddy movements and crawling with a weapon in your hand is a must. You cannot get hit, and, when the enemy starts firing, you better hit the ground and/or find shelter. Also…if you have come up in hopes of flanking the enemy…hopefully you have a team, and then, you will have to wait for your team to signal you to move.

Speaking of moving, terrains are never flat and even grounds. You will have trenches, you will be running around in building, up hills and down hills. You will be running through brush, you will be running on trails, you will trip, you will fall, you will get whipped in the face with branches, and by God you better get right back up and keep moving until you find cover.
these are just the basic of Airsoft. It takes the arm power to hold onto heavy guns, it takes will power to keep moving when you get sore, you better have the leg power to push yourself across that field in full-tactical gear when the terrain and weather are against you. This is a tough sport and takes a tough person to take on that challenge and enjoy it!

I trained for 2-weeks with my Army Veteran friend. I would work out 3-days a week with him right before work, running and learning military movements. It was so exhausting, and then I would have to go right to work and then walk for 8-hours. Pure…torture…but I endured and it made me a better person, a more confident person.

The Mental Benefits:
    Mentally, Airsoft can be really challenging. As said before, Airsoft is based off of Military movements, military operations, and military training. therefore, it's good to know codes. The pneumatic alphabet is one of the first things you will want to learn, second is hand signals used in combat and/or when engaging the enemy.
It takes a lot of mind power to listen to your objectives, figure out what you're supposed to do, where you're supposed to be, how you are going to fulfill your mission, and etc.
    It takes strategy, teamwork, skill...it takes mental preparedness so that you're not the one standing in the middle of the field picking your nose 😁 you have to have the mindset that this is the real deal and that you are really going to battle with real battle tactics. There is do or do not, there is not try. To try is to admit to the possibility of failure, and failure is NOT an option, soldier!!!

Patience is Key:
    Airsoft is a sport enjoyed by all types of people of all ages.
The youngest person I have ever had on my team was 8-years-old. Patience in key when playing with a younger audience because they will most likely not take the game seriously. They will run out in the middle of the field, they will cry when they get shot, they will yet at their friends and alert the enemy to your whereabouts because they weren't thinking, and some of them show up without even knowing how to really play...and yeah...that basically explains it all. Things can obviously get really frustrating, REALLY quick if you are not patient.

Leadership Opportunities:
    In Airsoft, there are always Leadership opportunities. they pop up all of the time.
    You will notice that when you are playing with a younger crowd that they will follow the people that are best-equipped and/or that know what they are doing. That leaves that person with a bunch of people to coordinate and give orders to. THAT'S a leadership opportunity.
    Sometimes the Leader of a group gets hit and has to go to the Respawn point. That leaves the rest of the squad without direction. Someone always has to step up to finish out the mission at hand. THAT is a leadership opportunity.

Sometimes you have been given a mission and you see that everyone else is doing the mission a single way. You believe differently and think it can be done better, so you set out to do it your own way. You have taken charge of yourself for the betterment and success of your team. THAT is a Leadership opportunity.

Even now, I am currently Captain of an all-girls group that is starting this Winter because I stepped up to the plate and said: "YES! I am a girl that is not afraid to get shot by a BB and I am willing to lead others into battle!" I might have over-exaggerated a bit...but I got the job anyways

Putting your trust in others:

Say you're not the leader-type or you happen to get stuck with a group that already has an established leader, and etc? You have to have faith in your squad and faith in your team. A lot of the time, the people you are playing with are complete strangers. New people come in every competition, and it's very rare that you get stuck playing with the same people twice. You have to learn to have faith in those around you to do the right things and to try their hardest for the betterment of the entire group.

Fitness
Talon
Real Jedi Enclave

A Jedi should be fit.

The first and most obvious area of fitness is physical fitness; a Jedi needs to strive to be as fit as physically possible. We're not all the perfect specimens of health and so we have to accept our own limitations and work with them. Jedi come in all shapes and sizes; so we can't set exacting standards of fitness because that would be like saying that Jedi shouldn't need sight correction like glasses or contact lenses. However, we should set a standard that a Jedi be as healthy as possible. The more fit an individual, the better they will deal with stresses and trauma's of life -- that is essential because if a Jedi is to be leader then they should be fit to lead when leadership is desperately needed.

This moves us on to knowledge. A Jedi needs to be fit to lead intellectually. Greater wisdom results in the ability to apply knowledge to a variety of situations. As much as we'd like to be able to know everything, though, like physical fitness we can not expect a Jedi to be experts in everything. The ability to think critically, solve problems and do research is far more important for the Jedi than having expertise in law enforcement or counseling skills unless those areas of knowledge are where the Jedi specialize.

A Jedi should be spiritually fit. Our spirit is impacted by both our fitness and our intellect; but spiritually we need to be solid in our ethics and morality. We might not all have the same moral framework, but whatever framework we work from, we need to have confidence in it and dig deep so that we fully understand why and how we behave a certain way.

Here at the Real Jedi Enclave; our ethical approach is derived from the Jedi Code. When it says something like 'There is no emotion' -- because we all come from a variety of different backgrounds we each have the spiritual responsibility to determine how that guideline interacts with our cultural, religious and familial values. If they mesh, then all the better. However, if there is a conflict, it could easily lead to spiritual instability.

While we segregate mind body and spirit into parts; remember that they are all integrated. An unfit body is a result of an unfit mind and has an impact on the spirit.

Iaido
Garm
Temple of the Jedi Order

I would like to give a description of a martial art that to me applies many of the beliefs and traditions that we as Jedi hold dear. The practice of this art is akin to meditation itself and can be enjoyed by anyone regardless of age or physical condition. It has more to do with the mind than the body. With luck I plan to continue this art until I can no longer stand on my own. The following is a mixture of my own views and information collected from other sources.

Iaido is the traditional Japanese art of swordsmanship specializing in the countering of surprise attacks. Iaido is translated approximately as 'Instant awareness', meaning one should be able to respond to any threat instantaneously and in a way to ultimately avoid being attacked. The modern martial art of Iaido is developed from actual Samurai combat practice. They not only practiced techniques for using the sword but also how to judge situations and opponents under all possible circumstances.

In the time of the Samurai, even the slightest cut could bring death, if not by the wound itself then almost certainly by infection. Speed and accuracy played a decisive role in the development of their techniques.

The practice of Iaido requires a solemn spirit, extreme concentration and skill, the technique is highly refined. Every unnecessary movement is cut away, simple and direct in order to increase speed and reduce the chance of the opponent's blade from finding its mark.

The secret to this martial art is in a calm spirit. With a tranquil heart you put your hand on the hilt of your sword "in a split second your hand moves to cut down your opponent and resheath your sword" then return to your composed mind. A serene spirit must be cultivated at all times. It is said that the sword is like the mind, and if the sword is upright, the mind is upright. But if the mind is not upright, the sword can never be wielded properly.

Iaido is an authentic art that has proved its martial values in a time of constant battle and warfare. The art has been preserved and passed down over the generations for over 450 years. Because Iaido has no practical use in modern warfare it has the unique character if being taught unchanged from ancient times, there has been no need to adapt if for use in the modern world.

The first schools dedicated exclusively to sword drawing appeared some time during the 16th century. Hayashizaki Jinsuke Minamoto no Shigenobe (1546-1621) is generally credited with being the originator of the first dedicated school. The two largest schools practiced today are Muso Shinden-Ryu and Miso Jikiden Erishin-Ryu (I practice this discipline) however both schools trace their lineage to Hayashizaki Jinsuke Minamoto no Shigenobe.

In practice, Iaido training consists of practicing Kata like in most martial arts. Each Kata consists of four parts:
NUKITSUKE (NEW-key-tsky) drawing the sword from the scabbard or Saya,
KIRIOROSHI (key-ree-oh-row-SHE) the cutting action,
CHIBURI (chee-BOO-ri) flicking blood off the blade, and
NOTO (NOH-toe) the sword is returned to the Saya.

There exist approximately 48 Kata between the two schools; however like most martial arts there exist subtle differences in the forms themselves.

The sword (Katana) is handled with respect, observing good manners at all times. At the beginning and at the end of training the student and master alike bows to both the

O-Sensei and then to their sword. One does not step over a somebody else's sword or touch it without the permission of the owner. Many Samurai believed that their Katana possessed a personality of its own, a spirit of a past warrior or a natural element (wind, fireâ€¦) instilled into the blade when it was forged, there are many stories depicting the acts of Samurai accomplishing great feats partially due to the influence of the spirit of the blade.

Iaido cannot be considered to be a sport; it may be better described today as an art form. The student tries to hit not an opponent, but something in him or herself. There is a pre-set form to an Iaido Kata, which is studied endlessly. This form is honed and polished until the result is a beautiful and harmonious whole. Iaido is never perfect, Masters understand that there is always room for their own improvement and that their students are human, the path of the Iaidoka being a lifelong journey.

An Idaioka is in harmony with his sword â€" the sword is part of him, in the past his sword was literally his life. I have owned my Katana for fifteen years, longer than two of my children have been alive. The feel of this weapon is ingrained into my being. In class during an exercise to prove this, while blindfolded, I could tell nine out of ten times if the sword handed me was mine or not. Also, if I use a another's sword during Kata my performance always sucks, the funny thing is after I return to using my own, it takes a couple of Kata before I regain my norm, almost like as if my sword is saying, use another eh?

Ranking in Iaido is similar as in other martial arts, differing only slightly. The following depicts a typical format: Generally children and younger teenagers will wear a yellow obi (belt) and will test for the white obi when ready. Adults and older teens will start with the white obi and will test for a Dan level when ready.

The Dan levels wear a black obi with embroidery colored to match the level, White for Shodan (1st Dan), Grey for Nidan (2nd Dan), Silver for Sandan (3rd Dan), and Gold for Yondan (4thDan), ranks Godan to Hanshi usually wear the black and gold obi, but change the color of the Keikogi (similar to the karate gi top).

I have heard rumor of schools that have no visible ranking at all, everyone wears the same uniform and trains with the wooden bokken in the dojo. When the Sensei decides that an individual is ready for Dan ranking a katana is presented symbolizing their advancement to Dan and therefore assistant teacher status. No testing, only time and effort, under observation of the Sensei's trained eye as to when adequate personal growth is reached. To me this way is probably the most traditional and also seems the most Jedi like.

Iaido does not actually mean the overcoming of an enemy, but overcoming one's own limitations. The only and most dangerous opponent is the Iaidoka himself as he / she trains toward human perfection. With endless practice the Iaidoka learns to understand his / her place in the universe.

MTFBWY

Connect to Your Center
Jackie Meyer
Institute for Jedi Realist Studies

I recently rediscovered this in my blog and it was just what I needed to read. from October 24, 2006.

Walks are good for thinking, and making connections on the grand scale. The road construction, while inconvenient, isn't all bad.

Tonight at aikido we were working on a technique against a punch. We learned the names of the techniques, but I've already forgotten them. Anyway, you simply step off the line, and with your front hand lay it on their elbow, nice and relaxed. Then you take a step, drop the arm, and they should fall. Sounds easy enough. But when doing it with an experienced aikido student, it wasn't working well, and I needed muscle. At times it didn't work at all. He reminded me to just connect my hand/arm to my center. It was so easy after that it was almost scary! I mean, night and day, and no muscle.

What's interesting to me is that, our arm is a part of us. We will all agree that our arm is not separate from us. Yet we act as if it is. We make it do things all by itself, or maybe with a few friends (the shoulder, back). And while this has it's place, it's certainly not the easiest way to go about doing things. As soon as you link your arm to your center, it is as strong as it needs to be, yet completely relaxed.

In many the same way, this is how we interact with the universe. We are not separate from it, yet we act as if we are. We go about doing things on our own, or with a few friends, using a lot of muscle, and sometimes going nowhere. But the solution is simple. We have the infinite power of the universe at our disposal, and all we have to do is connect with it. Connect with our center, and life becomes much easier and relaxing.

So in a sense, training in aikido is also training my larger spirituality, for as I connect with my physical center, I connect to my spiritual center. The training is one and the same. To unify the body and the mind is to unify the spirit.

As I finished my epiphany moment, the song that was in my head before came more fully in my awareness. "Suddenly I see, why the hell it means so much to me." (KT Tunstall)

Synchronicity.

Going Through Health101
Dineara
Institute for Jedi Realist Studies

PART 1

So, I'm working again on the Jedi weight loss program, though it appears to have taken the form of Health 101, possibly. I've basically rewritten most of the material already to better fit in this context and added new stuff there and also dropped some. It's a great deal of fun, I love to challenge myself intellectually. As I've learnt to use my tools better it has opened new possibilities and also means that I don't have to include so much stuff in that course - if I can get it, others can too. It's a good research project. If what I 'knew' already about self-esteem, well-being and health was working I wouldn't have to write this, but since the methods that are usually taught work for only a minority of people... I get to bring in something old, something new and something revolutionary and turn them into a package that will work for - guess what - everybody. That's the best part of this. There is no right or wrong way of doing things, but if I can successfully help somebody to get better in touch with themselves and find the ideal health, weight and fitness by teaching him to listen to his body, well, that's awesome. The challenge is to present the information so that everybody can benefit from it, and that's why getting feedback is crucial. If what I write is hard to understand or completely bonkers it'd be cool to know so that I could fix it. lol

You know, in the end taking care of oneself is really simple. We just think that it's hard. There's no right way to do it, so what the course will be about is to help a person find the way(s) that work for him. I've already benefited so much just from writing it. Actually I'm glad that this opportunity presented itself, for this is the area I've been struggling with the most. Slowly it's beginning to seem that I'm actually doing fine here but have to work more on other areas. Finding the ideal weight and all that will come naturally when the principles are taken care of. What's important is that I feel super good about myself. Being healthy and balanced doesn't have anything to do with struggling, resisting, pushing, pulling and forcing. Since I used to do that and knew no other way it's not a big surprise why I never got any results.

Now I don't care about results anymore. What's important is this moment. Every moment I can make a choice. I can do something, or choose not to do it. Either way is fine, I can always choose again. If something is hard, I let go of whatever is dragging me down and move forward easily. I don't have to worry about tomorrow, or the next five kgs, or that muffin I just ate that I didn't really need or want (didn't eat one but you get the point. Just had to say. lol). This is the state of being that I try to help others achieve as well. Heck, tomorrow I can be stressed out, worry about every single stuff in the world if I like and do stupid things, but so what? I am happy and balanced right here, right now. It's all that matters.

Wow, have I made some progress lately. lol

PART 2

Today I've noticed that I have a fundamental error in my way of thinking. As I am very convinced (and have been for ages) that everything is energy, that the Force is between me, you, the tree, the rock, everywhere, it just doesn't fit to think that I am somehow a separate being. There's a part of me that is strongly telling me that it's bloody silly to let me think of myself as the world, everything or the universe. But hell, if we in the end are just playing hide and seek, if there are things like telepathy, if sometimes you can feel that you've know a person for ages, if life is an illusion and the things we call ego and personality are just covers of the greatness that we share, that we are… I've really been just fooling myself. No matter how you look at it, we are energy. You take the tiniest particles and go even further and everything is waves and vibration… Everything. Doesn't that mean that fundamentally we are One? I used to think at some point (during my witchy years) that gods and goddesses I worked with were faces of the Force, presenting different sides and shades of it to be tapped on. Aren't we these gods and goddesses ourselves? I don't know, this would have seemed like the dumbest idea some time ago, but now it just seems so simple, so obvious, and somehow so relieving. I've really been savouring the illusion of separation for over a decade as I was depressed and "nobody could understand or want me". In a way, I still am. And here I am, realizing how utterly blind I have been, as this world is a marvellous play of Oneness that I'm happy to participate in. Suddenly even the vacuum cleaner looks more friendly to my eyes. Argh, I don't know. My brain partially exploded or something. I just feel that that's the way it is. It's like everything I do doesn't really matter at all, but at the same time is the most important thing in the world. I'm going to drop the subject for I am unable to comprehend or explain it. I think I'll just concentrate on feeling it.

No, I have to continue - it's all been a big lie. I mean, the Force. It's not something external I'm supposed to be connected to. It is me, the aware me, the actual self, and it has been there all along, and I've just made it so hard for myself since I've thought it's something I have to strive for. This is purely how I've made myself think, nobody told me to think that way. Everything has to be hard, so frigging hard, that when you've had your part you feel like you've earned it. And then, when you realize it, you see it's a big joke. I mean, really. I'm laughing, and tears run down my cheeks. I'm surprised and relieved. I should have known, but I didn't want to. At this moment I'm even loving the cats! In the end even love doesn't matter, for it doesn't change the fact that I am you and you are me. Instead of forcing love I should respect, for this all is just so gorgeous, so magnificent, so clever, and so right. There has been no problem to begin with, it's always been just the way it should, with all ups and downs and what have you. It's brilliant, a play of shadow and light, so hypnotizing and entrancing... And here I've been thinking that in case I ever wish to become enlightened I'd have to spend fifty years in a monastery and even after that I wouldn't be worthy enough, yet I've somehow strived for it, trying to 'get' the big idea. But the funny thing is, there is no idea. There doesn't have to be. Oh, my, goodness.

I'm so incredibly amused right now but more sane than I've ever been. A part of me is worrying what others will think about this rambling but it doesn't actually matter, for right now this is what I felt and wanted to say. If it's all gone in an hour, so be it. Even that is perfectly okay. Right now, with a little stretching, I can feel the whole universe, and there is this amazing tingling and vibration and sense of well-being.

What I am learning from Yoga
Jackie Meyer
Institute for Jedi Realist Studies

It's now been a few weeks of yoga and I want to summarize what I'm learning before I forget. These are in no particular order.

1. It's almost impossible to be distracted when learning all of these poses and challenging myself to do them better. Definitely a moving meditation.

2. It's easier to meditate after doing intense physical activity, especially when it includes the level of focus that yoga takes.

3. There are so many ways to breathe! Every week I learn a new way to breathe. I'll try to summarize them for my own reference. First was breathing and expanding out - in all directions, not just out and down. Do that at the base, belly, and chest level, and then reversing the process on the exhale. The next was imagining a balloon at the root chakra/tailbone that fills on inhale and then shoots the energy out the crown chakra on exhale. You can imagine the balloon anywhere though. Then today we learned about sealing off areas.

First, the perineum, then the belly button, and during an inversion (like shoulder stand) it's the throat. While focusing on closing these off on the exhale, make a small noise. On the inhale relax all those muscles.

4. If you don't learn to quiet your body you will never learn to quiet your mind.

5. You can place your hands on a chakra and breathe through that chakra and it becomes easier to sense. I was having trouble feeling the energy going through my chakras on Sunday, but it was really easy once we placed our hands where we focused. My hands are significantly more sensitive than other parts of my body.

6. Try. You won't know if you can do something until you try. I'm surprised every class at what I can do. I have pretty good balance and can do many things pretty well. And in the areas I am weak I feel myself getting stronger.

7. I think Yoga has an infinite number and combination of poses and flows. lol

8. With the right teacher, yoga is so awesome. Qualities I look for are not going too quickly through things, allowing me to really know what I should do for each pose, or how to modify. Also, the energy understanding of each pose is key. Then the modifications are still addressing the energy intent. It's not just a fitness program, it's an energetic one.

9. However, it has made a huge difference to my body. I'm getting stronger, my back hurts less, and I'm getting much more flexible. I'm a believer now!

   I'll probably think of more later. Or after the next class. How does it get any better than that?

Meditative Properties of Martial Arts
Grayson Dark
Temple of the Jedi Force

Patterns (forms) are a varied series of attacking, defending, sparring, power and speed techniques. These are performed as if the student is defending himself against an imaginary opponent's attack.

Enacting patterns is an extremely efficient method of teaching a student many different techniques and some subtle aspects of the art which cannot be learned so easily through other forms of training. These include effective breathing, rhythmic movements, extended coordination and a precise ability to focus.

Executing patterns requires a total concentration of effort, perseverance and strong self control. Mastery of the art cannot be obtained unless proficiency in patterns is first achieved.

By constantly practicing patterns a student will become aware as his body movements and his mind begin to flow as one. This will become an intuitive action. He will no longer have to work at summoning his total attention. As mastery builds, he will acquire an intense and impenetrable spirit which will automatically unite his whole being into a singleness of purpose at will. Such an ability of control can assist him in his daily life in a world which constantly challenges him to overcome its frantic pressures.

Basic Principles of Learning Patterns:

1. Students must have perfected each pattern before moving on to the next.
2. You must begin and end at exactly the same spot.
3. Pay careful attention to maintaining the correct posture and stance throughout the pattern.
4. Patterns should be performed with a rhythmic movement, never stiffly.
5. Students must understand the purpose and correct application of each movement in the pattern.
6. Continually practice all previously learned patterns in addition to your present pattern.
7. Strive to make each technique clear and defined.
8. Concentrate on achieving accuracy in the techniques, the build up speed.
9. The written interpretation of each pattern should be learned by heart.

Response to Cooling Down After a Workout
Kol Drake
Institute for Jedi Realist Studies

I ran cross country and track in high school and did a fair amount of extra physical training while in the military so, most of this is 'stuff I've learned' then and over the years since.

The 'cooling down period' after a work out is as important as the workout itself. And, sadly, mostly ignored in the 'hurry and get on to the next thing' pace of today's society... but that's another soapbox all together.

So, you've just completed your workout and are really feeling the tension in your muscles. You congratulate yourself on how hard you worked and dream about how much stronger you'll be as a result. What you're forgetting, however, is the second key component of a great workout: muscle relaxation. Not only do you need to stimulate your muscles to grow, you must also provide them with enough rest and relaxation to heal and repair themselves so they will grow stronger.

Consider these next 'steps' as part of a program you should follow no matter the form of exercise/strenuous work you do. Making it 'part of the program' insures it becomes a habit -- just as exercise does. By incorporating techniques such as the ones that follow into your daily routine, you will ensure optimum recovery and feel your best for every workout.

BREATHING
Duh.

Best performed during the cool down and stretching component of your workout. ((AND, before you go to bed at night. The whole JEDI body control thing of calm centering))

But first...

STRETCHING
This frequently neglected part of your workout is critical for promoting recovery and decreasing muscle stiffness. It also helps to prevent injuries if done BEFORE and AFTER each work out... so... VERY important! Perform these exercises right after your workout when your muscles are at their warmest and most limber.

Hold each stretch for a count of 15 to 30 seconds. Do NOT force muscles 'until they hurt'.... as you are trying for stretching; not tearing. Firm but not stressed flexing is best -- feel a good pull in your muscle without any significant amount of pain.

Hamstring stretch: Stand or sit and try to touch your toes.

Quadriceps stretch: Bending one leg at the knee and holding your foot behind you, slowly pull your knee backward.

Oblique stretch: Standing with your feet shoulder-width apart, lean over to one side, letting your hand slide down the side of your leg, and repeat on the other side.

Tricep stretch: Extend one arm over your head, bend it at the elbow and gently push that arm behind your head with your other hand.

Calf stretch: Find a step and place your foot so the back half is hanging off. Then, slowly put your weight on your leg and lower your heel until your calf muscle feels a slight pull.

Back stretch: Kneel on the floor and stretch your arms as far forward as you can. Round your back while doing the motion to release any built-up tension in your back muscles.

By including these stretches in your workout, you will increase your range of motion, thus allowing you to target more muscle fibers during your strength training.

As an alternative, you can go through some Tai Chi or Qi Gong movements which also incorporate slow stretching movements. Perhaps a little easy Yoga if that's your thing or something like the Eight Brocades -- though, doing all over the above stretches would be optimal.

BREATHING (again)

Can't get enough of it myself. 🙂

Focus on controlling your breathing; take slow, deep breaths. Some writings suggest a 4:4 second count -- in and out. ((work it and see what works to get you breathing slow and mellow)) As you exhale, imagine all the tension and negative energy slowly moving out of your body. Feel your muscles relaxing and, if you are lying in bed, growing heavier. Work your way through your entire body, focusing on relaxing one muscle group at a time.

Breathing this way will help to increase your mind-body awareness and focus your energy on muscle relaxation.

HANGING UPSIDE DOWN or YOGA STYLE HEAD-STAND

Believe it or not, it may seem like an unconventional way to get your muscles to relax, but by allowing gravity to do its work, you can achieve a deeper state of relaxation. IF it's available, find a bar that you can reach comfortably, lift your knees and wrap them around the bar. Then, slowly release your arms and let yourself hang for a minute.

Concentrate on completely releasing any tension in your muscles and letting gravity pull you downward. Do not stay in this position for an extended period of time, however, as excess blood accumulation in the head can cause many health concerns.

If a bar is not available, learn to do the good old yogic HEAD STAND. Place a folded towel or cushion where your head will 'plant' and do a head stand. It's even okay to cheat and go 'up' against a wall. The idea is to get inverted.

Here's a little side trip regarding how 'good' the head stand Yoga posture is for ya.

The head stand Yoga posture is often referred to as the King of the Yoga Asanas because of its numerous mental and physical benefits. If you have only a short time to practice, and want to maximize the benefits, do the head stand. There are four major systems in the body that the practice of inversions positively influences: endocrine, circulation / cardiovascular, lymphatic, and nervous. ((but, because I like to.. I'll stick in a few more systems it helps. AND, I'm not hand waving these.. these have been 'proven' by various doctors/institutional studies over the years... so nyah. 😛))

Endocrine System
Enables a favorable reconditioning effect on endocrine gland secretion. Allows for the system to withstand greater stress and strain. It also stimulates the pituitary and pineal glands on which the growth, health and vital strength

of a person depends. Nourishes and stimulates the pituitary and pineal glands. In particular, the head stand provides refreshed blood and bathes and nourishes the hypothalamus, pineal gland and the pituitary gland. These glands play an important role in the endocrine system. The endocrine system uses hormones to regulate the metabolism of the cells. Our growth, health and vitality depend on the proper functioning of these two glands that control the chemical balance of the body. The secretions of the pituitary regulate sexual characteristics and growth of the reproductive organs. It also regulates the function of adrenal, thyroid and the ovaries. It is the hormone which stimulates the production of milk in nursing mothers. Thus, pituitary is the master gland which plays a very important role in regulating menstruation and pregnancy. The inverted postures in turn regulate the functioning of this master gland.

Circulatory System

Inversion gives the old heart 'a break'... by taking a little of the load off of the old 'fight against gravity' which the heart combats 24/7. Inversion exercises the heart and encourages venous return. The head stand does much the same for the body that aerobic exercise does. Inversions use gravity to bring more blood to the heart - turning yourself upside down encourages venous return and reduces heart strain. The heart works persistently to ensure that freshly oxygenated blood makes its way up to the brain and its sensory organs. When inverting, the pressure differential across the body is reversed, and blood floods to the brain with little work from the heart.

Headstand allows a plentiful supply of oxygen-rich blood to reach your head and brain. Increasing the blood flow through the brain cells increases your thinking power, clarity, memory, concentration, and the sensory faculties and moreover minimizes disruption of brain tissues therefore, acting to slow cell degeneration. Fatigue of the brain cells is done through the rejuvenation of the brain cells with fresh blood and O2. Studies have also found doing head stands REGULARLY help to minimize risk of stroke and Parkinson's disease. ((the whole blood and O2 deal again !))

Lymphatic System

Again, it's a constant battle against gravity. Fluid build up is reduced. Lymph, like the blood returning to your heart via the veins, is dependent upon muscular movement and gravity to facilitate its return. Thus, in the headstand, lymph fluid is relieved from the legs and ankles and with regular practice prevents the buildup of fluid in the legs and feet.

This also strengthens the immune system. Because the lymphatic system is a closed pressure system and has one-way valves that keep lymph moving towards the heart, when one turns upside down, the entire lymphatic system is stimulated, thus strengthening your immune system.

Nervous System

Headstand stimulates the nervous system which increases mental alertness and clarity. The immediate change felt after performing this pose is an enhanced alertness which lasts through the day. ((morning head stands... yep. BUT, evening head stands can be a 'meditative' and 'relaxing' time also... as one sort of 'reverses gravity' at the end of the day / end of an evening work out.

Brain Blood!

No, I am not advocating turning into a zombie. 😐 The most important aspect of inverted poses is to soak the brain with blood for a fixed period of time which never happens in other systems of exercises.

According to Dr Raman (Raman, 2004): "This rejuvenates the brain cells and prevents age related cerebral atrophy. Senile changes in brain are prevented. And as mentioned before ischemic strokes can be completely prevented as the blood supply is enhanced without pressure."

It tends to calm the brain and helps relieve stress and mild depression. It is a centering, calming and soothing pose. A cooling effect is felt on the face in the pose. Heck, even Yoda had Luke doing a hand stand while levitating all the crap around him in the swamp!!!!!

And now, some of 'the extras'...

Respiratory System

Healthier lungs. Inversions also ensure healthier and more effective lung tissue. When standing or sitting upright, gravity pulls our fluids earthward, and blood "perfuses" or saturates the lower lungs more thoroughly. The lower lung tissue is thus more compressed than the upper lungs. As a result, the air we inhale moves naturally into the open alveoli of the upper lungs. Unless we take a good, deep breath, we do not raise the ration of air to blood in the lower lungs. When we invert, blood perfuses the well-ventilated upper lobes of the lungs, thus ensuring more efficient oxygen-to-blood exchange and healthier lung tissue, oxygen consumption and blood flow.

Being topsy turvy strengthens the lungs. When done properly, head stands help the spine become properly aligned, improving posture, facilitating good breathing and reducing muscular stress. The inversion rests the lungs which feel refreshed. The vital capacity increases as the lungs learn to breathe against the strain of the body organs resting on it in the posture.

Digestive System

Head stands increase gastric 'fire' and produces heat in the body. The weight of the abdominal organs on the diaphragm encourages deep breathing, which gently massages the internal organs. By reversing the pull of gravity on the organs, especially the intestines, it helps to cleanse them by releasing congested blood in the jejunum and colon. Fresh warm blood invigorates the cells and overcome problems of the liver, kidneys, stomach, intestines and reproductive system. The change in posture enhances peristaltic contractions and aids good elimination.

Musculo skeletal system

Head stands strengthen the spine, neck, shoulders and arms. The muscular system of the abdomen and legs are toned. So, this particular one is a WIN-WIN... no matter when it is done...... as long as it's DONE.

MASSAGE

A massage goes a long way when it comes to relaxing your muscles. Look for a certified deep tissue massage therapist and book a full-body treatment. A deep tissue massage reaches muscle fibers that you aren't able to target with everyday methods like stretching. During the massage, focus on the breathing technique described above to relax your muscles even more.

Ya ya.... I know. You can't get one of these every day blah blah blah. But, when and if you can... do it! It's worth it.

In the meantime, I do ---

BATH, SAUNA and/or STEAM ROOM

All of these options warm up your core body temperature and increase your blood circulation, transporting more oxygen and nutrients to your healing muscles.

These treatments work best right after your workout or later on in the evening, since they're also a great way to relax and unwind psychologically. If you're suffering from an injury, however, ice should be applied before heat immediately after training, as it reduces inflammation, which is a priority for injured muscles.

Stay in the bath, sauna or steam room for about 10 to 15 minutes -- enough time to fully relax but not so long that you begin to feel lethargic. If you want, you can also perform some stretching exercises during this time, as your muscles will be very warm and at their most flexible state.

Since I don't have a hot tub or home sauna, I 'just' use some major tub time. Nothing feels more relaxing than to slide into a tub of hot hot water and letting it melt the old muscles for a while. Afterward, a short cleansing rinse and presto.... instant mellow. 😊

Add to that...

MEDITATION

Meditation is great not only for stress relief, but also for muscle relaxation. Do it right before you go to bed, as it will focus your mental energy and prepare your body for rest. Do it as you normally do and find that calm, centered, relaxed spot. Reread and do the first year academy meditation exercises 😊

Try to completely relax your mind, freeing it of all thoughts. Establish a meditative 'healing routine' in your head. Visualize your muscles tensing and relaxing, and all the energy moving out of them. Once you've worked your way through your entire body, take a few deep breaths and slowly get up. Heck, you can even work on visualizing that much desired 'deep tissue massage' on a table/bed.... remember, the brain / body reacts to these visualizations 'just like' it is experiencing the real deal. ((there are a ton of studies proving this lately too... trust me.))

After ALL this, your muscles should now feel relaxed and your body should be in a state of calm.

BUT WAIT, THERE'S MORE !!!

GREEN TEA

This dietary method of muscle relaxation is great since it is something you can easily add to your daily routine. Green tea contains a number of antioxidants that serve to eliminate free radicals that have harmful effects on your body. By reducing the damage to your muscle tissue, you won't need as much recovery time and can hit the weights harder, sooner.

To fully reap the benefits of this herbal beverage, include a cup or two of green tea in your daily diet. Make it (or another calming tea blend) your 'unwind' tea ceremony.

MAGNESIUM

Another dietary supplement that aids in nerve signaling, as well as muscle contraction and relaxation, is magnesium. This can be taken either in supplemental form or obtained from foods rich in magnesium, such as brown rice, spinach, almonds, and peanuts. Aim for 400 mg to 420 mg daily.
****

And that, kiddies, is probably a lot more then you EVER wanted to know about all this..... but, it's all good advice.

Biggest deal is.. DO IT.... and reap the rewards.
****

References (and borrowing from)

www.lessons4living.com/progressive_muscle_relaxation.htm
www.sunandmoonstudio.com/Articles/headstand.html
theyogabarn.blogspot.com/2011/03/most-important-pose-you-are-not-doing.html
www.askmen.com/sports/bodybuilding_100/143c_fitness_tip.html
drbenkim.com/nutrient-magnesium.html

Choosing a Martial Art
Jackie Meyer
Institute for Jedi Realist Studies

When deciding what martial art to choose to study, we can feel overwhelmed by the options. However, I've realized what has worked for me recently, and I hope that by sharing this personal experience it will help you in your decision.

I started taking American karate when I was 8 years old. My parents say my brother and I begged them after watching Teenage Mutant Ninja Turtles. (this was 1986) Being from a small town there was basically one option for martial arts, but thankfully it didn't have a tournament focus, but self defense. Now, at 8 years old I was an incredibly shy kid. But, I took to karate quite well. Looking back, karate gave me important skills. It taught me self confidence, especially since we had a self defense focus. Even more important, it cultivated that warrior spirit that was inside me, but hiding. I earned my black belt at 13. Even now, 16 years later, I can turn on that side of me at a moments notice. I may not be able to do the same techniques as then, but that mindset remains.

When I returned to college after my time in the Marine Corps, I wanted to return to martial arts. Again I found myself in a small town and small university. However, there was a university Shotokan club. This was particularly appealing because, while I learned good self defense as a child I really desired that traditional element that was missing. Shotokan provided this, in addition to teaching me how to really cultivate power within my body. As a small person at 5'2", this was particularly nice to learn. What also made this club great were the instructors who are world champions and great teachers. Unfortunately, this was not the case when I moved to Texas and I quit shotokan due to time constraints and a dislike of the instructor.

Then, finally, I found the aikido club on campus. This was a huge departure for me after spending a huge part of my life with the 'hard' styles that focus on power and speed. Aikido instead focuses on blending with your attacker and staying relaxed. And when you do that, you find things work incredibly well. The reason I am drawn to aikido is that it reinforces my own spirituality. Blending rather than pushing. Minimize harm to everyone involved. These concepts, while practiced physically at aikido, also need to be applied to everyday life.

You see, when I was a child, I needed to learn strength and cultivate a warrior spirit. Now that I have a warrior spirit, I need to learn to blend and flow with the world or Force rather than push. The martial art I chose to practice reinforced the lesson I was learning in other areas of my life.

So, if you are a timid person, I would recommend a harder style, in general. Cultivate that warrior spirit first so that it's always available to you. If you are a person who pushes through life, forcing things your way, take up a gentler style. If you are in the middle, perhaps choose something that does a little of both! In this way you are balancing yourself and approaching growth from multiple levels. Granted, there are other limitations. You need to find a school where you feel comfortable. In many small towns that isn't an option. But, when you have the option, I hope this helps you choose.

SCHOLARLY ART

2012 Jedi Gathering, First Aide Course

The Road to Hell
Alethea Thompson
Heartland Jedi

While I was in Coast Guard Basic Training, I got stuck in regimental hold for a sprained ankle. Perhaps one of the biggest headaches of my time there was the mini series Band of Brothers. Some of the people that were in Regimental Hold had watched the movie so many times they could quote it word for word. But there was this one section that was heart wrenching, and I just couldn't help but watch it each time they reached that part in the series.

The story started out with the soldiers finding a recently abandoned Jewish concentration camp. When Easy Company enters they find that there are survivors that had been exposed to very horrifying conditions- and all of them starving to death. Easy Company, their hearts rushing out to the prisoners secure food for them and start handing it out. They felt blessed that they could do something for these people, an array of women, children, men, spread across various ages, all of them happy and squirming for the little bit of bread the soldiers were managing to obtain. Suddenly, a physician arrives on site and has to take control.

To the only Jewish soldier and german speaker within the ranks, Liebgott must have felt like the physician was the worst person in the world, and his commander the second worse for taking the physician's side. Liebgott was ordered to tell the prisoners that they had to get back into the camp. In order to gain Liebgott's cooperation, the physician had to explain that what Easy Company was doing, was in fact going to kill the people in this camp, because they would "eat themselves to death". Refeeding Syndrome was first described after World War 2. While this may not have been understood by the physicians arriving at concentration camps as the Holocaust was coming to a close, the scene in Band of Brothers drives home a very invaluable point to a Jedi's mission.

No matter where the heart of a Jedi is, it is nothing without the knowledge we have to cultivate in order to perform our jobs. Seeing someone that is starving can be horrifying for us, and we automatically want to reach out and help the person in need. But what if we, in the long run, cause that person to die five days later because we took them in and fed them without the knowledge or skill to help?

There are many examples over the years where being unprepared for the help you are willing to give can be detrimental. In search and rescue efforts, evidence can be lost or misconstrued because of untrained personnel going out to look for a missing person- ultimately losing the victim to death, kidnapping or worse- never knowing. When you talk with a friend who says they are suicidal, and you believe that your pep talk was enough, only to discover that they decided it was a good idea anyway to depart from this world. Is the the responsibility of a Jedi to to understand what our actions, even well-intended ones, can lead to if you do not take responsibility for your education. As Jedi, you owe it to the people you want to help to pick up every skill necessary to the contribution you hope you can give back to the world around you. Taking on a scholarly art is not about learning everything there is to know in the world, it's about taking an interest in perfecting your abilities in a particular field.

The Meaning of Training
Jeremy Cowan
Institute for Jedi Realist Studies/Chicago Jedi

I was recently watching a Japanese show on the different understandings of training in Japan and in other countries like America. It was interesting to see how training is generally viewed differently. Although I have the feeling that most Jedi have a view more similar to the Japanese.

The Japanese word being examined was 修行 shugyo. It is usually translated into English as training, but a fuller definition for how the Japanese usually understand this word would probably be more along the lines of, "to undergo a difficult process that will result in personal improvement." The Japanese usually assume it involves some type of suffering or self-denial, but that one will be a better person for it. The Japanese see shugyo as an ongoing activity and a lifelong pursuit. People from other countries tended to think of training as a onetime or short-term program to gain a particular skill or accomplish a particular feat.

There are certain Japanese traditions when it comes to shugyo. When you say the word shugyo to a person it often first brings to mind the image of the practice of meditating in nothing but a loin cloth under a cold waterfall. Martial arts is also thought of as shugyo. But when asked about shugyo that they are undergoing, the Japanese tended to say things like, "my job," or, "my relationship." They interviewed a sushi chef of 30 years who said that he is still undergoing shugyo in how to prepare sushi properly. Part of that is due to the Japanese desire to be humble and downplay one's own skill, but it also indicates how shugyo is thought of.

As I said above, in general it seems that Jedi think of training in much the same way. Training is an ongoing activity that can involve all aspects of our life and requires self-discipline and self-denial to accomplish. Though there may be certain skills that we train in for a short time, overall our training will go on for our entire lives.

I found the program to be thought provoking and I wanted to share it here. Feel free to add your own views or to comment on anything I have said.

Herbal Medicine
Kol Drake
Institute for Jedi Realist Studies

I am not certain if we have any 'Nature healers' among us. I am intrigued by those who can identify plants, flowers, and trees and know what 'works' and what does not. For whatever reason, my mind just can not seem to wrap around 'doing that'. Still, I think it's neat.

I am reminded that Hippocrates, who lived sometime between 460 B.C and 377 B.C., left historical records of pain relief treatments, including the use of powder made from the bark and leaves of the willow tree to help heal headaches, pains and fevers. Most major pharmaceuticals are artificial 'remakes' of what comes naturally from Nature. The works of Edgar Cayce also come to mind since he used poultices and compresses and teas and infusions in most of his readings so, it can't be all 'bunkum'.

The single most important factor when purchasing herbs for making remedies is recognizing and obtaining the best quality available. Buy your herbs from reputable companies, those that have a conscience and are concerned about both the quality of the products they sell and the environment. (A couple of friends highly recommend this place to buy bulk herbs from -- Mountain Rose Herbs) Whenever possible, use your herbs fresh. However, this is not always feasible - but quality dried herbs will generally retain all of their medicinal properties. A good dried herb should look, smell and taste almost exactly as it does when it's fresh.

Of course, the best way to ensure that you are getting quality herbs is to grow your own. Many of the plants that you use for medicine can be grown as part of your flower/vegetable garden. They might even be growing wild already in your backyard or in the woods. Incorporate them into your landscape and use them as they grow and thrive. Plenty of books on 'how to grow herbs' and even how to make it 'work' even if you live in an apartment with no yard and nearly zero space... even if it means setting up a container garden of herbs for medicine and cooking. Fortunately, most herbs thrive in a small container on a sunny windowsill. ((even for folks like me with a purple (and sometimes black) thumb))

Herbs retain their properties best if stored in air-tight glass jars, away from direct light, in a cool storage area (a kitchen cabinet will do). You can store them in all kinds of containers, but durable glass bottles do best. IF you try to re-use any kind of jar, make sure to wash it out REALLY REALLY

WELL. You do not want your herbs smelling like pickles or marinara sauce. And, remember to label all of your jars with the plant name and date.

Now, the stuff I hope someone might find useful. Or have available to help a boo boo at a Gathering someday!

Knowing what plants cure what illness is not enough. One must also know how to prepare the plants. So, before the natural medicines are presented here, the ways of preparing them is presented here now.

Infusion: Cut and crush the herb, pour boiling water over the herb, stir and leave to cool. Do Not strain, allow the herb to sink and leave the to cool. If no boilingwater is available, chew or suck leaves to extract juices, then spit out the pulp.

Decoction: Cut, scrape and mash the herb roots. Soak the mashed roots in water,about half an hour. Bring the solution to boil and allow to simmer till about 1/3 (half a pint) of the solution has evaporated.

Poultice: Mash the root, leaves or whole plant and compress the plant into a flat pad. Add water to the pad if it is too dry. Apply pad to the wounded area, cover with a bandage or large leaf and bind the poultice into position.

Expressed Juice: Crush the stem and leaves into a juice pulp with rocks, sticks or your hands. A commercial juice machine is excellent for working within your home. Squeeze only the juice into an open wound and spread the pulp around any infected areas. Bind the pulp into position the same way as before with the poultice.

<u>To Stop Bleeding:</u>
Giant Puffball Mushroom: Pack Spore as a poultice
Plantain: Pound leaves into a poultice

<u>Cleansing Rashes, Sores & Open Wounds:</u>
Use externally to bathe 2 to 3 times daily or, if indicated, as a poultice.
Burdock: Decoction of the root, crushed raw and mixed with salt for animal bites.
Chickweed: Expressed juice of leaves.
Comfrey: Decoction of root as a poultice
Dock Weed: Crushed leaves

Elder: Expressed juice of leaves.
Oak: Decoction of Bark
Scurvy Grass: Crushed leaves
Shepherd's Purse: Infusion of whole plant, except roots, as poultice
Sorrel: Crushed leaves
Tansy: Crushed leaves

Fevers:

These plants will induce perspiration to break a fever.
Elder: Infusion of flowers and fruit
Lime: Infusion of flowers

Aches, Pains & Bruises:

Use externally where indicated.*Birch*: Infusion of leaves
Borage: Infusion of whole plant except for the roots
Burdock: Decoction of the Roots
Chickweed: Infusion of whole plant except for the roots
Comfrey: Decoction of the Roots, applied to the area of swelling
Cowberry: Infusion of leaves and root
Dock: Crushed leaves, apply leaves to bruises
Poplar: Infusion of leaf buds
Sorrel: Crushed leaves, apply leaves to bruises
Tansy: Crushed leaves, apply leaves to bruises
Willow: Decoction of bark to relive head aches.

Colds, Sore Throats & Respiratory Illness:

Angelica: Decoction of the roots
Bilberry: Infusion of leaves and root
Borage: Infusion of whole plant except root
Burdock: Decoction of the roots
Comfrey: Infusion of whole plant
Horseradish: Eat the root raw, stepped in a tea
Lime: Infusion of the flowers
Nettle: Infusion of leaves
Oak: Decoction of bark, to be used as a gargle
Plantain: Infusion of leaves and stems
Poplar: Infusion of leaf buds
Rose: Decoction of hips

Willow: Decoction of bark

<u>*Upset Stomach:*</u>
Bilberry: Decoction of fruit
Bracken: Infusion of leaves
Bramble: Infusion of leaves
Dandelion: Decoction of the entire plant.
Horseradish: Infusion of the root
Mint: Infusion of entire plant, except root, with powdered charcoal and water.

***

Ya, I know it is 'smarter' to use 'modern meds' when possible BUT, if there was the zombie apokolypse or the magnetic fields do loop-de-loops or some other whacked out 'THING' happens and modern pharma 'goes away'... knowing which plant does what (and which ones won't kill you!) seems like a 'good thing to know'. (or have a good book with illustrations and which part does what. ((shades of Hogwarts' Herb-ology 101 classes...))

SPIRITUAL ART

Photograph by Nathan Thompson

Meditation Sermon
Alexandre Orion
Temple of the Jedi Order

Let's talk for a little while about meditation.

Many of us admit that it is a good idea …

… we study it briefly in the Initiates' Programme …

… some of us talk about doing this or that 'style' of meditation …

> But do we ever consider the question : *'why do I want to meditate ?'*
> What is this curious gesture of sitting, lying, standing or walking and just "being present" ?

Why do we do it ?
> It is a more serious question that it sounds … If we agree that meditation is a good thing to do, then we need to also agree that we need to be very clear on what meditation is, as well as what it is not …
> One definition of meditation concerns "the act of thinking about something". However, in this respect, it may be better to think of it as "observing the act of thinking about something" without holding onto it.

> So, the first thing that we would do well to bring our attention to is our INTENTION :

"Why do I want to meditate ?"
> There may very well be various means (*upaya*) for attaining a meditative state, but there are not so many moments that the meditative state arrives in ~ **only this one.**
> So, you see – meditation is not a means to an end ; it cannot be used as a vehicle or a utility for some **future** wish.
> Meditation is being present – fully present – in the here and now we say we admire so much. It is accepting that present however "catastrophic" it may be, as it is, without desiring, planning or plotting to change it in any way.

Now, this doesn't mean that we not going to act in and on our environment before or after our meditation. It simply means that during our meditation practice, we accept the present moment exactly the way it is ...and we remain present with it.

Meditation has no end goal. If there is something I am trying to attain, achieve or resolve by meditation (enlightenment, or some higher state of mind or being, or some folly such as that) then I am not meditating.

Clarity may come from a meditation practise, but one cannot 'meditate' to gain clarity.

(the 'clarity' was always there – one just gets rid of the clutter)

One cannot 'meditate' to become centred.

It is useless to meditate on the solution to a current problem – that is 'thinking' or 'intellectualising', no matter how relaxed one is.

Meditation is not relaxation neither, although it may be quite relaxing.

Meditation is not controlling the breath, however when one is meditating one may notice that the breath becomes very regular and rhythmic … Actually, one just becomes aware that it is when one becomes aware that the breath is always there …

Meditation is not 'concentration'. Concentration is selectively omitting most of what is going on from the field of awareness to narrowly focus on one detail of things – and usually not even 'how things are' but 'how one wants things to be'. So, it isn't meditating.

But what meditation is is the present awareness and acceptance of things as they are – without having to do something about it, nor having to react in any particular way to them, nor to change them nor even to perpetuate them.

Meditation is not 'controlling the mind' neither. You can't ; don't try – you'll just get discouraged. Even during meditating, the mind is going to wander. Minds **DO** that – it is normal. That is why having a mind is a cool thing ; that mental wandering and flittering and all of the circus performances our minds do is how they keep us alive and why we can be creative and interesting … So, don't try to 'lock it up' … Just let it do what it is going to do …

Therefore, when you've realised that your mind has wandered off somewhere, take notice of where it went, then just lovingly bring it back. If it is your breath you are using as an anchor, then bring the attention back to the breath … if it is the hearing, then bring the attention back to hearing … &c.

It is helpful to see it as weight-training : the mind wandering off is like the weight lowering – that is normal, gravity attracts. The mind gets attracted by many various distractions of thought in much the same way. Yet, as the "training" part comes in, we use our muscle to bring the weight back. Likewise, for "training" in meditation, we must bring our awareness back to the anchor (breathing, sound …)

And if the mind wanders off a thousand times, just bring it back, lovingly and gently a thousand times. Don't judge the wandering of the mind – and if you do, **then don't judge the judging** … just kindly bring the awareness back every time.

Now, this does require some practice, but at the same time, anyone can do it. We are all present in the present moment (where else could we be ?), just often our awareness is anywhere but where we truly are. Hence, all those rows we have with people, or buses we catch or meetings we attend – all when really we are just in the shower or walking somewhere …

And, anyone can meditate. Anyone. All of us can take the time to bring our awareness to the present moment, if only for just a few seconds or a few minutes. It is not necessary to sit like a Buddha for 45 minutes without flinching (although that is good too – whether one flinches or not). Whatever time one has to simply bring the focus back to where one is and what is really going on is fine too …

Anyone can meditate, but the mind can certainly come up with as many different excuses as there are ways of meditating. No one is too busy or too lonely and isolated, no one is too poor or too ill. No one has 'just too many problems'.

In the past 35 years or so, meditation has gained an increasing interest among medical professionals and studies have shown (do not call me on fallacy here if I do not provide a bloody bibliography for that ! This is a sermon and not a scientific conference) that there have been remarkable benefits for people with all sorts of disabling conditions – from advanced stage cancer to AIDS to mental health disorders … almost every serious health concern imaginable.

So, if even those with overwhelming, life-threatening, life-compromising conditions can be helped by a regular meditative practice – most of us certainly can be. And we can also understand that meditation is as essential a practice as diet and fitness for the over-all health of the body (including the organ called "*brain*").

So, when we meditate, let's be very clear on our intention. The only intention that can provide a true meditative state is "to be present" – let's not be setting goals for it. Not meditating 'on' or 'about' something – that is thinking. It is about being in the here and now, not trying to get something.

This is why just sitting, lying, standing or walking with our awareness simply on the present moment and the experience of all of its sensations (including our thoughts) is a very active engagement.

I wanted to talk to you this evening about meditation, for it is one of our basic studies we cover in the Initiates' Programme, yet thereafter we rarely pay it any attention (HA !).

Yet, it is one of the fundamental precepts of life as a Jedi.

Thus, when we meditate, the intention 'just to be present' is vital ; let's be sure that meditating is what we are actually doing .

Ergo : instead of the regular recitation of our Creed, let us take a few moments to be completely present, here and now, with whatever is going on being just whatever is going on. Observe, let our awareness include just whatever is present .

Thank you for taking these three minutes to meditate with me.

May the Force be with you all.

Building your relationship with the Force
Silmerion Skywalker

Each Jedi has a special relationship with the Force but it is not always easy to build it at the beginning, so I felt a lesson about this theme would be very useful.

It is good to consider first of all the nature of the Force:

The Chinese Masters saw three aspects of it:
-Jing (the essential energy given us by our parents)
-Qi (the energy we work with)
-Shen (the spiritual energy)

According to them, the Force is made of 3 Energies:

The Earth energy (energy of the Elements, Gravity, electro-magnetic energy, Earth). It is linked with our lower Tan-Tien.

The Cosmic energy that goes down to the Earth, attracted by the magnetic field created by the Earth and the Moon. It is said that human beings are the highest manifestation of the Cosmic energy. It is linked with our Heart.

The Universal energy made of the unconditional love, stars, galaxies, it penetrates everything and feeds the Cosmic energy in the nature. It is linked with our Third Eye.

(These energies are called the Three Pure Forces because it is said that they came from the Great Void before anything else)
They manifest themselves in our body as Jing, Qi and Shen.

The Jedi Masters saw two aspects of the Force:
-The Living Force (which comes from anything living and binds us to the here and now)
-The Unifying Force (which binds us to the whole universe without limit of time and space)

This is a quote from "The Phantom Menace" by T. Brooks about the Force:
"The Force was a complex and difficult concept. The Force was rooted in the balance of all things, and every movement within its flow risked an upsetting of that balance. A Jedi sought to keep the balance in place, to move in concert to its pace and will. But the Force existed on more than one plane,

and achieving mastery of its multiple passages was a lifetime's work. Or more."

Understanding the passages or aspects of the Force is not considering that the Force is divided, the Force is one but it exists in different planes.

The Living Force is the way the Force communicates with us in the here and now, allowing us to meet certain persons in certain places, helping us taking decisions, teaching us and allowing us to use it, to heal, to fight or to sense.

We should be aware that the Living Force also leads us to the Unifying Force, something we do in the present will affect the future and the universal flow of the Force.

The Living Force and the Unifying Force are very closely linked. The present is the result of the past and becomes immediately the future.
The Unifying Force can help us taking decisions in the present and knowing how to use the Living Force. The Unifying Force gives us a direction.

In the "Phantom Menace" Qui-Gon met Anakin, if he had considered only the Unifying Force, the goal of his Mission, he would have left Anakin on Tatooine. The decision he made led by his sensations through the Living Force allowed the Prophecy of the Chosen One to be fulfilled. Focusing on the Living Force brought him to serve the Unifying Force, because the two aspects are totally linked.

Each of us is naturally attracted more by one aspect than another but training taught me that the relationship a Jedi builds with the Force should be balanced.

I was closer to the Unifying Force, I worked on the Living Force and I discovered another way of seeing the world. I also became more balanced myself.

One thing a Jedi should never forget:
"An infinite mystery is the Force. The more we learn, the more we discover how much we do not know"

It is good to realize that the Force is beyond our understanding and the first step to take in order to deepen our knowledge of it is to learn to think with our heart.

This does not mean to rely on emotions, it means to learn to rely on our 6th sense, our feelings through the Force.

Practices:

-Jedi Breathing:

When we breath in, we breath oxygen and energy (Living Force), it happens naturally but being aware of it, can make it more powerful.
Breath in, thinking you are at the center of the universe, surrounded with the Force, (the energy of God for who is religious), you breath in it, it goes through your nose down your lungs until your Tan-Tien.
Breath out, the Force expands in all your body and out of it, all the energy you do not need goes out of you and joins the universal energy (Unifying Force).

-Meditation:

Meditate on these concepts :
How do you see the Force?
How is it present in your daily life?
Do you feel closer to one aspect of it? Why?
Do you have difficulties in building a relationship with the Force?
How can you define your relationship with the Force?
Has it evolved? Is it balanced? How do you feel about it?
The Force is the Jedi's Ally:

"For my Ally is the Force and a powerful Ally it is" (Master Yoda "Empire Strikes Back")

"An unwise Jedi might consider the Force a tool, a means to his own ends. But a true Jedi understands that the Force is a partner on a concurrent course, a common pathway to true harmony and understanding." (R.A Salvatore "Attack of the Clones")
Each of us has his/her own relationship with the Force, but the Force is much more than "a tool", it's an Ally, it is not a person, it has no mind, but it has a flow.
Just like most of the persons allow their emotions, which are energy, to guide them; a Jedi is in a state of inner peace to allow the Force to guide him/her.
I personally believe that seeing the Force as a tool may be dangerous

because it can lead a Jedi to use it for what he thinks is good, but what we as human beings think is good isn't always what is really good for everyone and for the universe. That is why it is important to be balanced, think clearly, rely on Force Guidance, Logic, Wisdom.
The Force flows toward the good of the universe.

The Force is a great Master if you open yourself fully to it and follow its guidance, considering it like a tool can stop a Jedi from learning from it. In the "Jedi Way" it is written that a quarter of the Jedi's knowledge comes from the Force.

"Jedi feel the Force as an ocean of energy in which they immerse themselves, floating with Its currents, or directing Its waves." (S.Barnes "A Cestus Deception")

A Jedi can have a dialogue with the Force, just as when we are in the sea: we use the water to swim and we can also float on the waves to go where they bring us.

Practices:

-Water Meditation:
If you can go to the sea or the ocean.
Alternate moments of floating with moments of swimming, trying to be one with the water.
Then meditate on having the same sensation with the Force.

-Spring Forest Qi Gong:
They are 5 exercises to do together.
During these exercises try not to move your back in order to allow the energy to flow better.
You can practice these exercises, standing, sitting on a chair or laying.

While doing these exercises, you can remember these concepts:
I am in the universe
The universe is in my body
I and the universe combine together

1-Beginning of the universe
Stand in the Qi Gong usual posture, knees slightly bent, relaxed, back straight, chin slightly down, head that is "pulled" toward the sky.

Your arms are at your sides, with palm facing backwards, fingers slightly open.
You breath in the Force and breath out anything you do not need.
Remain in this position for 2/3 min at least

2- Forming Yin and Yang
Your right hand rises until your throat without touching it, your left hand goes down below your Dan-Tien without touching it
You can imagine a column of energy going in your spine
Remain in this position for at least 6 min

3- Moving the Yin and the Yang
Your right hand goes down while your felt hand goes up until slightly above your head, then your right hand goes down passing above your left hand without touching it, and so on, up and down. (the hand that goes down is always external)
This movement evokes the little Celestial Circulation, also called Small Universe.
Do this for at least 6 min
Then put your hands on your Dan-Tien to store the energy
(right above left for the men, left above right for the women)

4- Breathing in the universe
Create a ball between your hands in front of your Dan-Tien, then breathing in open your arms, expanding yourself in the universe, breathing out, condense the energy between your hands, bringing your palms closer, again and again.
Do this for at least 6 min

5- Connecting Yin and Yang
Turn the ball between your hands to the right, to the left, to the right...
Do this for at least 6 min
Put your hands on your Dan-Tien, breathing in, you can do this in several steps as the energy gathered is very much

While practicing this technique, imagine you are immersed in the ocean of the Force, if you feel stable enough, you can close your eyes.
Be aware of your connection with the Living Force flowing inside of your body and between your hands, as well as the Unifying Force which connects

you with the whole universe.

Write a detailed report on each practice taught in the Class.
Do you consider the Force as your Ally? Why? Why not?
Do you have difficulties having a dialogue with the Force?

Working with the Living Force:

"Keep your concentration on the here and now, where it belongs. (...) Be mindful of the Living Force" Qui-Gon Jinn "The Phantom Menace" by T.Brooks

The Living Force flows inside of us, in our blood, in our breath, in our cells and so in every living creatures, it surrounds us and allows our universe to be alive.

In order to be in tune with the Living Force, a Jedi should live in the here and now, to perceive it, follow or direct it.

It is a strong link between all living things, it is through the Living Force that we can sense the emotions or state of someone, when we shake hands, we hug or only when we are in the same room.

The Living Force helps us also to be more aware of what happens around us and to have better reflexes, it is very useful to heal oneself or someone else and it allows us to feel at peace and fully alive when we meditate on it.

Practices:

-Mindfulness Meditations:
Take the posture you prefer to meditate
Focus on the here and now with your six senses, being aware of everything around you and inside of you
When you notice that your thoughts are wandering, just turn back focusing on the present moment
The present is a gift, live it fully

You can also meditate focusing on only one sense at a time, the sound, taste, sight, touch, smell and your 6th sense.

-Perpetual Meditation:

This is a Zen tradition which aims at living fully each thing you do.
You can meditate walking, concentrating on each step, how you feel, how is your body, how is your breath, how is the ground, the touch of the wind, the Living Force...
You can meditate typing at computer, focusing on each letter, each move of your body or what happens around you (a good way to do it is typing without watching the screen)
You can meditate this way doing anything, you will discover each simple action as if it was the first time you do it, and you will perceive the Living Force as part of everything.
 Practice these meditations and be mindful of the Living Force in your life and training.
Write a detailed report on each practice taught:
What is the Living Force for you?
How is your relationship with it? What can you do to better it?

Working with the Unifying Force:
 The Unifying Force penetrates everything, it has no limit of time or space. It links us with the past, the future and the whole universe.
Its flow is powerful and indicates a direction, what we may call the Will of the Force.
 As it encompasses everything, the Unifying Force is also the flow of our own destiny in the universal design.
 The Unifying Force is the spiritual part of the Force, it can make us feel closer to God (whatever name we give Him) and being closer to God/the Divine allows us to feel more in tune with the Unifying Force.
 Of course, each of us should build his/her own relationship with it, through religion, spirituality, art, practices...The first step is to be open to it. The Unifying Force can allow a Jedi to see the past or a possible future, it can help understand things beyond human logic, giving wisdom and enlightmnent, and more than anything, it can teach and provide guidance. Feeling close to the Unifying Force allows a Jedi to feel a part of the whole, closely linked with all the universe, past, present, future, here and everywhere, in eternity.

Practices:
-Meditation sessions focused on compassion, love, abandon and openess to the Force.

-Prayers (any form of prayer you are comfortable with)
-Listening to religious music
-Singing Gregorian songs or Spiritual music

These practices should be deeply rooted in the heart.

-Meditation:
Choose a place in the natural world
Find a comfortable position (any posture but your back should be straight)
Relax
Focus on the elements: Air (wind), Fire (sun), Water (sea, lake, river, rain, snow), Earth (ground, rocks), Space (everywhere in the universe)
You can focus on them one after the other in different meditation sessions.
Or you can focus on all of them in the same session.
Try to think of their true identity: the Force
Observe their power and the fact they give life, in the past, in the present, in the future.

Choose any place you feel right for you
Find a comfortable position (as above)
Focus on the universe as a whole
(Do not go out of your body, you should fill the fullness of the universe in the simplest way. Do not try to sense anything, just focus on the idea of wholeness)
Be patient.

Write a detailed report on each practice taught.
What is the Unifying Force for you?
How is your relationship with it? What can you do to better it?

Being one with the Force:
   "Years, it takes, to become a Jedi Knight. Years more, to become one with the Force."-Master Yoda "Attack of the Clones" R.A.Salvatore
   The highest goal of the Jedi is to become one with the Force. Of course we know that after death we transform into the Force. But it is possible to become one with the Force in this life, it helps us prepare for eternity, allows us to gain knowledge of ourselves and the universe through the Force as well as guidance and to direct it much better.

One of the best way to become one with the Force is to be deeply aware that the Force is everywhere, in everything. It is especially evident in the natural world:

"As much as the works of mortals could be, and often were, quite beautiful, there was always something about natural world that touched Obi-Wan even more deeply, as if a testament to the truth and depth of the Force that conscious efforts could never approach."
"A Cestus Deception" S.Barnes

It is good to spend time practicing Qigong with trees and meditate near animals to get closer to the Living Force around us.

It is also good to meditate focusing on the elements like in Lesson 4, but with the idea to become more united to the Force, it is important to realize that we aren't separated from the external world.

Our body is made of three energetical membranes:
-Our Tan-Tien (our inner energy center, below our navel)
-The energy membrane around our skin which is like a second skin
-Our Aura

Our Aura isn't made to separate us from the rest of the universe. It is made to unite us with the whole.

It is good to be aware that what happens outside of us can affect our inner self and what happens inside of us can affect the world around us as well as the whole universe through the Force.

With this idea, our meditation in the natural world can be made in a new light: The elements are outside our body but we are also made of them: water, air (breath), fire (warmth), earth (our material body), space. The energy of each element is linked with an emotion.

The Force is part of our inner nature as well as part of all things, all things are part of the Force and we are too.
This is how Master Yoda explains this concept to Luke:

"For my ally is the Force. And a powerful ally it is. Life creates it and makes it grow. Its energy surrounds us and binds us. Luminous beings we are, not this crude matter," he said as he pinched Luke's skin."
"Empire Strikes Back" D.F.Glut

We are made of the Force just like all the universe.
The Force is our true nature, it links us with everything and it is eternal.

Meditations:

-Any practice (Prayer, Holy Communion) that makes you feel in communion with God (the Creator of all things whatever name you give Him)
-Qigong exercises in the natural world
-The Force and the tree:

    To practice this Qi-Qong exercise, you have to choose a tree which is not very old or young, nor very tall nor short. Don't practice with a Magnolia or a Laurel, the ideal is an evergreen tree like a Pine.

    You have to come to the tree with respect, eventually "asking" the forest's permission, "greet"

    Assume a basic Qi-Qong position: feet shoulder wide apart, knees slightly bent, waist relaxed, head that "pulls" to the sky, chin "re-entered".

    Your arms should take a position as to embrace the tree but without touching it.

    Feel its roots, if you feel uncomfortable in some way, it means that the tree doesn't "accept" you so choose another one.

    If you feel good, relax even more so that a spontaneous movement may appear, (it is the Force that moves you) feel the tree's energy.

    The point of this practice is not taking the tree's energy, it's sharing the energy, as you too give something to the tree.

    After a while, step back slowly, bringing your hands to your Tan-Tien (the right above the left for the males, the left above the right for the females) to bring the energy to your center.

    "Greet" the tree.

-Meditation in the natural world (see above)
(it is recommended if possible to use the posture described in the "Self-Control" topic in the Jedi Talk Forum, it is made to balance the energy of the elements inside of us)

-The White Sphere Meditation:

    Find a comfortable place

    Choose a posture you like (with the back straight)

    Focus on the weight of your body on the floor for a few minutes

    Focus on your breath for a few minutes

    Visualize a sphere of white light at the center of your chest at the level of your heart.

It is made of the purest energy, the essence of the Force (it comes from God for who believes in God)

From the white sphere, rays spread in all your body, reaching each cell, each space and bringing exactly what you need now, peace, balance, harmony, anything you need.

The rays spread even more and fill your Aura

They spread in the room you meditate in, touching everyone there and bring them all they need-

The rays expand even further, filling all your house, then all your town, then your country, then your continent.

The rays reach all the earth, bringing light and what everyone and every place needs

The rays expand to fill the space around the earth, then the galaxy, then the whole universe.

Rest for some minutes in this state

If you know someone who is particularly in need, think of this person with the light around him/her

Slowly dissolve the visualization

Focus on your breath for a few moments

Focus on the weight of your body on the floor.

This is the last Class of this session.
Write a comment about the work you have done during this Classes and observe if your relationship with the Force has evolved.
Write a detailed report on each practice taught.
Are you able to feel connected with the Force at any moment? Why? Why not?
Are you feeling one with the Force and the universe?
How does it feel? What are you feeling about it?
Does it change your relationship with the world?

Understanding the Force is a lifetime work, a Jedi never ceases to learn. May the Force be with you always.

Force Delving
Charles McBride
The Labyrinth, Knights of Awakening

The Force Delve is the most basic of all meditations concerning gaining an understanding of The Force and yet it is perhaps the most intense of the experiences one can choose to take on when exploring The Force. What you will need to start this meditation is a comfortable seat, chair, or couch to sit in. A timer can be helpful to keep track of time as well but is not mandatory. Preparation for this meditation is simple. Prepare some tea, listen to some relaxing music, take a hot bath, anything to get you relaxed before the meditation. The goal is not to use the meditation solely for relaxation but to ease into the state having already relaxed and thereby increasing the productivity of this meditation for learning more of The Force. Use the bathroom before the meditation as much like a car ride, you will not have a opportunity to do so for some time. Once you are fully relaxed or nearly so you can begin the basic meditation.

Sit up straight in the comfortable position and begin to breath deeply. You should use long deep and steady breaths with long pauses to hold the breath in while doing the meditation and slow steady exhales and short pauses at the end of each breath. Focus on feeling The Force move through your body at first. You should feel The Force moving through the air, into your lungs, and into your limbs. Feel free to use visualization during this part if it helps. Focus on the feeling of The Force at first and slowly shift hat focus toward the center of your body and the core of your energy.

Keeping your attention focused on the core within your body visualize moving inward into The Force within as a long tunnel. This is the act of realization and understanding that all things are within and as they are also outside. Draw deep into yourself and continue to move inward until such time as you find you are no longer aware of focusing inward but are now focusing outward. During this meditation you will see images, places, people. Do not hold onto these images but instead let them flow freely to you. Do not focus on a single purpose the first times you do this but instead allow The Force to move you along its currents to see what is beyond your current sight.
When you feel you have reached the limits of how far you wish to go in this meditation, usually no less than thirty minutes no more than three hours, begin to bring your focus back toward the center again retracing where you have went to back to where you have come from. Take this opportunity to

make note of the visions, movements of currents, realizations, understandings, and thoughts that have come to you during this meditation. As you feel The Force in your body again take a moment to use it to clear out blockages, revitalize your limbs and strengthen your soul. Once you are settled again, relaxed, and now fully aware of your body begin to move about. Do some kind of physical activity even if only taking a small walk or stretching out.

The Basics of Ceremonial Energy Work
Charles McBride
The Labyrinth, Knights of Awakening

Ceremonial energy work has been a mainstay of the occult, eastern, and western religions for hundreds of years yet it is rarely discussed at its core components. The idea of energy work initially sounds daunting to most until they begin to step into the act of using energy. All energy works on simple guidelines and today we will explore those guidelines as well as how they interact with ceremony.

The first guideline one must consider when doing energy work is that of the focus. Wherever the focus of one person, or many, goes so does part of their energy. This causes a major misconception for most as they focus on parts of a broad range concept rather than the components necessary to achieve a goal. An example is the ever elusive weight loss in which one will focus their attention to their weight and watch themselves balloon in size. Within this the focus is then on weight, and not say on health, and as a result the energy empowers the increase in weight and mass. Likewise it has been known that a person focusing on weight loss might even achieve the loss of weight in muscle and bone mass yet not in actual fat mass. These are examples of poor case scenario focus though, a better example is often the use of focus to attract someone "just like this" in which case that person is attracted toward the focuser. Other examples include a calling out for help, generating an energy focus requesting help, and then mysteriously a teacher presents himself to assist a student. This is a known example of "when the student is ready the teacher will come" and is well known historically as having occurred enough to be a definite concept.

Next we should consider the rule of like attracts like. That is to say, however an energy is put to use it will attract other energies of a similar nature. Good examples of this in society are people maintaining a thought pattern or concept attracting like minded people to them. Likewise one who is in good humor will often attract others who are in good humor to themselves. This rule is not completely universal, as no rules are, but is a good basic guideline to consider during energy work of any kind.

Following the rule of like attracts like is the rule of attraction of need. This rule is very similar to that of focus however it often occurs without the direct need of focusing being done. When one has a deep need they are not even aware of they will attract others who can full fill that need on some level. This results often in friendships among people who compliment each others strengths and compensate for fellows weaknesses. The rule of need is a very basic one by its nature and often draws forth some of the most profound physical symbolization of spiritual power. When one needs something deeply enough they will find a way to manifest that which they need generally speaking.

Lastly is the rule of opposing opposites. This rule would seem obvious given all things mentioned above but in spiritual energy working most seem to over look it. This concept simply states that when two energies of a different type collide or clash they will force each other apart and/or attempt to annihilate each other. This rule is less strict than the others and has a wide berth of interpretation. However much this rule may be interpreted the basics of it remain the same. When two energies collide, much like two people of polar opposite personalities, tension and friction is created. While this rule can be, and is, used in many types of energy work it is always done so with caution. The unwise initiate who throws multiple energy types into a point is like the chemist who throws chemicals at random into a pot. Surely it is wise then for the beginner to consider any use of polar opposite energies with more caution than other energy types.

The Heart of the Ceremony

The ceremony is by its nature the symbolization of power in motion so that the mind may move the energies within, around, and externally from the body. Ceremonies come in many shapes and forms ranging from simple mantras to full blown mysticism. The choice of any one ceremony often is one based on time, preference, need, and comfort. Time is the most important of factors within any ceremony as preparation can be consuming even for a simple ceremonial chant. Preference and comfort are not directly synonymous nor lacking in consideration however. The preference of ceremony used is determined often by the type of work being done. Some ceremonies lend themselves better to some situations. Likewise comfort is of importance for doing any ceremony one is not comfortable with at all will likely have disastrous results. Lastly need brings up the end of power in motion and yet it is as important if not more so than time. Need is the purpose of any ceremony done and is of quintessential concern to the ceremony. One must be aware of the need being full filled by the ceremony be it power, action, or affect because it is the true need that is being fulfilled that will come into being the most even beyond the focus of the ceremony.

All ceremonies include symbolization that is recognizable to the subconscious mind. These symbols may be words, drawings, numbers, or any other such things that the energy worker decides is useful for the focus. Most ceremonies include the use of multiple symbol types relying on words, drawings, numbers, graphs, names, and often even other languages. This is done to provide a level of concentration and focus over top a level of distraction. When the conscious mind is in focus upon any goal it seizes it and halts its momentum, and thus if we can remove the conscious mind from a goal, yet hone the subconscious mind onto that goal we attain results. Ultimately then the resulting purpose of any symbolization is almost entertainment for the mind.

Most ceremonies have more than just symbolization and include repetition. This could be a repeated phrase, physical motion, or pattern of thought. Ceremonies making use of repetition often reap high benefits from the entertainment of the conscious mind. It is not uncommon for the repetition found within any ceremony, or the whole of the ceremony its self, be nothing more than a rhyme. The words acting as a symbol and the repetitive chanting acting as an entertainment this method has been used for years and is one of the most effective and easiest used when starting out.

Even without repetition, symbols, or even ceremony intent has much power on its own. It is no wonder then that by design or mistake all ceremonies include intent. The intent of a ceremony need not be written out or spoken so long as it is comprehended by its practitioner. Likewise intent must be strong, honed, and focus to prevent a ceremony from moving energy in an unwanted direction. Intent is perhaps the pinnacle point of any ceremony as it is the point at which all symbolization, repetition, focus, and energy meet.

Lastly after a ceremony is done is result. All ceremonies have a result, yet not all results are the intended ones. Wandering focus, distractions, intent not honed, and energy left undirected can all result in an undesired, or even undetectable, result. This does not mean a failure in the ceremony, or even the practitioner. This is simply a factor within any energy work. For best results of any energy work multiple uses of the same ceremony are suggested. Yet if a ceremony continues to fail it is wise to look back over the ceremony for mistakes that could be directing energy in the wrong direction.

Inner City Meditation
Alethea Thompson
Heartland Jedi

A long time ago, my friends and I talked about what goes on in "our little world". It's an inner city which you can retreat into and learn all sorts of things about yourself. Sometime this week, when I get some free time, I plan on visiting my own inner city to see how it has changed over the years (been a long time since I visited).

The meditation takes you on a journey to the depths of your soul, until you reach your "command center". For some, it is a labyrinth, for others it might be as complex as the New York skyline or even as simple as a tribal community. There may be people there, or it might be vacant. It could be in the air, in space, on land, under water or even underground. Whatever the case, it is something which speaks to you and only you.

Last I saw my "city", it was a lot like the underwater colonies you would find out of SeaQuest DSV. It had a lot of people willing to talk about everything that had happened over the course of their day. They inspired confidence, motivation to do things that I may not have done otherwise, and overall kept me sane while I was in the military (a place to vent frusterations I couldn't talk about because of my line of work- nothing too bad, just Operational Security type things).

My city told me that I am a social person, and had a deep connection to the ocean I so love. There was a lot to be learned there.

Have you seen your own city? What did it look like? What does it say about you as an individual?

Meditation to get you there
- Close your eyes and pick up a steady (not to slow, not to fast) breathing pattern.
- Once you are comfortable, let the scenery around you change to an element of your choosing (air, fire, water, earth, light, void, etc), in the midst of this is a gate.
- Take in the emotions you have when you see the gate- are your afraid, happy, indifferent, etc?
- Open the gate and watch as your city is painted before you. Take the time to walk around, and take in the sights, sounds, feelings and such.
-

Energy Healing Using the Mind
Kol Drake
Institute for Jedi Realist Studies

All doctors acknowledge the power of your mind to heal your body. They use terms to explain away such healing using terms such as the "placebo effect" or a "state of remission," but *they know* it is your mind that is creating such an effect on your body. Your body has a natural ability to protect and heal itself on a day to day basis. All so-called "cures" that take place are basically stimulation of your own immune system.

When your energy is high, so is your health. When your energy is low, so is your ability to heal itself, and it's at this time that you're most susceptible to ill health. How is the process of self-healing done? How can you reduce or eliminate your susceptibility to ailments with the power of your mind?

First of all, you should realize that every particle and atom in the universe is connected in some way to every other particle, and all the particles of your body are closely associated with each other. *Your body is especially responsive to the programming of the mind.* There is no thought or emotion you can experience that does not affect the body in some way. That is why care must be taken to 'see' yourself in the best possible way. With the power of a visualization, you can work with your mind and body to produce a healthy condition or an ill condition. It depends on how you see and program yourself.

When you see yourself in a better light, and program yourself with positive self-talk, you automatically transfer the benefits to your body and mind. When you begin feeling better, give yourself credit. Congratulate yourself and thank the Force for your better feelings. Gratitude is a large part of continuing to feel better about yourself. As we state all over here at the IJRS, YOU create your own reality.

After all, if you think things happen by chance, how can you be responsible for what happens to you? If you have a low self-image and don't like yourself, how can your body produce a perfectly healthy structure? How can you fulfill in your body what you are not thinking in your mind? Many people take the stance: "I'm not going to be sick today, I don't have time for it", and go through life without any maladies? Or, "I only get a cold once or twice a year", and that is all they 'get'. Conscious choice and will power do make a difference, so tune into yourself and make good choices!

You can consciously manipulate your cellular structure through the power of your thoughts. You can visualize the ailment diminishing and diminishing until finally the excretory system carries it away. By imagining the process, you complete the connection between your mind and your body. Of course, the prayers of others can also help to resonate the process to make the metamorphosis more complete. A book I highly recommend which is written by a doctor who did 'self healing' using visualization and positive 'healing' -- Guided Imagery for Self-Healing by M.D. Martin L. Rossman. I posted on it a bit when I was covering creative visualization. His studies over several decades document that this stuff WORKS.

In the East, yogis and lamas perform similar visualizations to achieve the same result. They may even add to the process by vibrating their inner tissues with a chant, like the sound, 'Aum-m-m.' Any number of visualizations can be created to combat and conquer internal disorders and disease. Imagining a swarm of healthy and powerful white blood cells (sharks) doing battle and eliminating the unhealthy disease cell (weak little fish) has worked for many people. Visualizing a funnel of white energy swirling over a troublesome spot has worked as well. In the book referenced before, a kid used the image of X-Wing fighters zapping the 'Death Star' tumor in his body to fight it. Verbalizing and affirming to yourself what you want healed, and then allowing the body to complete the task with an open receptivity to the process is also good.

When you have an ache or a pain, it is the body's signal to you that an area of the body needs addressing.

As an exercise, bring your conscious awareness to the painful location and dwell on the area for a while. The connected mind of those cells has to respond to your healing, soothing, energizing thoughts. By 'focusing on a specific spot, research has shown that your blood volume increases markedly in an area of the body you are consciously thinking about, and with the blood also comes helpful body chemicals and ailment-fighting antibodies and leucocytes. Real science backs up what we try to teach here; your mind can do some pretty amazing things IF you are willing to do the work!!!

Stay mindful and focused on the painful area and feel it respond. Talk to the area and discuss what you want to take place there. This process often relieves emotional blocks that are tied to the cells there. It is good preventive practice to give yourself a nightly visualization/affirmation for all your bodily parts to heal and repair themselves. Do this while consciously bringing your awareness to each area of the body in a methodical, relaxed way, and holding it there for several seconds. (Oft times, I do this while under a nice, hot shower or basking in a hot tub... the 'relaxing' is almost automatic.)

Unfulfilled needs create chaos and imbalance. Our bodies suffer. It often only takes a few minutes to make time for what we need to do in our lives. Of course, in this fast paced 'everyone and thing wants it NOW,' it is easy to become out of touch with our bodies and our health. Most people want a pill or injection to "fix" them because they have been told that that is the way to 'fix' most disorders. Imagine -- if they were told that they had to think differently or have a more positive attitude towards themselves, they might not understand the process! "I came to YOU to fix me -- NOT to tell me I can fix myself!" Imagine if we had as much 'faith' in our own healing ability -- as we seem to have in lotions, potions, and pills. Maybe 'health care' might not be the big issue it is today IF we had not gone 'the easy way' with health and healing?

Whatever your behavioral patterns are, if you do the same thing throughout your life, you will get the same result. When you change what you are doing, saying and thinking about yourself, you change the result you get afterwards.

The Five Principles
Kol Drake
Institute for Jedi Realist Studies

We, as Conscious Beings, are always moving along a continuum between life-giving and life-taking actions, thoughts, and feelings, and energies. When our responses to experience are life-giving, there is more energy generated by what we are doing, whether it be conversing, drawing, walking, or daydreaming. When we are responding in ways that are life-taking, we are trying to repress something, disconnect from someone or something, push it away, or tighten down. Our bodies tell us when we are doing too much life-taking by developing symptoms.

So "life giving," in a larger sense, means being connected to the Life Force/Living Force all around us -- the sea of energy we live in -- so that we have access to whatever is nourishing for ourselves. With that definition, "life taking" then means closing off to some degree from that sea of energy that can and does constantly nourish us on all levels.

You are More then a Hollow Container

as our pain deserves acknowledgement and respect (for letting us know 'something is wrong'), the body itself deserves respect. After all, it is the container for our life force, for our spirit, our soul. So the term "container" can be used to refer to the body -- not in the sense of an empty vessel, but as a vehicle or medium for all sensations and the flow of the Living Force through us. As we allow ourselves to feel these life-force sensations, we will have more and more of them. And as we do so, the strength of our "container" grows, so that no matter what life gives us, we can accept it. We can stay grounded and centered so that we make wise choices.

It is important to realize, as we are now learning scientifically, that the body is naturally integrated; that is, our emotions and feelings are not just specific parts of the body. Rather, they exist throughout the body. Furthermore, in order to have vibrant health we need to be "in" all the cells of our bodies. We operate best when all our parts are integrated, working together on our behalf. Yet religions and cultural standards usually give permission to men and women differently regarding which parts of the body they are allowed to be "in." For example, in our culture men have more freedom to be in their heads and their pelvises, whereas women have more permission to be in their hearts. Of course, those examples are generalities for the purpose of example, and fortunately the situation is changing. But when I refer to the container of the body, I am referring to a system where, when everything is happening optimally, the physical, emotional, and spiritual all blend into one.

Five Principal Principles

These are 'principles' we have scattered all over the IJRS web site and they pop in posts and threads all the time. Pretty basic but all interconnected if you use them wisely. To steal from the movie, <u>The Lion King</u>, I suppose you could call this the principles of the "Circle of Life," because all the principles are equally important -- like points on a circle, they are not hierarchical in nature.

Principle #1: Recognize the connection/separation continuum in your life, and where you are on that continuum at any given moment.

This is the ability to know at any moment whether you are headed in a life-giving or life-taking direction by the sensation of connection or disconnection that you have with your life force and with the world around you. When you are connected, it feels right.

If you do not currently have this ability, how do you develop it? One of the first things is -- how to develop a connection to the ground. Take your shoes off and feel the sensation of its firmness under your feet. There is energy there, and you can feel it nurture and support you. You can draw upon this unconditional energy whenever you need to, using your intention and sensation signals. Grounding can enable you to feel what you need to feel so that you are not overwhelmed by life's experiences. Second, ask yourself "Am I present/connected now?" You might be amazed at how often you drift into the past or future.

Principle #2: Acknowledge and widen your perceptual lens.

We all develop a perceptual lens, or worldview, based on our experiences and sometimes *just based on what other people tell us*. We create a whole set of assumptions and conclusions about life based on what we have experienced, what our family has experienced, what we have been exposed to in our culture, our religion, our gender, and so forth. Everything we experience is filtered through that lens and our head gives an interpretation of it. It is important to realize that it is just a lens and that we can change it if we choose. If we have a narrow perceptual lens, we might miss or misinterpret what is going on in the present moment. Or, if we always 'see' everything through a 'lens' of negativity; then we might never 'see' the good in anything.

To open or "widen our perceptual lens", we can start by connecting with the intelligence in our bodies. When we are connected in the sense just mentioned, that intelligence informs us -- for example, of situations to avoid (danger) or situations to approach (synchronicity). However, it cannot inform us if we are caught in a perceptual lens that limits how we see the situation, like blinders on a horse.

We must acknowledge our thoughts and feelings as allies. This intelligence is everywhere in the body, not *just* in the head. Some studies have concluded that there are endorphin-producing molecules in the gut as well as in the finger, ready to create the sensation of pleasure. Similarly, there are adrenaline-producing molecules everywhere in the body ready to create a response to fear. When we listen to that intelligence (that 'body awareness') and, say, get out of a situation in which our body is signaling fear instead of listening to our narrow perceptual lens that is telling us that it is not polite to leave a party 10 minutes after you arrive, then the lens has been widened.

Principle #3: Recognize that you have a Core -- your spirit -- which is uniquely yours, and that you need to create a 'container' that integrates your body, mind, emotions, and core essence/Spirit.

Perhaps it is inaccurate for me to say, you have a core, as if it were somehow separate from you. More correctly you ARE your Core. Your Core, as it flows through your container, is you. It is hard to pin down the nature of Core because it is flowing continually. It is made up of Life Force, and is often strengthened through the practice of many of the 'activities' we highlight here at the IJRS in our lessons -- things like chi kung (qi gong), t'ai chi, or yoga and meditation and energy 'awareness' exercises.

The IJRS lessons also point out that 'we' can amplify and change this energy by doing certain movements, breath work, or even having certain thoughts. It is always there, it is what connects everything with everything else: your head with your gut, you with your spouse, your feelings with your actions, that rock, that tree, even the X-Wing in the swamp. Your Core integrates your experience such that when your gut says "Danger, get out of here"; your head formulates the best way out, and your body moves in accord. When you listen to your body and it's innate connection to the Living

Force, take its signals seriously, and not let your perceptual lenses get in the way, you have attained the ability to trust yourself.

Principle #4: Connect your Core to the Force.
Because your Core is the flow of Life itself, it is not separate from the flow of all Life. The Force.

So you are not separate from the flow of all life. You are not an island. If you start feeling like an island, it is time to go to your perceptual lens and ask "What am I believing about myself right now such that I am not drawing in the energy I need?" This can be done by the process of grounding and centering yourself, so you can restore the flow of energy and thereby heal. It is the process of shifting from life-taking to life-giving.

Principle #5: Know that there is an ever-present Source of nourishing life energy.
The Source is called by many different names in the different spiritual traditions, but it is the same Source to which they all refer. This Source never runs out. It is unconditional in its giving, in its Flow. When we truly trust in our bodies and know that in all things we are supported, life takes on a whole new resonance, an aliveness. We become 'One with the Force' and be aware of how it flows around and through us and our actions.

+++

Upledger, John E. -- Your Inner Physician and You: CranioSacral Therapy and SomatoEmotional Release (1997) .
Scurlock-Durana, S. (Speaker) -- "Healing From the Core: A Journey Home to Ourselves" (1996).
Pert, Candace B.-- Molecules of Emotion: Why You Feel the Way You Feel. (1999).

Force Consciousness and 'True Seeing' is all about being aware of what is going on around you at any one moment.
Kol Drake
Institute for Jedi Realist Studies

You do not, for example, need to be able to 'see' the colors of someone else's aura to be aware that they are depressed, angry, or otherwise affected emotionally. You can assess someone's mood from a multitude of different cues - such as facial tension, gestures, posture, tone of voice, etc. Of course we tend to 'read' each other in this way automatically, and think nothing of it, but it is surprising how many people seem to lose the ability to do this, and often the reason is that they are too wrapped up in themselves to take notice of what is actually going on at any one moment. It is cool if you can 'see' colors, etc but not necessary.

In my view, awareness of one's immediate surroundings, and how one interprets what is going on, is a major step in developing one's Force senses. It is important to realize that we should not passively take in information through our senses about the world around us, but that we should interpret this information in particular ways, more in accord with our Jedi training and nudges from the Force itself.

I barely mentioned some of what can arise from honing your Force Consciousness but, some can seem pretty darn esoteric and glamorous abilities. Of course, a wise mentor would shake a finger and warn you that ... gaining odd and neat 'new abilities' is not what this is all about -- rather it is about learning about yourself, the Force, and the inter-relationship gained. (Even so, those 'side effects' of training can be pretty cool on their own -- just do not get sidetracked from the main goal... being one with the Force).

So, rather than striving to develop such senses in isolation to anything else, these Force abilities tend to arise out of one's experiences and practices spontaneously. I am certain many would agree -- for the most part -- if people consciously pursue the development of Force abilities they are often inhibited by their own expectations of what they think they should be hearing or seeing. Do not get bogged down in expectations nor in trying to make things happen. Relax. Enjoy the experience. Make mistakes and laugh when you do. Success or failure, it is all a part of the learning curve.

Developing Force senses then, is very much a matter of allowing impressions and perceptions to arise in you, and to take notice of these impressions without necessarily attributing any cosmic or grand significance to them. To be able to acknowledge the possibility of flashes of intuition or foreknowledge of events is useful, but can easily become a source of obsession or self-delusion.

Here are a couple more exercises which you can use --

1) Coincidence Control

All you have to try to do here is notice coincidences when they happen. Do not try and explain them or attach some cosmic meaning to them - just be aware of them happening.

We tend to behave as though coincidences are somehow 'outside' normal life or some otherworldly 'something' messing with us. What is really unbelievable is how much we can dismiss what is happening around us. So notice your awareness that someone is going to say or do something, or that something is going to happen - no matter how trivial. (Kind of like me posting about spies and then having a movie on 'psychic spies' pop up and...) (another personal story -- having someone email me and mention some specific concept and later walking up and down the aisles of a bookstore and having a book literally fall off a shelf at my feet.... and the book is specifically about what the email / topic had been all about. 'Coincidences' are not always so 'thwap him with a two by four' but... The Force sometimes has to work hard to get my attention. 😊)

2) Unconscious Seeing

This is a simple technique for seeing images arising out of everyday phenomena.

All you have to do is choose some everyday object - it is helpful if it is somehow textured - such as a whitewashed window, a brick wall, a patch of moss on a stone, a plant, etc and look at it, stilling your mind. Forget what the object 'is', and let forms arise out of it while you study it.

This is a very ancient magical technique for allowing meaningful images to arise out of flames, the passage of birds, the swarming of bees, cloud formations, etc. Leonardo Da Vinci called it "Eidetic Vision", and it is said that a friend of his discovered the technique when staring at a wall upon which superstitious folk, particularly the sick, would stop and spit. The man is said to have gazed at the wall for hours, amazed at the shapes and forms which arose out of the blobs of phelgm. (yuck)

Any object which is sufficiently complex, from manufactured items to natural growths can be used in this way.

I have had many a time when I have seen some VERY specific images / faces in the random patterns of floor tile or swirly paint patterning on a wall. Same as I mentioned for those who can see 'nature spirits' in the bark of trees or the clumping of leaves on a shrubbery.

Working your Force Consciousness 'muscles' gets you into the proper mindset to explore the deeper aspects of the Force and Force related abilities as you progress along the Jedi Path. An added plus is... working those same 'Force muscles' helps to create, modify, and strengthen the neural connections in your head which opens new Force possibilities which helps to... love those self improving circles!

Mysticism Without Gods
Taijibum
Institute for Jedi Realist Studies

Mysticism Without God?

Do you need a belief in a god or gods to explain mystical experiences? It is my intention to show traditional Western mysticism with its "god-centered" three ways of purgation, illumination and union, from a strongly-rational and materialist point of view, in order to argue that it is materialistic psychological processes and not a gods grace that initiates and determines the process of mysticism. It is my argument that supernatural forces do not cause the mystical experiences of advanced meditators and that they have their source in neuroscience, or perhaps in some advanced, but not yet discovered cosmological physics.

Defining "Mysticism"

In the Western mystical tradition, which comes to us from from the Neoplatonic school through St. Augustine and Pseudo-Dionysius, we are told that there are three stages in the process of mystical union (Garrigou-Lagrange, 2002, Intro. pg X), and it has been associated with seeking a direct experience of God through Gods grace. It is taught that we do not initiate our seeking God on our own, but that it is God who calls us and we answer. Our answer to Gods call is to cooperate with grace and reform our character as well as pray and meditation on the life of Christ.

The traditional divisions in the mystical life go by the names of purgation, illumination and union. Purgation begins the traditional Western mystical life. Most often it starts with a personal tragedy or some other powerful and profound reason to seek the meaning of life, a direct experience of something divine or enlightenment. Daniel Coyle writes in The Little Book of Talent (2013, pg 3), a manual on skill development that,
Talent begins with brief, powerful encounters that spark motivation by linking your identity to a high performing person or group. This is called ignition, and it consists of a tiny, world-shifting thought lighting up your unconscious mind: "I could be them."

At this stage we most often seek out a religious guide who teaches us the basic prayer techniques and meditation of our religion. Religions East and West begin with focusing on something such as your breathing or a word repeated over and over. Buddhist's have their Mala beads and Catholics have their Rosaries, but they serve the same purpose. This is called concentrative meditation and it is the easiest part to learn and also the most crucial. The main difficulty with meditation is when a person is told to count their breaths from one to ten and then from ten to one for twenty minutes, there is no way to observe their level of attention unless they are being observed by an fMRI or other brain scanning device. What happens is the meditators may sit there and not do the work. That is why those who have a profound reason to meditate most often get the best results.

Phase two on the purgative path and the beginning of the Dark Night of the Senses is the movement from focused meditation to mindfulness meditation. The reason behind the necessity of focused meditation before mindfulness meditation seems to be to strengthen the ability of the mind to hold its attention. Otherwise meditation is just daydreaming, or worse (Johnston, 1973, pg. 53-61).

After a period of mindfulness meditation the mind begins to let go of things. This is a painful period where we actively eliminate from our lives things that are not in line with our newly chosen vocation of mystic. Moral virtues are increased and our character flaws are decreased. Strictly speaking, the Dark Night of the Senses is the period after the happy, wondrous, thrilling and euphoric inner mental experiences beginners get in mindfulness meditation fade and they are left with nothing consoling or rewarding. This is just a baby crying for milk. As can probably be surmised, this is a painful process for the beginning meditator to go through.

Illumination is the stage that begins with the vision of ultimate reality. Thomas Traherne perhaps gives us one of the best examples of this vision of ultimate reality in Centuries of Meditations (1908) and Dr. Richard Bucke who wrote the book calls it Cosmic Consciousness (1901), also has a detailed description of the vision of illumination. What the reports of the vision of illumination seem to have in common are three things:

1. Illuminated Visual Perception- Vision changes from seeing the the surface or outer appearance of things to seeing the totality of a thing, inside and out. A sort of living, intelligent light is seen as the source of the existence of all things.
2. Serenity of Emotion- The emotional state of the mystic changes to serenity. All things seem to be in their proper place and it is "good" and this seems to be related to the feeling of timelessness. Instead of knowing you are so many years old you now feel eternal.

3. Revelation of Knowledge- Discursive thinking stops and all knowledge is revealed. Often the mystic actually states that all the study and books read seem insignificant to what is known in this state of being.

What follows the vision of Ultimate Reality is the Dark Night of the Soul, and it is this soul rending experience that separates the natural mystics such as the poets from the mystic masters like St John of the Cross, Jesus, and Buddha. While on the path of Purgation, the mystic felt the pain of withdrawal from the things of this world as they actively try to purify themselves. Now, on the path of Illumination, the mystic feels the pain of withdrawal from the sense of self and passively endures the self-abnegation that is happening without conscious effort on the part of the mystic.
This Dark Night of the Soul is the result of the withdrawal of the vision of Ultimate Reality. From here the ecstasies happen less and less until they finally cease as the Dark Night of the Soul comes into full effect. It is at this point that most mystics quit the mystic way and fall back into their past character flaws and suffer temptations such as have not been felt since before they began the path of Purgation.

The Dark Night of the Soul is the psyche reorienting itself to find a stable center after the mind-blowing experience of illumination. The vision of Illumination is not just a visual event. Illumination is an overload of knowledge, love and every other sense perception that we have including the knowing that we are just small finite beings in an infinite cosmos. In a very real sense, the Dark Night of the soul is our minds reorientation to the directly experienced fact that we are nothing. (Underhill, 1990, pg. 380-412)
The way of Union begins slowly after the Dark Night of the Soul. When at first the mystic desired to see God or experience Ultimate Reality, now the mystic simply seeks to be. The Dark Night of the Soul, if passed through, becomes the furnace that has removed all the impurities from our sense of self. It is at this point that the mystics say, "I am nothing", but at the same time, they become brilliant engines of creation. At first they may have hidden away and sought solitude, but now they fully engage the world in whatever work the world seems to need at the time.

We can only observe from the outside looking in on what this stage is like. Here the consciousness of the mystic is advanced to the point that communication with other people is difficult. The mystic in "Union" will often speak in parables, koans or in the case of Socrates, in questions. It seems at this level the mystic has as his or her only purpose the uplifting of mankind. They do not teach truths like mathematics, but they are passed to other people in whatever way that is expedient so the other person discovers the truth for themselves. Union is the stage where the mystic is made one with God and deified as it is said, God "assumed humanity that we might become God" (Athanasius, 1989, sec. 54).

The final end to those in the true state of union is called ascension. In the Western mystical tradition, a person need look no further than the Judeo-Christian scriptures to find incidents of ascension. The first being Enoch (Genesis 5:22-24), the second Elijah (2 Kings 2:11), and the third was Jesus (Acts 1:9-12). In the Western mystical traditions this last stage has fallen out of favor.

Does Meditation Cause "Mystical" Visions?

I will be using the following definition of meditation as, "a family of techniques which have in common a conscious attempt to focus attention in a non-analytical way, and an attempt not to dwell on discursive, ruminating thought" (Shapiro, 1980, p. 14).

The answer to does meditation cause "mystical" visions, may lie in the psychological studies of perception. As an analogy, take the hollow face illusion, which a concave mask of a human face appears to our visual perception as a normal convex face. The late Richard L. Gregory, formerly Emeritus Professor of Neuropsychology at the University of Bristol, in the article, Knowledge in Perception and Illusion (1997) says, "The strong visual bias of favoring seeing a hollow mask as a normal convex face is evidence for the power of top-down knowledge for vision." What this means is that our eyes are unaccustomed to seeing a concave face, so our minds fill in the gaps and turn it inside out so we see something familiar. Our brain is literally superimposing what it wants us to see upon what we are actually seeing. There is a striking exception to this rule. At the Hannover Medical School in Germany and several other neuroscience institutes it was discovered that people with schizophrenia seem to be immune to this illusion. It seems that in healthy people the connectivity between the parietal cortex, the top-down control center, and the lateral occipital cortex, the bottom-up control center, increased during the visual test. In the group that had schizophrenia, this same communication between cortexes did not occur and it has been suggested that this disconnection is what makes them immune to optical illusions.

I am not suggesting that mystics are suffering with the illness called schizophrenia. What I think this suggests is that what the mystics teach us about the world being one unified living being is in fact entirely possible. Perhaps we do not see this fact because our minds hide that reality from us. Schizophrenics often report that the can feel the walls are breathing and watching them. Perhaps those with schizophrenia are just open to ultimate reality, but in an unhealthy way. Mystics often spend years preparing themselves for the mystic vision of union, whereas a person with schizophrenia may have the vision thrust upon them without warning and completely out of context.

Another exception to the optical illusion are those under the influence of drugs that mimic the symptoms of psychosis, such as THC, according to Dr Jonathon Roiser of the UCL Institute of Cognitive Neuroscience, and this may be because THC causes the same disconnection between the lateral occipital cortex and the parietal cortex, just like those with schizophrenia. Dr Michael Persinger is a cognitive neuroscience researcher and university professor at Laurentian University, who has done ground breaking work in the area of neuroscience as it relates to mysticism. In the article, Quantitative Discrepancy in Cerebral Hemispheric Temperature Associated with "Two Consciousnesses" is Predicted by NeuroQuantum Relations,(2008), suggest that in normal living our left brain hemisphere is dominant and we get our sense of self from this hemisphere as well as our normal intellectual processes. Intrusions from our right brain hemisphere are noted in intuitions and in rare instances, during "mystical" experiences. At such times the sense of self is altered from a left brain discursive cogito ergo sum, to a right brain non-discursive intuitive timelessness and non-judgmental awareness of self.

Are Mystics just Experts in the Soft Skill of Meditation?

In order to define mystics as experts of meditation in any meaningful way we need to apply some type of metric to the word "expert". For example, in chess there are standard deviations and rankings which define a players ability from Class C with a ranking under 1600 up to a Grandmaster with a rating over 2600. 200 rating points differentiate each ranking of which there are seven and they are listed in this order; Class C, Class B, Class A, Expert, Master, Senior Master and Grandmaster.

Chess is considered a hard skill, meaning you need training to learn it. Soft skills are those skills that need minimal training such as soccer or public speaking. No game or vocation is totally one skill or the other, of course, and deliberate practice is required to master both types of skills. Those with a basic understanding of chess and who have sufficient motivation may enter a tournament. They enter at a ranking of 1600 and depending on how they do, either increase or decrease their ranking. With deliberate practice, experience and enough time, a person may advance from a Class C player to a Grandmaster.

There was a study on chess by Chase and Simon, (1973), that reported its findings of it taking an average of ten years to advance to the level of Grandmaster and further suggested it took a similar time frame in other areas of learning, such as the violin. Ericson, Krampe, and Tesch-Romer (1993) found that top level violinist practiced an average of 10,000 hours to reach their status. Progression through these seven levels of rankings occurs over time with experience and deliberate practice. Deliberate practice is defined as purposeful, engaged and intense. This is the type of practice where we consciously improve our ability instead of the rote, automatic practice we find in those who are content with their level of skill.

According to Fitts & Posner (1967), it takes only about 50 hours to become proficient in soft skills such as tennis or driving a car. You start with just learning the basic requirements of the activity. You focus on doing the activity, but mistakes are common and it is slow going. In the second phase of learning mistakes become rare and it is relatively easy to maintain the activity without too much thought and the activity becomes automatic. This is where most people stop progressing and enter a comfort zone. Those who progress to the realm of expert and mastery enter the third phase and continue learning after this point using deliberate practice.

Therefore, an expert by my definition, is someone who has spent approximately ten years or 10,000 hours in deliberate practice of a skill and they are seven levels of standard deviation above the median norm of ability, as it is normally tested.

What this suggests is that meditation as a soft skill that may be increased to levels far above normal levels of the average. These expert meditators may have access to ways of perception and thinking that normal people do not, much in the same way that an international grandmaster chess champion sees the chess board differently than someone who just started playing.

Conclusion

In ancient times, humans looked at the sun, stars and even storms and said, "These must be gods." Later, people became more sophisticated and did not say things were gods but looked at the entire universe and said, "What ever made all this, must be God." There have even been so called "mystics", who practiced ascetic practices such as fasting and meditation, and although they gained deeper insight into human consciousness and the universe, they once again pointed at visions or experiences they did not understand and said, "This (fill in the blank) must be God", and think that these experience prove the dualistic nature of the universe and the existence of God. I think they do just the opposite.

If these reports are true they suggest a universe that completely materialistic, however complex it may be. The mystic's perception is opened to experience more of the universe and not another "separate" universe as the dualists claim. It is much like the light spectrum that we can normally see and the much greater portion that we can not see. When the scientist builds a machine to look into the infrared spectrum or builds a radio telescope to detect gamma rays he is not detecting another universe. What the scientist is seeing are levels of our reality that just normally go unseen, but they are still part of this material universe. In the same way, when the mystic perceives the universe as a single living-mind, they are perceiving a deeper aspect of our material universe that normally goes unnoticed. Therefore, we do not live in a dualistic or idealistic universe, but a full-spectrum materialistic one.

Bibliography

Athanasius, Saint. (1989). On the incarnation. Crestwood, NY: SVS Press.
Bucke, R. (1901). Cosmic consciousness: A study in the evolution of the human mind. Innes & Sons, Penguin Books. 1991 edition.
Chase, W. G. & Simon, H. A. (1973). Perception in chess. Cognitive Psychology, 4, 55-81.
Coyle, D. (2013). The little book of talent: 52 tips for improving your skills. New York, NY: Bantam
Ericsson, A. Charness, N. Hoffman, R. Feltovich, P. (2012). The cambridge handbook of expertise and expert performance. New York, NY: Cambridge University Press
Ericson, Krampe, and Tesch-Romer (1993). The role of deliberate practice in the acquisition of expert performance. Psychological Review. 100(3), 363-406
Fitts, P., & Posner, M. I. (1967). Human performance. Belmont, CA: Brooks/Cole
Garrigou-Lagrange, R. (2002). The three conversions in the spiritual life. Rockford, Il: TAN

Gregory, R. (1997) Knowledge and perception in illusion. Philosophical Transactions of the Royal Society London B: Biological Sciences. 352, 1121 - 1128

Hick, J. (Ed.) (1990). Classical and contemporary readings in the philosophy of religion. Upper Saddle River, NJ: Prentice-Hall, Inc.

Johnston, W. (1973). The cloud of unknowing. New York, NY: Doubleday.

John of the Cross, Saint (1542-1591). The collected works of st. john of the cross. (K. Kavanaugh and O. Rodriguez, Trans.) Washington, DC: ICS Publications

Kohn, L. (2010). Sitting in oblivion: The heart of Daoist meditation. Dunedin, FL: Three Pines Press.

Persinger, Meli and Koren (2008). Quantitative discrepancy in cerebral hemispheric temperature associated with "two consciousness" is predicted by neuroquantum relations. NeuroQuantology. 4:369-378

Peterson, M., Hasker, W. Reichenbach, B., Basinger, D. (2013). Reason and religious belief: An introduction to the philosophy of religion. New York, NY: Oxford University Press.

Shapiro, D. H. (1980). Meditation: Self-regulation strategy and altered state of consciousness. NewYork: Aldine.

Traherne, T. (1908). Centuries of meditations, London: private publication.

Underhill, E. (1990). Mysticism: The preeminent study in the nature and development of spiritual consciousness. New York, NY: Doubleday

Spirituality Exercise
StormyKat
Institute for Jedi Realist Studies

I went to Catholic school from Kindergarten through Graduate School. How that happened I am not quite sure, because I am not Catholic. Well, the Catholic grammar school was the best school in the area, so that's how I ended up there....but the rest were just flukes. Most of my spiritual beliefs come from my Catholic grammar school education. The Catholic faith was drilled into us (or perhaps it was just that one teacher in 7th and 8th grade....) I didn't agree with a lot of it. So while a lot of my spiritual believes may be said to originate from a Judeao-Christian background (I went to a Presbyterian Church when I was little) I do not hold with most of the Catholic religion. I remember being violently against some of the things that were taught us in school, specifically that animals do not have souls. That pissed off little StormyKat, who knew her cats and her grandparents cats and her friends' dogs had souls.

What I did get from my Catholic school education was a believe in the "Golden Rule" to treat others as you wish to be treated. The belief that others are to be treated kindly and it is a blessing to give what you can in service to other humans as well as the believe in the power of love. (I question that last sentence as I type, but I keep feeling the word "love" coming up as I think, so I know it must go in here, just perhaps not the way I worded it). I was more enamored with the stories of how Jesus lived--giving to others regardless of society's view of them, etc. This is what has shaped my conscience. Which is how I determine what is right and wrong (though I think some of that good ol' Catholic guilt creeps in too).

I was introduced to Buddhism in high school and I fell in love with it. The 4 Noble Truths and the 8 Fold Path spoke to me in a way no religious teaching had. I went to some Buddhist meditations for a while (I don't remember what branch of Buddhism it was though). It was there that talk of reincarnation popped up and in the context it was talked of left me feeling uncomfortable about the concept. I have a hard time accepting that a small child who is abused or murdered is a soul who was actually coming back and earned this from a previous life. I don't know what I believe about death. I have tried to sort that out for years and I just don't know. I would like to believe there is life in some form after death. I don't believe in the concept of heaven that was taught me in childhood, that all our souls go and sit around of fluffy clouds etc. I don't believe in hell. I believe if there is a god/God s/he is caring and would not punish us eternally. I feel like there is something though. Whether it is our energy being redistributed throughout the universe, or our souls being released into the universe for reincarnation, or heaven where we all sit on fluffy clouds, I believe there is something.

Last year I went to talk to an Animal Communicator for the fun of it. The night before I spoke with her my Sam cat came to me in a dream. It was not just a dream of him, it was him. I could feel him, he was more vibrant than the dream itself. He was almost three dimensional. It was proof to me there must be something after death. I have since had that happen once or twice with my cat who passed away on New Years Eve. She has come to me in my dreams. I have had strange experiences with animals sending me signs from "beyond the grave" so I know if my animals are still around in some form that my grandparents and other humans souls must be around too.

For me, spiritual practices are as simple as going outside and enjoying nature. When I am outside late at night, taking the garbage out or whatever I like to just stop and stare at the sky. It is so calming, peaceful and centering. It refreshes me and reminds me of my place in the universe. Besides that I feel that whether there is a God, a creator, an all powerful force that started life and holds it all together, whatever the spark was s/he/it created the universe and nature so what better way to be in touch with this all powerful force than by being in its creation.

Meditations of a Jedi
Zanthan Storm
Temple of the Jedi Order

Balance. Everything is balance. Ying and yang, day and night, sadness and joy. The universe in balance.

A Jedi must seek balance in themselves each day. Without balance we would be out of control, unable to concentrate, out of sync with ourselves and therefore the world.

We see loss of balance everywhere in the world. Everyday you can see it on the news. Simple observation of the behavior of humanity that there is a loss of balance in people's lives; Balance of power, of ego, humility and heroism. Most of all emotion, our teaching and meditation teach us to control and suppress our emotions.

In some cases it is necessary to compartmentalize how we feel in order to achieve a greater good or complete a goal. Sometimes we push aside small bits of emotions and just let them stay there, this too is dangerous because the more emotions are left there the more potent and powerful they become. Meditation helps us identify these emotions through self examination.

Eventually to keep those emotions from controlling us there must be a release of some kind. This release can not be using the dark side, lest you fall prey to it. However, the release allows our emotions, our bodies and our minds to balance from the potent affects of those emotions. This balance is essential to Jedi, with it we achieve greater wisdom and understanding of both ourselves and the universe.

Through the force and meditation a Jedi or any person can begin to balance themselves. The creed says, "there is no emotion, there is peace" I take this to mean that emotions are powerful forces to Jedi especially. Anyone who has seen a great emotional moment has felt it, the world trade center, a baby being born, a child's first step or even an achieved dreams in life. These can be felt by anyone who was there. A Jedi ruled by emotions even happy emotions is not leading the Jedi way. There must be wisdom, experience and knowledge to govern the mind and body; to hold back unwise and re-enforce good decisions. Unfortunately wisdom is very hard to find. Many claim to have it and those who do have it seldom say so.

So we must temper ourselves with our knowledge, gain experience and wisdom from life. Learn it from our mentors and use our abilities and ourselves for the good of all humanity.

Service, true service is voluntary. You can not be forced to serve. You can be forced to work, to be confined to complete an objective. True service is selfless and the Jedi must be so.

The Jedi are easily recognizable by the use and ownership of a light saber. The light saber and it's value to a Jedi's life were taken from the samurai warriors. Samurai means, "to serve." Service can be many things, as Jedi we have chosen a life to serve others, to protect them, and to heal those who need it.

On my own experiences, as an Eagle scout and in the medical field I have seen and felt much of the force. I have also felt the want to just not care anymore, to move on, to let someone else take care of it all. It would be much easier to just let everything be and not care about it, why not?

The answer is simple: We are Jedi.

We are the guardians of peace and justice and therefore, in my eyes, of life. At the end of the day I sleep well. I am exhausted and my body hurts from working. Its nice to have a day off work and that happens sometimes, but we cant stop being Jedi. Nothing is done well without work, dedication and effort. It know it is hard and there is little thanks, but like many I have embraced it.

Easy is not for Jedi.

Jedi Meditation: An Overview
Katie Mock
California Jedi

Meditation is a practice common to most philosophical or spiritual paths. Whether it is the common image of Buddhist or Hindu meditation, or the Christian or Muslim practice of reflective prayers, or even the non-religious practice of self-reflection and relaxation, all Jedi practice a form of it.

Meditation is meant to unclutter and calm our minds, and help us look at ourselves, our problems, and the world around us with objectivity and clarity. As the Jedi Code says, "There is no emotion, there is Peace". When we can learn to clear our minds of extraneous detail and emotion, we can act, not react, and view our lives and problems objectively, which is the first step to improving them. No matter your spiritual or religious leanings (or lack thereof), most Jedi practice a simple form of meditation that I will go over here. For some of you this will be a great review of the basics, and for others it may be your first time meditating: this method works for both.

Make yourself comfortable, whether that means sitting on a chair or the floor, standing, or lying down. Try to have your spine in a natural position (no slouching or twisting). Close your eyes, or if you wish to keep them open keep them unfocused. Let the tension drain out of your body, especially in the back and shoulders.

Take a deep breath in, feeling your lungs and belly expand as your diagphram pulls air in, feeling the coolness of your breath on the inside of your nose. Exhale slowly, feeling your body relax as the warmer air exits your nose or mouth. Repeat as many times as you like.

Your thoughts will wander, this is perfectly normal and expected. Don't stress about it, just casually bring your attention back to the physical sensation of your breath. Do this as long as you want to or feel like. Set a timer, or do it free-form. As you practice more, it becomes easier to meditate for longer periods of time. Especially with a regular practice, you should start to feel more alert, calm, and bright, with better focus and emotional stability, although most people feel better even after the first time.

There are many many apps to help you meditate, but the one I use most often, especially when I am feeling too fidgety and distracted to focus well, is calm.com. Just a little nature white noise and a timer.

How do you meditate? Did you like this exercise? Do you think meditation is important for a Jedi?

JEDI MEDITATION: KNOW THYSELF
Katie Mock
California Jedi

There is an ancient proverb: in Greek it is *gnothi seauton*, in Latin, *temet nosce*. In English, it is usually phrased "Know Thyself". Last week, I posted an overview of Jedi meditation with a simple exercise that is the first step towards this goal, and that is the core purpose of meditation: to take control of your mind and emotions.
The core of each Jedi's path, no matter how diverse, is deep self-understanding. Emotions don't come out of nowhere. We become angry or sad or happy not because there is some set response to each moment, or because people "make" us feel a certain way. Our emotions are clues to our internal landscape. This landscape is shaped by all our experiences, and in turn shapes our ideas, emotions, and tendencies.FRespect the L

If someone says something to make me angry, my first reaction as a Jedi isn't just to squash down the anger, and certainly isn't just reacting with knee-jerk rage; the first question I need to ask is "Why am I angry?" What about this person, this statement, this moment is making me see red? Is it actually that I am hurt by their opinion of me? Why do I care about that opinion? Is it that I find their statement offensive? Why am I offended? It is when you can take a moment and find honest answers to those questions that you can begin not only to act instead of merely react, but begin to shape your own emotional landscape.

This ability to see and sculpt our biases, tendencies, and problems internally is a human trait; we have both reason and the power to choose our actions. However it is the responsibility of each Jedi to know themselves deeply, in order to fulfill our objective of acting objectively, not influenced by hidden emotion or unfounded bias. The Jedi code says 'There is no emotion, there is peace'. To act peacefully, serenely, and objectively we must first understand ourselves deeply, to see what makes each of us tick. This process requires frequent, frank self-examination, and meditation is the most effective way to do that. So to that end, here is another exercise in Jedi Meditation.

Again, carve out a little time where you will not be disturbed, where you can be by yourself and think. Sometimes it helps to write, or speak aloud what your thoughts are, or you can keep them in your mind.

Also keep in mind that as you do this it will become a faster and more natural process, and you can start to practice it before, during, and after moments of stress or high emotion to help you act instead of react.

Close your eyes, and breathe naturally and deeply. Let the darkness behind your eyelids and the air in your lungs calm your mind.

What are you feeling, right now at this moment? What ideas or emotions begin to float to the surface of your consciousness? Try to tease apart the ball of tangled feelings that is normal for most people. Don't let this stress you out: all you are here to do is look at who you are, not who you were, or could be. You are not here to judge or regret. Examine your emotions as you would the horizon, or a familiar but new object in your hands. What is there?

Likely there will be one or two things that pull your attention in particular. Let yourself be pulled, examining those closely. How do you know that you feel this way? Are there physical sensations, like a tightness in your throat, chest, or shoulders? Are there memories or events associated with these feelings?

Remember to keep breathing and relax as you continue.

Next, delve a little deeper. Why are you feeling these emotions now? What sparked them? It could be something specific, or as nebulous as a rough week. Think about what parts of yourself could spawn these emotions. Are you nervous about your position at work? Worried about a friend? Conflicted about who you are, or what you want? No judgement is attached to whatever you reveal, you are merely following a stream back to its source.

Lastly, what is this emotional reaction based on? We feel emotion, especially strong emotion, as a response to fundamental needs that are either being filled or not, such as our need for love, stability, approval, and independence. When we lack a fundamental need, or feel it threatened somehow, we are often swamped with emotions like fear, insecurity, and anger. If you find that your emotion comes from a lack or need, how can you fill and stabilize that need? Is it good for you to do so? If not, how can you learn to be less dependent on that need?

Give yourself space to feel the emotion and recognize it, and make a note of all you've learned. As you do this more, you will start to understand yourself and your reactions in a new way, and start to be able to predict and control how you react or will react; this is the key to balancing objective Jedi behavior with proper emotional self-care. All this meditation is about is self-understanding, gaining knowledge that will help you shape yourself and your actions in the future, so anything you learn is important.

What did you think? Does this work for you, or help you on your path towards emotional wellness and objectivity?

Guide to Studying the Metaphysical and Mystical:
By: Connor L., also known as Laxus

Introduction to Version II:

So, weary traveler, you have come to this temple to learn about the Metaphysical and Mystical. I am glad you have come because this article is really an eye opener, for me included. I wrote this document in late 2013, which was ages ago in my book. I remember I actually wrote this close to the beginning of my journey into the occult and mystical. Now, two years later, my whole perspective has changed. And, looking back on this document, I now see things that my past self can teach me in addition to the things that I would like to change. This version was specifically prepared to go with my friend Seta's project. I hope you enjoy it.

Disclaimer:

I am not an expert. I have studied healing modalities for the better part of a decade. From Qigong to Access Consciousness, my methods have evolved and grown enough to where I think I understand how almost anybody can get involved in energy work.

SECTION ONE: I WANT LIGHTNING SHOOTING OUT OF MY HANDS

Well, I'm sorry... It's unfortunately not going to happen for you.

There is no reason to learn techniques that overly control the atmosphere around the body. Moving objects, reading minds, etc. these are tools that can be useful at certain times, but most of the time are not worth the sacrifice. When choosing a metaphysical art, you should not choose one that will force you to devote your whole life then end up dying without even knowing you'll achieve the result. Because of this, I respectfully advise against the following arts: Energy Projectiles, Immortality, Neigong, Any form of Taoist alchemy, Mind reading, Telekinesis, Pyrokinesis, and Psionics. Some of these arts, like mind reading and pyro can be applied in techniques like it, but to find documentation and work for 20 years on developing a technique is a waste of time, I believe.

Of course, if you are looking for a moral code, I would direct you to the Wiccan addage: "An it harm none, do what ye will."

That being said, if you are hell bent on finding a magical art that will take your life as a sacrifice, I won't try and stop you. I just won't teach it to you here in this document.

SECTION TWO: FINDING THE RIGHT ART:

Ok! Here's how you get to the fun stuff.

1. Find an art form that suits your passions!
Do you like healing people? Making them feel better? Empathetic Healing is probably for you! So, ask yourself: Why do you want to learn a mystical art? The answer will give you a starting place.
2. Take your time and do some good research on the art.
Read all the literature you can find. Read criticisms especially. Find out why people disregard things that are improvable. Usually it will be because of two reasons:
One, they can't do it him/herself.
Two, they have found empirical evidence and testify without giving it a go him/herself.
3. Make the decision: is it something you want to devote a portion of your life to?
Maybe do an intro course on it somewhere. Find out if it's the right art for you!
4. Once you've done your research, make the investment.
Time, money, whatever it takes. Do not half-do anything. Really get into it. If you aren't fully engaged, you'll never make any changes.

On Money: I used to be of the mind that nobody should pay for training. But, this is a ludicrous thing to ask for in a world where money is the primary exchange of energy. In this world, we should not keep people from knowledge, but we should expect to be paid for our teaching. It may not be in the form of money, per se. You might work in their house. You might tend their garden. You might serve them food. But, there should be some sort of energy exchange. It keeps things in balance. There will be people who disagree with me. That is simply my opinion. It is alright to pay for a class. It is ok to give back to your teachers.

SECTION THREE: WHAT IS THE FORCE?

In order to fully understand what Metaphysics and Mysticism entails, energy must be defined. Healing. Mind reading. Anything like that... it all has to come from the energy we have here on our planet and throughout the universe. I will reproduce an article I wrote in 2012. It follows the idea that Chi and Energy all stem from the principles of Kinetic and Potential energy. See below:

"Spirituality: is a term that has been around forever, I'm sure. I don't know precisely when its use became effective, but it is a word common to anybody who was brought up in a faith-based environment. To be honest, the population in America who was not brought up in this milieu is a small minority. I was brought up in the Christian Faith, and my first encounter with the term Spirituality was, of course, the Holy Spirit. Growing up in a Judeo-Christian household, the Holy Spirit was a big part of my childhood and adulthood. Father, Son, and Holy Ghost (spirit) are the Trinity. I was a United Methodist, and their insignia (cross and flame) shows two of these things. The Father is not shown because the Father is manifested in the form of the Son and the Holy Ghost.

Spirits, in a way, were not a part of my childhood. Spirits were not talked about in my house because the only talk really allowed was talk of God. This is not to say that other forms of religion were not discussed, but serious talk of other faiths was not a part of my childhood. I wouldn't even say that my house was closed-minded: my father is Jewish and my mother is Methodist. Now that you know this, I can say: we just didn't ever talk about it. Spirits and other metaphysical phenomenon just never came up for me until I was in my early teens.

Spirits can manifest themselves to us through tuning into frequencies. That makes perfect sense because all spirits have a frequency (just like the rest of the things in the universe do), and if you can tap into them, then you can channel them like a radio... all the experiences, memories, etc. It provides comfort to those in our world. Granted, I wouldn't go so far as to say there is a physical world in the life after death. To be honest, I think the spirits are in OUR world, but not manifested into humanoid form. I think this comes with our need to view things in human form to identify objects. This is why Angels appear to be human in the mythology. Why Kami look human.

Why Chinese Ancestors are animals and humans. This rich history of communication with the spirit world is Universal. What I want to get across is this: there is probably not a physical Heaven after death. Our human bodies are a product of evolution, but the Life Force inside of us comes from the Spirits.

    Spirits are the Universe. There is nothing bigger than the Universe itself (that we need to consider, anyway, for this to be). Therefore, when the first organic thing came into being (like an organism), there must have been a wisdom instilled in it: reality. There is a distinct reality of things. Reality shows us that we are all Star Dust, and are all one... so why wouldn't we consider that Wisdom and Knowledge aren't already there? They must be. We just have to discover it. So, this Universal Conscious is made up of infinite vibrations around all things. Different levels, different understandings. You must understand that, like Light (and the visible spectrum), there are an endless amount of colors we cannot see. But, just like radio waves, we can interact with them on a different level. Well, Spirits could very well be a Collective Conscious that lives on various vibrational levels. Like Chi, when we learn to interact with these vibrations, we can commune with these Spirits.

    When you feel tingly in your meditations, could you attribute that to tuning into higher frequencies? I think so. I think it could also be using Chi to transform this vibration.

    We are to train in Mind, Body, and Spirit. But, in reality, if you think about all this: the Mind and Body are part of the Spirit, yes? There is no separation except by what your sight, hearing, feeling, tasting, and smelling tell you. Those senses are limited. This is why I am starting with Spirituality. I want you to know that when I leave this behind to go into the other two fields, never let go of the Truth that we are all Spirit, and the division is mainly for human convenience and lack of understanding. So, why is it that hard to conceive that you could talk to deceased? I think it would be a fabulous way to gain true Knowledge while in life. Bring the truth to the people. Speed up the growth process. Spirituality is important to a Jedi because it provides a link to greater growth and wisdom. Would you really be ok turning that down? I know I wouldn't." [end of article]

    And, from an article on the Force itself:
"...we should begin by [de]mystifying the Force.

There are two types of things that can be measured in the world: those that interact with the physical (which can be measured with physical things) and those that do not interact with the physical. Physical things, which can be measured, tend to be the things that Scientists love. And, when it is immeasurable and not "supposed" to be there, then Scientists and logical thinkers tend to disregard it as unnecessary and improvable and get rid of it. The difference between internal Chi and the Higgs Field is that the Higgs Boson has to be there. Without it, the Universe would not work, so Scientists knew there was a hole there, but kept it open. But, Chi was a different matter.

We are looking at two different things. Again, I want to make this crystal clear: You have things that can be accessed through the physical realm; you also have things that are beyond physical understanding, yet interact with the physical world. I read an article that talked about how time might be able to flow backwards, so do not tell me that my assertion is even farfetched.

Some people swear by Qigong. Testimonies are only so strong, though. Eventually, it melts into an argument about proof. One of my favorite things I've seen on the topic thus far has been here: http://askville.amazon.com/believers-chi-give-proof-existence/AnswerViewer.do?requestId=4701690. They seem to really get into the whole mind effect. I was reading an essay on Chi Sensativity here (www.matzkefamily.net/doug/papers/tucson2b.html), and I saw these wonderful sentences "The major proof that Chi exists today is the fact that people are sensitive to Chi and describe it in consistent and repeatable terms across many subjects. This subjective experience is no different than people who are wine tasting experts with highly "calibrated tongues" or perfume experts with highly "calibrated noses". In fact, apprentices who have been trained to become very sensitive and aware of Chi are called Chi masters." Because, if you think about it, it's true! Chi is like wine tasting in a way. There is no scientific proof that one wine is better than another. There may be better ways, but also tastes differ. However, there are some foods that if you have a tolerance for the type of food, everybody at the table will have an inexplicable desire to "mm" and attempt to describe why they like it. There is no science for that. It is the same way with Chi sensitivity. Not everybody in the world is open to Chi. They may just not like the idea. But, in the end, people who at least accept the idea have always given positive responses to Chi treatment or practice. So, in conclusion about Chi, there is no scientific proof that Chi can be measured by physical means.

But, does that mean that Chi is not measurable by non-physical means? We'd have to buck up and define Chi first. So, I will try and explain what I think Chi is: I believe that everything in the entire Universe is Energy (big e, for all-encompassing dramatic effect). The Universe began with energy (read Lawrence Krauss's *A Universe from Nothing*). Big Bang, yeah? So, it would make sense, since energy can neither be created nor destroyed, that it must transform and manifest in different ways. This goes from the beginnings of uncollected universal dust to the electrical energy and gravity that began to form around energy centers and planets with stars being formed, etc.. I said a couple of days ago that we are Star Dust. Did you ever think about how it was possible to go from dust to skin to cells to brain to complex thinking? Science puts Chi right in the middle of all that and everybody has MISSED it! That's the best part. People keep saying: Chi isn't real, it's a myth! But, there is something about the transformation of energy that people just don't really understand yet, and this is where my definition of Chi lies. In the brain, nothing becomes possible unless an electrical connection is formed. Two nodes that form a bond become a memory. A pulse is sent to a nerve to say: "move". These things are learned, and the electrical connection is strengthened. The stronger the electrical connection, the easier the action is to repeat. Same with a memory. The more you think about something, the stronger the electrical connection is and the harder the memory is to forget. Get it now? In acupuncture, the needles are used to move the energy of the body to help the Chi become balanced (not static, but flowing evenly). I mean, for crying out loud, it should be obvious to you what's going on. The brain controls the body, but the body is also an independent entity. Without the brain, the body would not move. Without the body, the brain would not grow and have the ability to intake information. What bonds the brain to the body besides the physical nerves? Electricity, Chi. I am not saying Chi is directly this "electricity", but it is Life Force. It is energy. It is the act of this connection between the mind and body to the Higher Consciousness. Chi is in every living thing because every living thing is connected by Energy. Kinetic to Potential. Mechanical to Electric. Chi. It's all laid out in front of you, you just can't measure it because it isn't a "physical" thing. It is the act of connecting energies from one to the other resulting in such a large Field of Energy that the name must be given: Chi.

    No, it doesn't have a physical manifestation. I have seen testimonies of people who move things with their "mind". But, they aren't doing so. They have taken a hold of Chi and realized that they can manifest energy changes with their will. What does this mean for the brain? It means that Chi lies within the body as it does in the brain. But, consciousness lies in the brain. It lies in the will for change. I don't mean "life" change. I mean change in energy. When you get up, your body has potential energy stored up and ready to use. Your brain sends an electrical signal to innumerable parts of your body to say move. Your electric energy moves to mechanical energy. Your potential energy to kinetic. This act of using the brain to change the stasis of an energy is called Chi, to me. So, of course, you cannot measure Chi. It's not a real thing! It's a connection of various energies to other kinds of energy. When people have a heat in their stomach, it isn't because Chi is there, it is because Chi is there that the energy changes to heat energy and the body leaks it. What you are doing is willing the body to change energy just like you use electrical impulses to move your arm. There is no difference. When people measure Chi, they finagle the ability to measure electricity coming from seemingly nothing. But, what does that say to you?

"But, Connor… If it's so simple as moving your arm, then why does Chi take years to learn?" Another easy question, my friend. How long did it take for you to develop the willpower to develop muscles and bones and strength to hit a ball at 80 MPH (I know that's not fabulous, but you get the point, yes)? You kept mirroring those around you and used instinct, and you developed strength and natural growth over a long period of time before you could completely control your movements all the time. Chi is the same. When you are born, you have the natural ability to influence the Chi in your body. But, many around us are not in touch with our Chi, so we don't use it. And, if a child didn't use their arms at all until they were 9-10 years old, do you think the development would have been as dramatic? No! It would be lax. And, the future strength of the arm would be hurt. Luckily, we DO use our brains to send signals ALL the time, and working with this connection is ingrained into us, we just don't really know how to focus on it.

At this point, you're probably thinking, what does this have to do with the Force… and why the heck is there so much pseudo-science surrounding this subject and not enough spirituality? I'll tell you: Dude, Chi isn't spiritual. It only seems that way because of how history has been mangled with. 5000 years ago, Chi was SCIENCE in China. They used the flow and change of energy to determine the imbalances of Yin and Yang. What seems to be lost is the knowledge that Chi isn't a "thing", it is a bridge between things.

So, is Chi the Force? I think so, but on a larger scale. I think the Force itself is the Tao. The Tao that can be said is not the true Tao. Why? Because the Tao is not an object that can be measured, but it is a non-physical bridge between everything, keeping all things in balance. When you are not in line with Chi, Tao, Force, then you are out of sync with the Universal Perspective. You have taken on the job of moving your Chi around into imbalance. It is unnecessary, and all you have to do is learn to be at peace with Reality and learn to use your energy. Personal, Living, and Unifying Force. These levels of Energy are the truths of our lives. Personal is the brain saying: "this is how I want energy to change". Living is the energy in transit and interacting with the rest of the world. And, Unifying is the true encompassing Force. It is the combination of limitless strings of connections bound together to keep the Universe from being Energy-less and stagnant. A static universe would end. It would simply stop. All life would cease and time wouldn't even exist.

To say that Chi does not exist. To say that the Force, or even Energy, or EVEN Life Force does not exist is to say that the Universe is a stagnant and empty place.

Luckily, in my opinion, that is NOT the case. "

SECTION FOUR: THE PROCESS

So, you've picked an art, you've defined your energy. Now, you need to be able to feel it.

Step one: Relax and find a good place to sit or lie down.
Step two: Do some counting meditation for blood circulation. Breathe in for five, hold for five, and let out for five. Repeat for 5 minutes.
Step three: Begin feeling your energy in your lower dan tien (this is the area behind your belly button and a little lower). You can do this by clenching your ab muscles, releasing, and remembering how that feeling is and just focusing on it.
Step four: hold your left arm out, and begin clenching a fist, and then opening it. Back and forth for a long time. Slowly, though. Keep your focus on the lower Dan Tien.
Step five: the energy will naturally make a connection from the fist to the energy center, and your whole body should feel tingly.

SECTION FIVE: EXPERIENCING V. STUDY

So, by now, you've felt the Force. You've picked an art to study. You believe you are ready to go about practicing your art or going through a program. How can you deal with the world around you that is so cruel? Remember, society is all about things we can see, and things we culturally identify with. So why is it that we're always so weary of programs we're not familiar with? Articles constantly discredit programs like Reiki and Qigong because of their lack of "physical" change. What about programs that do not claim to have any direct influence? Oftentimes, these programs are not personally in accordance with the art because they do not experience it firsthand.

When was the last time you tried to meditate and did not do it your OWN way in your own body?

In each of our lives, we all learn to throw a ball. We can all breathe. But, each of us experiences this in individual ways we cannot communicate on a sub-molecular level. So, when scientists try to tell us how we experience metaphysics within our own bodies, it makes no sense to discredit them because no change is observed. And, even, so, mental changes can occur in the body. See studies on Tummo Meditation.

So, when doing exercises involving "metaphysics", I advise using experience as a guide rather than empirical data alone. If you are using Reiki to heal somebody, a prescribed method might not work! You might just not be feeling it correctly. Altering the method to become personalized destroys the notion of reproduce-ability. If you notice, many professional practitioners of metaphysical arts develop their own style of practice. Have you ever wondered why that is? Because we all experience the universe through our own lens.

SECTION SIX: RESONANCE:

Resonance is why metaphysics works. This is not a new idea, either, but it is often overlooked by many scientists.
What is Resonance?
The phenomenon that ideas are personalized to each person.
How can you use it?
When speaking about topics, find words and actions that feel "Light" to you. That feel as though they do not bog you down.
This kind of individualization is important to people's success on the path.
How can we apply resonance and make the connection between study,

experience, individualization, and resonance together to make successful study?

CONCLUSION:

It all comes down to applicability. Whatever works for you is what works for you. That's it!

Find the things that work, and ignore the opinions of those against you. But of course, don't fall victim to ignorance and disillusionment. It takes a healthy criticism to truly scrutinize find what works.

Good luck.

Orders Represented in These Pages

Temple of the Jedi Order
templeofthejediorder.org

Temple of the Jedi Force
templeofthejediforce.org

Force Academy, Light Aspect
forceacademy.co.uk

Institute for Jedi Realist Studies
instituteforjedirealiststudies.org

Jedi Knights
jediknights.b1.jcink.com

California Jedi
californiajedi.org

Heartland Jedi
www.meetup.com/Heartland-Jedi/

Aurora Borealis
www.theaurorainitiative.com

Jedi of the Noble Order
www.facebook.com/groups/413378692153694/

Real Jedi Enclave
rjenclave.b1.jcink.com

Jedi Church (the Original)
www.facebook.com/groups/28586881121/

Kharis Institute
kharis.kharisinstitute.org

Jedi School
www.facebook.com/groups/jedischool/

J.U.S.T. Jedi
www.facebook.com/groups/JustJedi/

Ashla Knights ashlaknights.net

Jedi Path Academy
jedipath.academy

Knights of Awakening
www.koaaxiom.com

Chicago Jedi
chicagojedi.com

Coelescere Enclave
No Longer Active

Setanaoko's School for Jedi (Book Series)

The Nomad Jedi (Dave Jenson's Title)

Thank you also goes to the Church of Jediism and Jedi Academy Online for their contributions to the original outline referred to as "The Jedi Compass By the Jedi Community", and to Jedi Realist Radio's continuing support of this project.

May you find guidance and strength as you navigate the Force

/bows

Printed in Great Britain
by Amazon